Routledge Revivals

New Technology

First published in 1989, this book presents a unique comparative perspective on the relationship between technological change and human resource management. Following a detailed introduction, chapters deal with a variety of issues, including managing change, industrial democracy and employee involvement, gender and structural change. International and well-renowned authors provide an authoritative analysis, which will be of particular interest to students of Business and Management, organisational and technological change, Economics and Sociology.

New Technology

International Perspectives on Human Resources and Industrial Relations

Edited by
Greg J. Bamber
and Russell D. Lansbury

First published in 1989
by Unwin Hyman Ltd

This edition first published in 2014 by Routledge
2 Park Square, Milton Park, Abingdon, Oxon, OX14 4RN
and by Routledge
711 Third Avenue, New York, NY 10017

Routledge is an imprint of the Taylor & Francis Group, an informa business

Publisher's Note
The publisher has gone to great lengths to ensure the quality of this reprint but points out that some imperfections in the original copies may be apparent.

Disclaimer
The publisher has made every effort to trace copyright holders and welcomes correspondence from those they have been unable to contact.

A Library of Congress record exists under LC control number: 88027970

ISBN 13: 978-0-415-73681-7 (hbk)
ISBN 13: 978-1-315-81831-3 (ebk)
ISBN 13: 978-0-415-73684-8 (pbk)

NEW TECHNOLOGY

International Perspectives on Human Resources and Industrial Relations

---

Edited by

Greg J. Bamber
Russell D. Lansbury

London
UNWIN HYMAN
Boston Sydney Wellington

Published by the Academic Division of
Unwin Hyman Ltd,
15/17 Broadwick Street, London W1V 1FP, UK

Unwin Hyman Inc.,
Winchester Place, Winchester, Mass. 01890, USA

Allen & Unwin (Australia) Ltd,
8 Napier Street, North Sydney, NSW 2060, Australia

Allen & Unwin (New Zealand) Ltd in association with the
Port Nicholson Press Ltd,
60 Cambridge Terrace, Wellington, New Zealand

First published in 1989

British Library Cataloguing in Publication Data

New technology: international perspectives on human resources and industrial relations.
1. Personnel management. Implications of technological innovation
I. Bamber, Greg J. II. Lansbury, Russell D. (Russell Duncan)
658.3
ISBN 0-04-445123-7

Library of Congress Cataloging in Publication Data

New technology: international perspectives on human resources and industrial relations/edited by Greg J. Bamber and Russell D. Lansbury.
p. cm.
Bibliography: p.
Includes index.
ISBN 0-04-445123-7
1. Labor supply—Effect of technological innovations on. 2. Industrial relations—Effect of technological innovations on. 3. Industrial management—Employee participation. 4. Trade-Unions. 5. Personnel management.
I. Bamber, Greg, 1949- . II. Lansbury, Russell D.
HD 6331. N493 1989 88-27970
331.12—dc19

Typeset in 10/12pt Palatino by Fotographics (Bedford) Ltd
and printed in Great Britain by Billing and Son, London and Worcester

Contents

List of Figures

List of Tables

Contributors

Anders Bäckström is a senior economist with the Landsorganisationen i Sverige (LO, the most important Swedish union confederation). After graduating from Uppsala University in 1968, with a degree in economics and statistics, he worked for two years in the field of national accounts at Statistics Sweden. Since 1970 he has been with the LO, except for a break in 1976–77 when he worked in Zambia for the Swedish International Development Agency (SIDA). He has published many articles and been a co-author of several books, most of them in Swedish.

Greg J. Bamber is an Associate Professor, Graduate School of Management, University of Queensland, Brisbane, Australia. Previously he was the Director of Research, Durham University Business School, England, where he was also an Arbitrator for the Advisory, Conciliation and Arbitration Service (ACAS). In the 1970s, in Britain, he worked for the Commission on Industrial Relations, and for the Steel and Industrial Managers' Association. He holds degrees from the University of Manchester Institute of Science and Technology, and Heriot-Watt University, Edinburgh. Dr Bamber's publications include *Militant Managers?* (Aldershot: Gower, 1986) and, together with Russell Lansbury, *International and Comparative Industrial Relations* (London and Sydney: Allen & Unwin, 1987).

Margaret Cove became Editor in Chief of the International Labour Organisation's (ILO) *Social and Labour Bulletin* in August 1987 having been responsible for the English edition since 1979. She has also worked in an editorial role in the ILO's Training Department. Before this she worked in the private sector and carried out research for Monsanto and Imperial Chemical Industries Limited. She holds degrees from Trinity College, Dublin. She is the co-author of several papers and articles on industrial relations topics with special emphasis on the repercussions of technological change, and is co-editor of two publications on the impact of technological change (both published by the ILO).

Peter Cressey is the Convener of the Centre for Research in Industrial Democracy and Participation (CRIDP) at the University of Glasgow. He was educated at Coleg Harlech, Wales, and the University of York, England, where he gained undergraduate and postgraduate degrees. He has been involved in full-time research since the late 1970s, primarily in the area of industrial relations and industrial sociology, and has acted as a research fellow, rapporteur, and expert on a number of British and European research projects. He has published extensively in the areas of worker participation and the introduction of new technology and in mainstream industrial relations.

Edward M. Davis is Associate Professor and Director of the Labour-Management Studies Program in the Graduate School of Management at Macquarie University, Australia. He holds a Master of Arts from Cambridge University, England, a Master of Economics from Monash University, Australia and a doctorate from La Trobe University, Australia. He is author of *Democracy in Australian Unions* (Sydney: Allen & Unwin, 1987) and, together with Russell Lansbury, he is co-editor of *Technology, Work and Industrial Relations* (1984) and *Democracy and Control in the Work Place* (1986), both published in Melbourne by Longman Cheshire. He has acted as a consultant on industrial relations to employers, unions and government, and he has also undertaken assignments for the International Labour Organisation.

Vittorio di Martino works with the International Labour Office. He was previously Research Manager at the European Foundation for the Improvement of Living and Working Conditions, Dublin, with special responsibility for the areas of Industrial Relations, Social Dialogue, and Technological Change. He holds degrees in labour law and industrial relations (University of Rome) and in European Community law (University of Bologna). He has been visiting fellow at the University of Newcastle-upon-Tyne, England, and at the Commission for Human Rights and Fundamental Freedoms in Strasbourg. He is author and editor of several books and other publications on industrial participation, quality of work life, industrial relations, social impact of information technology and biotechnology.

Gert Graversen is a Senior Research Fellow at Åarhus University, Denmark, and former director of the Department of Industrial Psychology, Technological Institute, Copenhagen. He has many years of consulting experience with private and public organizations on job design and organization development. In the early 1970s, he was a teacher and research fellow at Leeds University, England, and Copenhagen University, Denmark. In 1984 he was visiting fellow at the Australian National University, Canberra. He has published books and articles on industrial and organizational psychology, especially in the fields of job development, industrial democracy and quality of working life. He is currently doing research on individual coping and adaptation to technological and social change.

Rose Marie Greve is a sociologist at the International Institute for Labour Studies (IILS), Geneva, since 1977. She is the IILS Focal Point for Women's

Questions and the editor of its journal *Labour and Society*. Her main areas of interest are industrial relations, participation, social perspectives and the quality of working life. She has published many articles and papers in these fields.

Frank A. Heller is Director of the Centre for Decision Making Studies at the Tavistock Institute of Human Relations, London. He took an engineering diploma and worked in the motor car industry for six years before taking an economics degree at the London School of Economics and Political Science, followed by a PhD in psychology. After a stint as head of a department of management, he took a six-year consulting assignment in South America and Visiting Professorship at the University of California at Berkeley, USA. Since 1970, when he joined the Tavistock Institute, he has been involved in six major cross-national studies in Europe, the USA, Japan and, most recently, China. He is currently President of the Organizational Psychology Division of the International Association of Applied Psychology, and is author of several works on the psychology of work, managerial decision-making and industrial democracy.

Everett M. Kassalow is Professor Emeritus of Economics and Industrial Relations, University of Wisconsin, Madison, USA. He has also been Visiting Professor at Carnegie Mellon University, Pittsburgh, USA, and is currently attached to the University of the District of Columbia (Washington, DC). He has been Research Director for the United Rubber Workers of America, Economist for the Congress of Industrial Organizations, and Director of Research for the Industrial Union Department, American Federation of Labor–Congress of Industrial Organizations. He has served as Senior Labor Specialist in the Library of Congress (USA), Senior Research Associate, International Labour Organisation (Geneva), and Labor Adviser to the US Mission in Paris, France. He is past president of the Industrial Relations Research Association (USA). He has lectured abroad extensively.

Thomas A. Kochan is a Professor of Industrial Relations at the Massachusetts Institute of Technology (MIT) School of Management, USA, and Head of the Behavioral and Policy Sciences Area of the School. His past and current research focus on industrial relations theory and policy, human resource strategies, and the relationships between human resources and technology. From 1973 to 1980 he was a faculty member of the New York School of Industrial and Labor Relations at Cornell University, USA. He holds degrees from the University of Wisconsin, Madison, USA. His publications include *Collective Bargaining and Industrial Relations* (Homewood: Irwin, 1980) and, together with Robert McKersie and Harry Katz, *The Transformation of American Industrial Relations* (New York: Basic Books, 1987).

Russell D. Lansbury is Professor of Industrial Relations at the University of Sydney, Australia. He was previously a faculty member of Monash and of Macquarie universities, Australia. He holds degrees in psychology and political science from the University of Melbourne, Australia, and a doctorate from the London School of Economics and Political Science. He has worked in personnel and industrial relations for British Airways in London, and has held visiting positions at various universities in Europe and North America. In 1984 he was a Senior Fulbright Scholar at both the Massachusetts Institute of Technology (MIT) and Harvard University, USA. He has acted as a consultant to governments in Australia and to the International Labour Organisation on industrial relations issues. He is the author and editor of numerous academic articles and books on topics such as industrial democracy, technological change and the role of management in industrial relations.

Hedva Sarfati is Chief of the Salaried Employees and Professional Workers Branch of the International Labour Office (ILO). Formerly she was Editor in Chief of the *Social and Labour Bulletin* (ILO, Geneva), 1973–87. She holds degrees in economics and political science from the University of Geneva, Switzerland. She is the co-author of several papers and articles on industrial relations topics such as technological change, workers' participation and labour market flexibility. She launched a new ILO series of comparative studies dealing with topical labour market trends in 1982 and is a member of the International Industrial Relations Association and of the International Association of the Public Service.

Boaz Tamir is an Assistant Professor in the Department of Political Science at Tel Aviv University, Israel. He received his doctorate in political science from the Massachusetts Institute of Technology, USA, in 1987. His research focuses on the political economy of organizations and industrial relations strategies.

Anil Verma is Associate Professor of Industrial Relations and Human Resource Management at the University of Toronto, Canada. He holds a BTech in electrical engineering from the Indian Institute of Technology, Kanpur, India, an MBA from the University of Saskatchewan, Saskatoon, Canada, and a PhD in management from the Sloan School of Management, Massachusetts Institute of Technology, USA. He has taught previously at the University of Saskatchewan, University of British Columbia and the University of California, Los Angeles (as a visiting professor), and worked in the steel industry as an engineer for five years. His primary research interests are in the area of management responses to unionization, participative forms of work organization, employment stabilization practices and contingent compensation such as profit/gainsharing.

Wilfred Zerbe is Assistant Professor, Management of Organizations and Human Resources at the University of Calgary, Faculty of Management, Canada. He received his PhD in commerce and business administration from the University of British Columbia, Canada. He also holds a Master's degree in social psychology. Professor Zerbe's research interests include investigating structural and temporary influences on employee motivation, and identifying sources of occupational stress, particularly among employees in service organizations. He is also interested in organizational research methods.

Preface

There was an informal symposium, 'Technological Change and Industrial Relations', at the Sixth World Congress of the International Industrial Relations Association (IIRA) held in Kyoto, Japan, in 1983. The papers were subsequently published in a special issue of the *Bulletin of Comparative Labour Relations* (Belgium: University of Leuven/Holland: Kluwer, vol. 12, 1983, eds G. J. Bamber and R. D. Lansbury). At the Seventh IIRA World Congress, held in Hamburg in 1986, technological change was one of the main themes. The IIRA also formed a special study group on this subject, which met at the Hamburg Congress. The chapters in the present book were given in their original form at the Hamburg Congress either in the plenary session or in one of the workshops, but most have subsequently been revised. We particularly thank all the contributors who have travelled a long route with us from their first drafts! We apologise to those whose work is not included, for this book is a selection. It was not possible to include all of the many relevant Congress papers. (Some of the others are being published by de Gruyter, Berlin.)

Given that this book arose directly from IIRA activities, we appreciate the kind cooperation of its successive presidents: Friedrich Fürstenberg, Roger Blanpain and John Niland; its secretary, Alan Gladstone; and all his colleagues in the IIRA and the International Labour Office (ILO). The ILO provides a good vantage point for comparative analysis. (The ILO is based in Geneva and supplies the secretariat and staff of the International Labour Organisation, an agency of the United Nations.) Three chapters in this book are written by ILO staff, though the views expressed are personal and not necessarily those of the ILO.

We appreciate the professional advice of Carolyn White, Patrick Gallagher and their colleagues, who have guided the publication both of this book and its predecessor: *International and*

Comparative Industrial Relations: A Study of Developed Market Economies (London: Allen & Unwin, 1987, eds G. J. Bamber and R. D. Lansbury). Technological change was also a theme of that earlier book and has been the subject of comparative research on which we have collaborated in several countries. The current book broadens the focus on technological change, however, to discuss some wider implications for the management of human resources.

Of course we accept responsibility for the errors that inevitably creep into such a book as this, in spite of all the help we have received. We cannot thank everyone by name, but some specific acknowledgements are mentioned in several of the individual chapters. Barbara Henson and Susan Reilly corrected the proofs. More generally, we appreciate various forms of encouragement from several mentors including David Dror, Geoff Kiel, Yasuo Kuwahara, Hazel Imison, Joe Isaac, Sol Levine, Rod Martin, Jacques Rojot, Bruce Rowe, Taishiro Shirai, Ken Tucker and Di Yerbury, and from our colleagues at our present (Queensland and Sydney) and former (Durham and Macquarie) universities.

For all their support and encouragement, we are most grateful to our immediate families (including Jim, Joan, Doug, Betty, Val, Alex, Katie, Freda, Consie, George, Gwen, Owen and Nina) and to our extended international families of friends and colleagues.

Greg Bamber and Russell Lansbury
Universities of Queensland and Sydney
August 1988

List of Abbreviations

ACARD	Advisory Council for Applied Research and Development (UK)
ACOA	Administrative and Clerical Officers Association (Australia)
ACTU	Australian Council of Trade Unions
AFL-CIO	American Federation of Labor-Congress of Industrial Organizations
ALP	Australian Labor Party
AMWU	Amalgamated Metal Workers' Union (Australia)
ATEA	Australian Telecommunications Employees' Association
AT&T	American Telephone and Telegraph Co.
BCA	Business Council of Australia
BIAC	Business and Industry Advisory Committee (OECD)
BLS	Bureau of Labor Statistics (USA)
BNA	Bureau of National Affairs (USA)
CAI	Confederation of Australian Industry
CBI	Confederation of British Industry
CFDT	French Democratic Confederation of Labour
CGIL	Italian General Confederation of Labour
CITCA	Committee of Inquiry into Technological Change in Australia
CSS	Council for Science and Society (UK)
CWA	Communication Workers of America
DVLC	Driving and Vehicle Licensing Centre (UK)
EC	European Communities
EI	employee involvement
EITB	Engineering Industry Training Board (UK)
ETUI	European Trade Union Institute
FIET	International Federation of Commercial, Clerical, Professional and Technical Employees

FRG	Federal Republic of Germany
GDP	gross domestic product
GM	General Motors
HRM	human resource management
ICFTU	International Confederation of Free Trade Unions
IIRA	International Industrial Relations Association
ILO	International Labour Office/Organisation
IMS	Institute of Manpower Studies (UK)
IOE	International Organisation of Employers
IRI	Institute for the Reconstruction of Italy
IT	information technology
ITS	international trade (union) secretariat
JIL	Japan Institute of Labour
LO	Landsorganisationen i Sverige (Swedish Confederation of Trade Unions)
MIT	Massachusetts Institute of Technology
NLCC	National Labour Consultative Council (Australia)
OECD	Organisation for Economic Co-operation and Development
OTA	Office of Technology Assessment (USA)
QC	quality circle
SPRU	Science Policy Research Unit (UK)
TAB	training advisory boards (USA)
TDC	Trade Development Council (Australia)
TUAC	Trade Union Advisory Committee (OECD)
UAW	United Automobile Workers (USA)
UFCW	United Food and Commercial Workers (USA)
VDTs	visual display terminals
VDUs	visual display units

I
Introduction

CHAPTER ONE

Technological Change, Industrial Relations and Human Resource Management

RUSSELL D. LANSBURY and GREG J. BAMBER

This introductory chapter discusses some key concepts: technological change, industrial relations and human resource management. It also considers several analytical frameworks: the socio-technical approach, the labour process approach, and a neo-human relations approach by those who prescribe 'excellence'. Against this background, the Introduction summarizes the main issues which arise in the following chapters. These include: changing approaches to collective bargaining, new technology agreements, employee participation, gender, skills, structural change and flexibility.

The issues associated with new technologies are becoming increasingly important for practitioners and scholars in many fields, including industrial relations, personnel/human resource management and organizational design, and for those concerned with the broader issues of public policy and political economy.

Which are the appropriate management styles and organizational structures for dealing with technological change? What are the policies and practices of employers, employees and unions in different countries? Which frameworks of analysis are available? Do women generally benefit or suffer when new technologies are introduced? How is the structure of industries and skills changing? Are new divisions emerging in the workforce? Current technological changes raise many such questions, which are considered in this book.

This introduction sets the scene for the chapters which follow. First, however, it is important to clarify what we mean by technological change, industrial relations and human resource management.

Some Key Concepts

Technological Change

The concept of technology encapsulates not only machinery, materials and equipment, but also their economic and social organization: the processes of control by managements, workers and the state. Technological change can be defined broadly as 'the process by which *economies* change over time in respect of the products they produce and the processes used to produce them' (Stoneman, 1983; our emphasis). Technological change may involve a variation of the output or of the application of knowledge and skills which results in a significant alteration in the management techniques, work organization, raw materials and the relationship between capital, labour and the state. Technological change can be defined more specifically, for example, as alteration in physical 'processes, materials, machinery or equipment, which has impact on the way work is performed . . . or on the efficiency or effectiveness of the enterprise' (CITCA, 1980).

The broader definitions are philosophically more satisfactory, but they embrace many variables, both independent and dependent. For practical analysis, the definition that focuses on physical machinery and equipment is more useful. The authors of most of the chapters in this book generally see new technologies as independent variables (more or less). Then they focus on issues of industrial relations and human resources as dependent variables (more or less) (cf. Batstone *et al.*, 1987, p. 2).

Although we use the more specific definition of technological change, we do not accept the notion of technological determinism, which holds that technology tends to determine organizational arrangements and a particular pattern of management, structure of work and industrial relations. We do not deny that technology may be an important influence, but there are other important influences, including the markets for raw materials, labour and products, and the traditions and policies of employers, managers, engineers, governments, workgroups and unions (Bamber and Lansbury, 1988).

Four key technologies that have become prominent in the 1980s are microelectronics, new materials technology, biotechnology (genetic engineering) and new energy resources (Commonwealth Secretariat, 1985). Microelectronics appears to be the most pervasive of these technologies and it has been described by Sir Ieuan Maddock, former British Government Chief Scientist, as 'the most remarkable technology ever to confront mankind'. The electronics industry is not new, but it has been revolutionized by advances in the design of microprocessors, which have recently been generating a ten-fold increase in information-processing capacity per unit of cost every five years. The uses of such technologies are having a significant impact on employment levels, skills, work patterns, occupational boundaries, job design and so on (Gill, 1985). There has, moreover, been a convergence of various computer and telecommunications technologies, which are transforming specific processes as well as the structures of whole industries and economies. Some of these transformations have been accelerated by the energy crises, and, in many developed market economies, have been accompanied by a decline in manufacturing industry and a rise in the level of unemployment.

Industrial Relations

Early students of industrial relations (e.g. Webb and Webb, 1897; Commons, 1910) were particularly influenced by the descriptive approach of traditional labour history and institutional economics; they were preoccupied with unions, especially their central leadership. When defining industrial relations, Dunlop (1958) and Flanders (1965) focused on systems of formal institutions and rules. Dunlop, in particular, was influenced by contemporary attempts at grand theorizing (Parsons and Smelser, 1956; cf. Mills, 1959). When Dunlop and Flanders were formulating their ideas, most industrial relations practitioners and scholars seemed concerned with such institutions of job regulation as unions, employers' associations, collective bargaining, industrial disputes, economic rewards, arbitration, and other forms of third party intervention by governments and independent agencies.

The Dunlop and Flanders type of approach now appears too restrictive. Concentrating on systems of formal institutions and networks of rules, it tends to overlook less visible controls, such as informal groupings of managers or workers, temporary political alliances, personal attitudes, beliefs and antagonisms. Further, 'a focus on rules and regulations may lead us to expect order, where order may not exist' (Palmer, 1983, p. 2). Disorder may characterize the uncertainties and contradictions associated with new technologies, in particular. Rather than expecting order, it might even be argued that 'conflict is the basic concept, and should form the basis of a study of industrial relations' (Margerison, 1969, p. 274).

Most of the chapters in this book adopt a broader approach to industrial relations than those of Dunlop and Flanders. Broader definitions have been devised by several writers. For Bain and Clegg (1974, p. 95), industrial relations is 'the study of all aspects of job regulation – the making and administering of the rules which regulate employment relationships – regardless of whether these are seen as being formal or informal, structured or unstructured.' Hyman's definition is more succinct, yet wider in scope. He sees industrial relations as 'the processes of control over work relations' (Hyman, 1975, p. 12), while for Kochan (1980, p. 1) it is 'the study of all aspects of people at work'.

Rather than focusing on unions, a few scholars have studied employers' associations (Gospel, 1974; Plowman, 1986). However, given a wide range of attitudes among their members across different industries and firms, any policies on new technology adopted by employers' associations tend to be broad and vague. Most national employers' associations see technological change as both necessary and inevitable. In general, employer groups emphasize the benefits of new technology, which can be used to increase productivity and quality, while making work less repetitive, more interesting and safer. The Swiss Employers' Association, for example, argues that, since microelectronics offers benefits for everyone, the material conditions of life and social status of employees will be improved as a result of technological change. Similarly, the French Employers' Federation emphasizes the positive role of computers in the workplace, as well as in improving the competitiveness of enterprises.

Windmuller (1984) notes that 'the issue of co-determination has been of foremost concern to employers' associations in several countries, in part because it has involved the state in the shaping of new modes of industrial relations through legislation which affects the system of collective bargaining, threatens management prerogatives and usually increases union power'. For most employers, 'the acceptable degree of consultation is strictly limited' (Rojot, 1988). International employers' associations generally argue that technological changes should not be used as a basis for the imposition of additional requirements for 'information, consultation or bargaining obligations'.

In those European countries with a centralized collective bargaining structure, the employers' associations may have considerable influence (Sisson, 1987), though they are rarely involved in making decisions about technological change. Individual companies usually wish to decide about new technologies themselves. Moreover, given that most employers' associations are far removed from the workplace, they inevitably have little or no direct role in managing people at work.

Human Resource Management

Many practitioners' job titles were changed in the 1980s; for instance, managers of industrial relations or personnel were retitled as 'director of human resources'. Often, such changes were merely cosmetic. Managerial behaviour has generally not kept pace with the terminology and rhetoric. However, students in this field also became less preoccupied with employers' associations, unions and other formal institutions, and turned their attention to the important role of corporate management (Purcell, 1983; Edwards, 1987). Thinking about management and industrial relations has been changing. It is now less influenced by labour history and institutional economics, and draws more on sociology, psychology and organizational behaviour.

Such influences are not new, but can be traced at least as far back as the First World War and the subsequent work of Elton Mayo and his colleagues (e.g. Roethlisberger and Dickson, 1939). Arguably, however, such social scientists were more concerned with human *relations*, rather than with the broader issues of managing people in organizations. The human resources approach is not just a passing fad. In 1981, the Harvard Business School introduced its first new compulsory course for a generation: human resource management (HRM). Harvard conceptualizes HRM as constituting four policy areas: employee influence, human resource flow, reward systems and work systems (Beer *et al.*, 1985). Taken alone, none of these areas is new. But, the general HRM approach can be contrasted with the three areas of the Institute of Personnel Management's (UK) syllabus: employee relations, employee resourcing, and employee development. As Guest (1987, p. 506) puts it: 'The difference which is apparent in, for example, the Harvard emphasis on reward and work systems becomes even greater when employee influence and employee relations are examined in more detail.' HRM embraces the whole range of recruiting, selecting, appraising, training, developing, educating, communicating with, rewarding, motivating, and retaining employees, together with such issues as incentives, quality of output and of working life, work restructuring, equal opportunities, health and safety, skill formation, team-working, flexibility, shaping the corporate culture and managing change.

The older-style industrial relations practitioners and personnel administrators are generally regarded as operational specialists, who engage in 'fire fighting – the imposition of short-term solutions on critical business situations' (Miller, 1987, p. 349). Such operational specialists are too rarely involved in formulating corporate strategies, but are asked merely to implement them and to settle the unanticipated disputes that arise. Industrial relations, then, is characterized by its critics as reactive and operational, or tactical. Typically, in the English-speaking countries, few companies have an executive director on their main board with responsibility for industrial relations (though in the UK they may have a non-executive director who keeps an eye on, say, industrial relations, personnel and administration).

By contrast, the advocates of HRM often add the adjectives proactive and strategic (e.g. Sparrow and Pettigrew, 1987). The HRM executive is seen as a board-level appointee who, ideally, plays an active role in formulating corporate strategies. Furthermore, those who follow the new HRM approach aim to work closely through, and with, line management. They characterize the old industrial relations practitioners as pragmatic 'staff specialists', who were often too distant from line management.

Of course, managing people in most large organizations still involves many elements of traditional industrial relations. But the gathering momentum towards HRM reflects several changes in the political and economic context. Recent governments in the USA, Britain and elsewhere have been seen as anti-union. This perception has been reinforced by their public policies and legislation, though this political context is arguably less significant than the economic one.

In the early 1980s, with increasing unemployment rates and decreasing inflation rates, union density and power were at a low ebb in many countries. Managements afforded formal industrial relations issues a lower priority than previously. In addition, increasing international competitiveness in *product markets* focused management's attention on the quality of output, on identifying market niches and on corporate restructuring, partly to deal with such market niches more directly, but also as a defence against aggressive corporate takeovers. Managements appeared to be gaining renewed confidence and assertiveness. This assertiveness was being displayed not only in marketing and in corporate takeovers, but also in relation to employees, unions and the management of change. HRM specialists thus tend to concern themselves with many more facets of people at work than traditional industrial relations specialists. The chapters in this book reflect the beginning of the movement towards this wider perspective, particularly those from North America.

From Industrial Relations towards HRM

Chapters 2 and 3 illustrate the current influence of HRM in North America. Interestingly, both these chapters touch on some of the same examples, but generally Kassalow writes from an institutional industrial relations/economics perspective, while Kochan and Tamir are more influenced by the HRM/organizational behaviour literature. Nevertheless, both chapters question whether traditional patterns of industrial relations and collective bargaining can deal effectively with issues arising from technological change. They highlight characteristics of the American approach, whereby management seeks to determine most basic decisions (including the introduction of new technology) possibly leaving unions to negotiate the impact of these decisions.

Kassalow cites several cases where unions and management have cooperated with the introduction of new technology. For many unions, this has been a defensive move, to preserve job security for their members; for the employers, it has often been a way of minimizing the degree of union resistance. The long-term impact of new technology on employment is yet to be seen, but Kassalow argues that collective bargaining is still a viable method of negotiating change. However, he also acknowledges that the North American approach to collective bargaining on a company or plant level (rather than the industry-wide approach of most of Western Europe) does make the unions more vulnerable when employers move to establish new non-union plants.

Kochan and Tamir seem less sure about the continuing viability of American-style collective bargaining. They argue that new technology is inducing unions to become involved in areas of decision-making that they previously saw as outside their domain. Furthermore, employers who provide a role for employee representatives at earlier stages of the decision-making process are more likely to respond more effectively to the increasingly rapid changes in the environment. The new Saturn division of General Motors, which was established (with union cooperation) to build a small car on a competitive basis in the USA, is cited in both of these chapters to illustrate a new approach to labour–management relations. Kochan and Tamir advocate that stronger links be forged between collective bargaining at the workplace or micro level, where the focus is on immediate on-the-job issues, and the national or macro level, where the emphasis is on policy issues such as economic growth and employment. They hold that if unions in the USA are to cope effectively with technological change, they will need to play a stronger role at the strategic level of decision-making.

The analytical framework used by Kochan and Tamir is derived from research on industrial relations and management conducted at the Massachusetts Institute of Technology (MIT). Their tentative model is a significant development from the Dunlop tradition (see Kochan *et al.*, 1987). They hypothesize that the outcomes associated with new technologies will depend on the interaction of changes in external markets, the political arena and employers' business strategies, which effect changes in the institutional structure of industrial relations. For the present book, with its international flavour, a key proposition is that national industrial relations systems that are less wedded to job-control unionism can more easily accommodate expanded union participation in strategic decision-making.

Dunlop's systems approach is less appropriate in the current context of rapid change. In the past, for example, banking, finance, education and most public sector enterprises were highly regulated in many countries; the managerial task was to organize and control stability and *continuity*, rather than change. In more dynamic segments of the economy, including some manufacturing industries, managing *change* has long been important. Organizations are increasingly exposed to change. Many cartels and monopolies are confronted by greater competition. This has been prompted by several forces, including the growth of international trade, changing patterns of protectionism, deregulation, privatization, energy shortages, and the accelerating pace of technological innovation. This last is often exploited most effectively by new small and medium enterprises (SMEs) finding novel markets (Roberts *et al.*, 1987). Thus, whether or not they use HRM terminology, most managers of people are increasingly concerned with planning and implementing technological and organizational change.

Unions and New Technology

Since the nineteenth century, unions have sought to exert some degree of control over technological change, through both collective bargaining and legislation. As unions tend to be defensive, often they appear to be suspicious about technological change. Many employers are opposed to unions participating in decisions about new technology. When unions are not consulted in advance but are merely confronted with a *fait accompli* about new technology, it is not surprising if their initial response is negative.

Where there have been serious industrial disputes about technological change, the conflicts have often involved traditional occupations which are threatened with extinction or at least a transformation, such as railway firemen, miners, dockers and printers. Thus, working with hot metal was the basis of the newspaper printers' old craft. The craft workers and their unions feared the prospect of extinction by the introduction of computerized typesetting, with direct keying by journalists (Martin, 1981). However, several newer occupations have also been involved in disputes about technological change, including computer staff, TV technicians, air traffic controllers and chemical workers. In such cases, the disputed issues include job security, economic rewards and the forms of control of the labour process.

Despite the media's focus on such industrial conflicts, complete resistance by unions to new technology is relatively uncommon; in recent years much new technology has been introduced, and most of it peacefully. Most technological innovations are not accompanied by industrial disputes (and are, therefore, less newsworthy). Only 7 per cent of a large British sample of managers of manufacturing establishments using new technologies reported opposition from the shopfloor or unions as a major difficulty (Northcott *et al.*, 1985, p. 37).

New Technology Agreements

In some European countries, unions have sought to challenge management's assumed prerogative of introducing technological change unilaterally. Unions representing white-collar staff have been especially active in promoting technology agreements (Evans, 1985). Accordingly, among the international trade secretariats (ITSs), the International Federation of Commercial, Clerical, Professional and Technical Employees (FIET) has played a leading role in coordinating unions' ideas for technology agreements. FIET has issued a model technology agreement (see the Appendix to this book). Where practicable in such agreements, the unions aim to cover both the procedural processes and substantive contents of the technology. The *procedural aspects* include provisions for joint regulation and reviews of technological change, information disclosure, technology representatives, access to outside expertise and the employers' research, monitoring personal data collection, and information for and consultation with employees. The *substantive aspects* include provisions for employment security, temporary and casual work and sub-contracting, redeployment and redundancy, job content and skills, job grading, pay and conditions, work environment, training, equal opportunities, and reductions in working time. Most of these concerns may arise from other issues besides technological change, but the perceived threats associated with microelectronics prompted many unions to review and update their earlier policies.

Such policies have inspired several hundred new technology agreements in Britain at local, company or, occasionally, industry level, mainly in relation to white-collar staff (Williams and Steward, 1985). In practice, most of the agreements fall far short of the particular union's policy or the FIET model; furthermore, the impact of these agreements has generally been marginal.

As cautioned earlier, much managerial rhetoric is not fully translated into action. Similarly, when examining union behaviour in relation to new technologies, it is important to distinguish between union *policies* and *behaviour*. Policies are often conceived in the rarified atmosphere of union congresses and reflect long-held ideological orientations, which are difficult to sustain in practice. Unions have rarely been able to translate such new technology policies into practice, for reasons associated with the employers as well as with the unions themselves (Dodgson and Martin, 1987).

First, employers' representatives have generally aimed to treat technological change incrementally, as merely another form of change. Therefore most employers in Britain have wished to avoid entering into special new technology agreements. Moreover, in the 1980s, the employers have generally had a strong position in the labour market. Some employers have been persuaded by worker representatives to sign a new technology agreement that reflects at least parts of the FIET-type model. (This has been most prevalent in the public services sector, where worker representatives may have more influence at higher levels than in the private sector.) However, such agreements have rarely been fully honoured. They have not prevented redundancies, subcontracting and deskilling, not least because employers invariably proceed to implement technological changes more or less autocratically. In consultations they argue that 'circumstances have changed since the original agreement was signed', and few union representatives have either the countervailing power or expertise to resist such arguments.

Second, the manual workers' unions in Britain have generally preferred to rely on workplace power, and on custom and practice, rather than on special new technology policies or agreements. Union thinking about new technology policies crystallized in the late 1970s and early 1980s. But these policies rarely distinguished between goals that were attainable and those that were not. In addition, although the technologies, economic context and other matters continue to change, few unions have revised their policies to accord with the circumstances of the late 1980s and early 1990s. This is partly because few unions continue to see new technology as a priority. In many countries, unions have been rather preoccupied with other issues (which may or may not be associated with technological change), including high levels of unemployment, declining levels of membership, inter-union conflict, hostile governments, and economic and industrial restructuring. Moreover, few unions have sufficient resources to continue to research and formulate policies about new technologies. This is especially the case in countries with fragmented and occupationally oriented union structures (like Britain, Australia and New Zealand).

In practice, unions facing technological change tend to respond pragmatically, without necessarily adhering to their own policies and agreements. However, we can classify union responses into five broad categories, which range from complete resistance to participative involvement.

1 *Complete resistance* by unions is rare and usually relatively short-lived, but may occur if the union leaders and members believe that the change will have unmitigated deleterious consequences for them and that these cannot be sufficiently ameliorated by negotiating or consulting with management. This position also implies that the union can exert some power in relation to the employers.

2 *Reluctant acquiescence* again means that employers make the decision, but present it to unions on a 'take it or leave it basis', implying that the stark alternative is unemployment. This has increasingly been the case during economic recession, when unions may not have enough power to oppose decisions successfully.

3 *Unconditional acceptance* also means that employers make the decisions unilaterally, but that they may then successfully 'sell' the change directly to employees and their unions. In spite of their leaders' policies, some workgroups may not want to participate in decision-making, but accept that 'employers should manage'. This position may be found with unskilled workers and in new establishments where there is no union with which to bargain or consult.

4 *Negotiated trade-offs* means that unions accept a technological change in exchange for certain trade-offs, with pay and conditions, for example.

5 *Participative involvement* occurs where unions positively welcome technological change, and have a real input into the fundamental decisions about choices and design at the formative stage. This rarely happens. In practice there is little or no union or workgroup involvement in making the formative decisions, which are made rather autocratically by managers and technical specialists (Bamber, 1988; for a similar approach to classifying union behaviour, see Francis and Willman, 1980).

These categories represent 'ideal types' and are designed to illustrate the range of different approaches. Any particular union response does not necessarily fall precisely into one category, but such ideal types can be helpful when analysing the variety of union responses.

Particular union responses are influenced by several considerations, including the management style (and the union perception of it), the union structure and government, the product and labour markets, the type of technological change and the stage of the innovation process (Slichter *et al.*, 1960; McLaughlin, 1979).

International Comparisons

Different types of union responses can be found in most countries, depending on the above-mentioned influences. Nevertheless, there are broad contrasts in the general approaches of unions in different countries. Where traditions are adversarial, as in most of the English-speaking countries, unions are more likely to oppose technological change than are their counterparts in West Germany, Austria and the Nordic countries. It is significant that unions in the English-speaking countries are the most wedded to job-control unionism (see the proposition by Kochan and Tamir in Chapter 3).

Social Partnerships and Accords

There have been conflicts about new printing technologies in many countries, including Australia, the USA, the UK, Canada, Sweden, Denmark and the Federal Republic of Germany. However, in the last three countries especially, the conflicts were eased by managements that seemed to give a high priority to HRM (without necessarily using this term). In particular, they engaged in advance consultation and retraining. These processes were facilitated by the presence of a relatively centralized and well-organized labour movement.

The term 'social partnership' is used to characterize many of the post-war industrial relations traditions in Germany, Austria and the Nordic countries. With industry unionism and strong central union confederations, the unions in such countries have generally been more successful in gaining influence in strategic decision-making about new technology at both the national and sectoral levels. However, influence on decisions at the corporate or plant level also requires strong union organization at the workplace, which is sometimes lacking in countries that have centralized industrial relations. In the Federal Republic, for example, attempts by unions to strengthen the role of the works councils at workplace level were thwarted in 1983 by a Federal Labour Tribunal, which ruled that works councils at Pan Am had no general right to co-determination on the layout of visual display units. This decision was reversed in a subsequent case when it was shown that the introduction of technology could be used to monitor employee performance and productivity. Nevertheless, unions cannot always count on favourable decisions by tribunals.

In the Federal Republic, the co-determination laws have not resulted in a profound shift of power from capital to labour, though they have affected employer behaviour. Managers have had to devote more time and resources to the process of consultation, to the issues of workers' skills, and to the quality of working life (see Chapter 4 in this book). Managers have to give even more attention to such issues and to consultative processes in Sweden, which is more of a social partnership than the Federal Republic (see Chapter 11 in this book).

The Swedish approach, in particular, has been adopted as a model for economic and social change by some key opinion leaders in the Australian labour movement. This was especially evident in the controversial report by the Australian Council of Trade Unions (ACTU), *Australia Reconstructed* (ACTU/TDC, 1987). The authors of the report were critical of the post-war British experience with incomes policies, social contracts and other corporatist policies, which were aborted by the 1978–9 'winter of discontent' and the consequent advent of Thatcherism. Instead, they looked to the Swedish labour movement for their inspiration.

As discussed by Davis and Lansbury in Chapter 5, in Australia the Labor government established an Accord with the union movement on economic and social policies (also see Lansbury, 1985). Although the Accord mainly focuses on wages and prices, it also includes several 'supportive policies' which promote consultation between the unions and the government, for instance on industrial development and technological change.

The Accord was the outcome of negotiations between the Australian Labor Party, while in opposition, and the ACTU, which represents approximately 90 per cent of Australian unionists. This Accord was a key issue in the election of the first (Hawke) Labor government in early 1983 and has been hailed as a new experiment in social contract bargaining (see Dunkley, 1984; Niland and Turner, 1985). Although far from permanent, the Accord's advent in 1983 had a significant influence on the way in which technological change and other issues have subsequently been addressed.

Following the Accord, the Hawke Labor government supported the Amalgamated Metal Workers' Union in an important test case on job security. As a result of the subsequent decision of the federal arbitration tribunal, protection from unfair dismissals was made available to unions covered by federal awards, notice of termination of employment has been extended and, if sought, severance pay increased. Furthermore, the consequent metal trades' award requires employers to consult with unions before making major changes in production, organization or technology.

The unions generally welcomed the award. It remains to be seen, however, to what extent the new rights to information, consultation and participation are implemented in the workplace. The extent to which unions are able to influence decisions about technological change and other matters is restricted by their lack of expertise and the limited scope for job regulation at the workplace, where most managers cling to their managerial prerogatives. In the Australian system of industrial relations, other unions may apply for similar awards. As yet, however, not all unions have sought to take advantage of the opportunity to have these provisions inserted in their awards.

Employee Participation

Technologies that place a premium on flexibility in the workplace put the stereotypical North American and British job-control unionism at risk, as employers aim to introduce new approaches to work organization. These approaches include quality circles (QCs) and other managerial techniques designed to foster employee involvement at the workplace.

Many employer-initiated schemes have been introduced to encourage greater employee involvement in task-related decision-making at the enterprise and workplace levels (Wilpert and Sorge, 1984). Employers' motives for introducing such initiatives include enhancing worker identification with corporate goals, facilitating the introduction of new technology, achieving greater flexibility in work organization and increasing productivity levels (Walton, 1985).

Few studies have focused on workers' perceptions of new technology, but the data in Chapter 6 provide some useful insights into worker attitudes towards QCs and other employee-involvement programmes in North America. Verma and Zerbe conclude that such programmes tend to enhance worker acceptance of new technology, but may also raise employees' expectations of influencing managerial decision-making, not least about technological change. To adopt these programmes successfully, managers will have to encourage genuine employee participation in decision-making. Many QCs and other employee-involvement programmes appear to wither away, precisely because they lack such genuine encouragement.

Cressey and Di Martino report in Chapter 7 on a series of cross-national research projects in Europe. They argue that a participatory approach towards technological change by both managers and employee representatives tends to elicit a higher degree of satisfaction by all those concerned. They add that regulatory legislation may not provide an adequate spur to participative management. Hence they explore alternative ways of fostering participative management. To some extent, their exploration is influenced by the socio-technical approach.

The Socio-technical Approach

The socio-technical approach to organizational analysis is derived from a wide range of work initiated by the Tavistock Institute of Human Relations (London), from Durham coal mines to Indian textile mills. A socio-technical system consists of two elements:

1 *technical factors:* mechanical equipment, technical processes and the physical environment;
2 *social factors:* the relationships amongst the work people and their individual and collective attitudes to it and to each other.

Although the socio-technical approach was published in the 1950s, relatively few managers in the English-speaking world seem to take its message into account when embarking on programmes of technological and/or organizational change. The message seems to have had more impact in Scandinavia. By contrast, more managers in the English-speaking world seem to invoke such books as *In Search of Excellence* (Peters and Waterman, 1982). This is ironic, given that such books are underpinned by less substantial research than the socio-technical approach, as discussed later.

How can 'social' objectives be incorporated into the design of a technical system? How can the development of a social system be provided for in a technical design? What is the importance of employee participation in the design process; and how early should different parties be involved? Such questions apply in general to the design of work organizations and the use of new technologies. They are considered by Graversen in Chapter 8, who draws on the socio-technical approach in a Danish study of the phases of the design and commissioning of a brewery that uses new technology.

With regard to the design of new organizations, Graversen identifies four different patterns:

1 Technical systems are designed without regard to social systems.
2 Objectives for, and the design of, social systems are separated from the design of technical systems.
3 Objectives for, and the design of, social systems are introduced after the design of technical systems.
4 Technical and social objectives and solutions are *integrated* in the design process.

In the Danish case, the management initially aimed to plan according to pattern 4. However, some aspects of their behaviour accorded with each of the other patterns instead.

Practitioners, as well as scholars, can learn a great deal from such studies, particularly if they are systematic and are of sectors or organizations that are similar to their own. Such studies can be facilitated by involving independent researchers, who are detached from the inevitably distorting prism of organizational politics (cf. Pettigrew, 1985).

Chapter 9 draws on French and British examples to argue that engineering solutions ('the technological fix') are often designed to maximize technological effectiveness, on the assumption that people, being almost infinitely adaptable, will make all the necessary adjustments to work with the technologies. Heller shows that such one-sided solutions can fail completely and advocates the socio-technical approach as appropriate for analysing the range of choices available when designing technologies.

The technological imperative tends to ignore the requirements of people and thereby usually fails to realize its full potential. The socio-technical approach implies an integrated solution rather than a compromise. Both the technical–economic system and the social system may operate at sub-optimum levels, but overall efficiency may be maximized by allowing the social as well as the technical factors to operate in coordinated harmony.

Although to some extent constrained by national and corporate cultures, managers still have considerable scope for choices, for instance about corporate strategies and management styles, organizational structures (including centralization or decentralization), the extent to which decision-making is participative, and how new technologies are introduced and maintained.

Alternative Perspectives

The early work of the Tavistock Institute was criticized, among other things, for sometimes confusing the distinct roles of consultancy and research, and for apparently ignoring the work of others in similar fields (Brown, 1967; Rose, 1975). Also, as is often the case with work from a primarily psychological frame of reference, it pays too little attention to unions, industrial conflict and industrial relations, and to the structure of the wider economy and society. Such criticisms are more applicable to the pioneers of the socio-technical approach than to later writers such as Graversen and Heller. Nevertheless it is worth examining two other approaches: the labour-process theorists, and those who search for excellence in a neo-human relations tradition.

A Labour-process Perspective

Braverman (1974) inspired a revival of interest in the labour process (cf. Marx and Engels, 1968). This is the management function which converts people's potential for work into productive work effort, under conditions that permit capital accumulation. Braverman's major criticism of the earlier scientific management approach (Taylor, 1964) is not of the technological imperative as such, but of the underlying drive for capital accumulation and control (Thompson, 1983, p. 73).

Since the mid-1970s there has been much debate about technological change and management from a labour-process perspective (e.g. Wood, 1982; Storey, 1983; Knights *et al.*, 1985; Blackburn *et al.*, 1985 – though this last work prefers the term production process rather than labour process). Such research has made an important contribution by directing attention to managerial strategies and the importance of skills. Braverman and some of his followers, however, tend to regard new technology as inevitably causing deskilling and the degradation of work. They appear to assume that managers invariably follow a technological imperative, use scientific management principles and give the utmost priority to maximizing the control of labour.

Some have criticized Braverman for underestimating the potential for worker resistance, for union action and even for worker control of some aspects of labour regulation (Batstone *et al.*, 1987, pp. 19ff). Others have argued that most of those following his approach have concentrated too narrowly on the point of production and exaggerated the pervasiveness, coherence and conspiratorial nature of management. In reality, business strategy specialists tend to focus on finance, marketing, research, production and corporate structures, while neglecting industrial relations, human resources and the labour process. Despite the legacy of scientific management and the current advocacy of HRM, much managerial behaviour can still be characterized as unscientific, tactical and opportunist. Rather than having a coherent strategy, management seems rife with ad hocery, office politics, internal conflicts, functional rivalries and personal clashes (Dalton, 1959; Hyman, 1987). Notwithstanding the growing number of textbooks on strategic HRM (e.g. Heneman *et al.*, 1986), most managements do not appear to have a consistent *strategy* for controlling human resources and their industrial relationships.

It may be true that the principal reason for introducing new technology during the early stages of assembly-line manufacturing was to reduce direct labour costs through economies of scale and standardization of production. In the more advanced stages, however, the main objective for introducing technological change in manufacturing is to achieve greater quality and flexibility in the production process, through the use of innovations such as computer-aided design, computer-aided manufacturing (CAD/CAM) and robotics. Although most managements aim to achieve consistent profitability and thereby retain the goal of minimizing labour costs, increasing emphasis is being given to customizing products and achieving fast reactions, in terms of changes in specification, delivery times and so on (Rojot, 1988).

When deciding about new technologies, most companies are primarily concerned with achieving greater control over production processes, improved product quality, and cost reduction (Northcott *et al.*, 1985). Labour processes, human resources and industrial relations are invariably of secondary importance and are often considered only in the implementation stage, rather than initially when making high-level corporate decisions about technological innovation.

More recent writing on the labour process has taken account of such criticisms and aims to adopt a more sophisticated view of managerial strategy. Some writers have moved away from a narrow focus on the point of production towards a wider political economy of work relations (e.g. Bray and Taylor, 1986; Littler, 1987).

One merit of the labour-process approach is that it does provide a clear analytical framework, but such a radical analysis has little appeal for practitioners and most of those conducting applied research on new technologies. Consequently, the labour-process approach has not yet had much direct impact on the way new technologies are introduced in practice.

A Neo-human Relations Approach

Despite the growing volume of literature on socio-technical systems and on the labour process, many American managers, in particular, have been impressed by such popular books as *In Search of Excellence* (Peters and Waterman, 1982). Several of its prescriptions are consistent with elements of the human relations school of the 1950s, as popularized by writers such as McGregor (1960), but following the traditions of Mayo and others. Peters and Waterman do not formulate a new behavioural model, but include a series of rather facile prescriptions, apparently based on their observation of America's most successful companies. They recommend, for example, that employees should be trusted:

> Treat people as adults. Treat them as partners; treat them with dignity; treat them with respect. Treat *them* – not capital

> spending and automation – as the primary source of productivity gains. These are the fundamental lessons from the excellent companies research. In other words, if you want productivity and the financial success that goes with it, you must treat your workers as your most important asset. (Peters and Waterman, 1982, p. 238; emphasis in original)

The excellence prescriptions have a fashionable appeal, not least because they are built on simple maxims. The other well-known ones include phrases that have been absorbed quickly into the management language: 'loose–tight organizations', 'stick to the knitting', 'close to the customer', 'bias for action', and so on.

Peters (1987) later tried to distance himself from such apparently simple formulas, by arguing that the world was changing too quickly for them to have universal application – an echo of Burns and Stalker's (1961) analysis of organic organizational structures. Hence Peters concluded that 'there are no excellent companies', yet went on to list forty-five breathtaking prescriptions for companies to follow in their quest for success.

Although their book has also been a best-seller internationally, outside the USA many scholars regard the remedies of Peters and Waterman as inapplicable, on the grounds that they are too prescriptive and too American. Even within the USA, the management issues for such renowned 'excellent' companies as McDonalds and Walt Disney Productions in the private service sector are very different from many of those confronting most managers in the public sector, mining or manufacturing. Within manufacturing, the issues differ greatly, for example, depending on the technologies, methods of production and the type of business strategy. Even within the private service sector, business strategies may range from concentration on specialist market niches with emphasis on high quality (and high pay) as the basis for a competitive advantage, to a concentration on mass markets with an emphasis on the quantity of low-cost output (and low pay), which gives a fundamentally different competitive advantage (as discussed by Kochan and Tamir in Chapter 3).

In Search of Excellence has inspired similar studies in Britain (Goldsmith and Clutterbuck, 1984), in Australia (Limerick *et al.*, 1984), in New Zealand (Inkson *et al.*, 1986) and elsewhere. Serious international and comparative research, however, reinforces the view that there are no universally applicable prescriptions for success, or for handling technological change (or for any other element of management). The most effective managers draw selectively on others' research and experiences, analyse their own national and corporate cultures and constraints, diagnose the opportunities and problems that they face, then devise the policies and practices that are most appropriate in their precise circumstances. This is the 'contingency approach' (Child, 1984), which is more demanding than buying 'off-the-shelf' prescriptions. For most managers, however, such an approach is more likely to be successful in the longer term. An important aspect is that those who are involved in conducting their own investigations and devising their own solutions tend to feel a sense of ownership and to be committed to their success.

Despite the common perception that they prescribe one-best-way to achieve excellence, Peters and Waterman themselves criticize the rational one-best-way scientific management approach (cf. Kelly, 1982). Yet their own work appears to advocate a highly prescriptive approach to the management of people. A combination of the socio-technical approach with a sophisticated approach to labour-process theory is likely to yield more useful insights into technological change, industrial relations and HRM.

Gender, Structural Change, Skills and Labour Market Segmentation

There are several areas of concern about women and new technologies. First, in Britain, there is a debate about the lack of women engineers (e.g. EITB, 1983). Second, there is concern about the effects of new technologies on domestic work (Schwartz, 1983). Third, and most importantly in the present context, there is concern about whether women tend to benefit or suffer as a consequence of structural or technological change, both in terms of redundancy and employment opportunities (SPRU, 1982; Martin and Wallace, 1984), and in terms of work organization and the labour process (Cockburn, 1986). In spite of such concerns, the implications of new office technology for a predominantly female workforce have been accorded relatively little attention, compared with all the studies of technological change in manufacturing, which have focused mainly on male workers.

Chapter 10 emphasizes that new technology can have a more or less beneficial effect on employment, skills and work organization, depending on how it is introduced, the speed of diffusion and its economic context. Greve observes that in many developed market economies women are proportionally over-represented in less-skilled, lower-paid segments of the service sector, parts of which are currently being transformed by microelectronics. Although this does not mean that women necessarily lose their jobs as a result of technological change, they are invariably required to adjust to changes that are introduced by (predominantly male) managers, with little or no consultation. Greve also emphasizes the impact of new office equipment on the structure of work traditionally performed by many women.

Restructuring, Education and Training

Chapter 11 offers an unusual union perspective on economic restructuring. When explaining the decline in importance of the agricultural sector as a major employer, for instance, Bäckström argues that 'restructuring of the workforce has occurred as a result of the children choosing different jobs from their parents' (i.e. the *supply* of labour). We would explain the structural change illustrated in Table 11.1 in terms of changing patterns of international trade and the shifting *demand* for labour rather than in terms of changing preferences by potential employees, who 'have chosen better-paid, indoor occupations, sheltered from wind and weather . . .'.

Notwithstanding the variety of possible explanations, Bäckström's analysis is valuable in showing that Swedish unions have consistently urged governments to give stronger support for technological development. He explains that the Swedish unions generally exercise a strong influence in the formulation of economic and technological policies. Any employment consequences arising from technological change have been dealt with by social and labour market measures; this has included retraining workers for alternative jobs. But if governments were to accord a lower priority to full employment as a political goal and if the influence by unions on decision-making was reduced, unions in

Sweden would be much more likely to resist new technology. While Bäckström concedes that many individuals fear that computerization may lead to greater unemployment and a loss of control by the individual at work, he argues that such fears reflect lack of experience of, and ignorance about, technological change.

At an international level, competition has intensified in the production of manufactured goods, partly as the result of prolonged periods of economic recession and partly because of the emergence of strong producers from the newly industrialized economies, especially in South-East Asia. Using new technology is one of the means by which many companies attempt to gain a competitive edge. It has also been associated with the international restructuring of key industries such as steel, vehicle building, electronics and clothing, whereby Taiwan, South Korea, Hong Kong and Singapore have industrialized and Japan has further strengthened its position. As Kuwahara (1988) observes, much of Japan's economic success has depended upon the development of new products in high-technology industries, such as electronic machinery and precision instruments, to offset 'jobless growth' in manufacturing. In Japan (and Sweden and the Federal Republic), alongside the widespread use of new technologies, substantial resources have been devoted to maximizing the skill formation of those people working with these technologies.

Against this background, Sarfati and Cove (Chapter 12) illustrate the extent of the challenges faced by managers, governments, unions and those who provide education and training in new skills. Following their review of a wide range of international evidence, they conclude that the traditional approaches are no longer appropriate, whether in managing people and industrial relations, or in education, training and other aspects of HRM. This conclusion echoes those of many of the earlier chapters.

Flexibility

Flexibility is a theme that emerges in several chapters and has been discussed repeatedly at the International Labour Organisation and in many other international arenas. Atkinson (1985) distinguishes between three types of flexibility that he sees as increasingly apparent in employing organizations.

1 *Numerical flexibility* refers to the number of workers who are employed to meet fluctuations in the level of demand.
2 *Functional flexibility* is achieved where the tasks performed by workers can be adjusted by multiskilling, for instance, which may help to reduce labour costs and the number of demarcation disputes.
3 *Financial flexibility* occurs where the level of pay reflects performance, so pay is raised or lowered in accordance with productivity, profitability or some other indicator.

As shown in Figure 1.1, Atkinson argues that 'the flexible firm' tends to divide its labour force into two categories. In the centre of such organizations, there is a small and numerically stable core

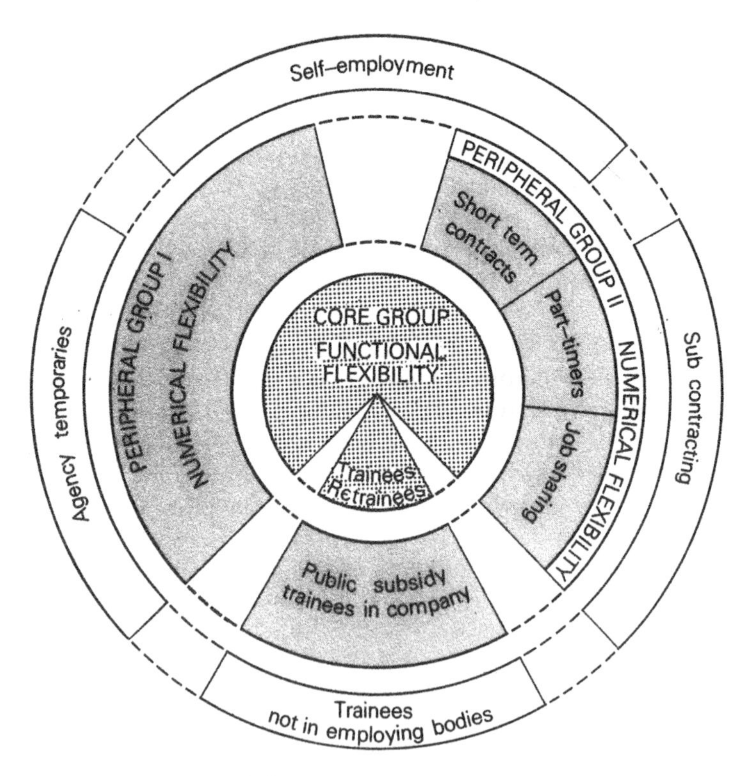

Figure 1.1 *The flexible firm*
Source: Atkinson, 1985 (reproduced with the permission of the Institute of Manpower Studies).

group of employees who are involved in the organization's key activities and who enjoy a high degree of training, job security and other benefits. By contrast, around its periphery, there is a larger and fluctuating number of workers who are not employed on a permanent basis, but are hired on a variety of part-time, temporary or sub-contract arrangements. Such flexible firms are thus dividing their demand for labour into fixed and variable components.

This model of 'the flexible firm' has been influential in the debates about flexibility during the 1980s. However, such managerial concern with labour flexibility is not new. It was a main aim of those who initiated productivity bargaining in the 1960s (McKersie and Hunter, 1973) and labour market segmentation was analysed by the dual labour market theorists (Doeringer and Piore, 1971). Many have inferred from Atkinson's work that segmentation of the labour market has become a significant managerial strategy.

This inference has been criticized, however (e.g. by MacInnes, 1987; Pollert, 1987; Industrial Relations Services, 1988). Pollert analyses evidence on temporary and part-time work, self-employment, sub-contracting and homeworking. In some cases she re-examines the evidence used by Atkinson (Institute of Manpower Studies, 1986). Pollert holds that such developments cannot be explained as a deliberate managerial strategy to create an employment periphery, except in the public sector (though Atkinson himself applies the model to the private sector). In the private sector, according to Pollert, the expansion of insecure and irregular employment can be explained by sectoral shifts in the structure of employment, cost-cutting, general rationalization and the difficulty many employers face in recruiting some types of skilled labour on a permanent basis. She finds little evidence of widespread moves towards functional flexibility or employment security of a core workforce. Hence she concludes that Atkinson's model should be abandoned in favour of a 'clear, historically informed sectoral analysis [which] . . . does not attempt to force the uneven and complex nature of the evidence into a simple mould' (Pollert, 1987).

In spite of such criticisms, several observers use the model in their discussions of current changes in the labour market. Moreover, there is little doubt that, when introducing new technologies, many employers are seizing opportunities to segment their workforce. It is increasingly feasible to locate elements of the periphery at some distance from the organization's centre. Being linked by electronic computer networks, sub-contractors may work at their own homes on a casual rather than a permanent basis. The spread of such 'telework', however, is generally still over the horizon.

Nevertheless, a continuing polarization seems likely between those employed at the core and those on the periphery. Core employees tend to have *careers* in large firms and to be the beneficiaries of new technologies (which they themselves control). The peripheral groups have *jobs* (not careers), often as sub-contractors, and technological change is less likely to be beneficial for them (especially as they generally have no control and little influence over the design and use of the technologies, and are less likely to be organized by unions).

Working Time

Debates about flexibility and new technologies are linked with the debates about working time (cf. Blyton, 1985). The West German unions have been campaigning for shorter working hours. This campaign was largely an attempt to counter the growth in unemployment. Following a major industrial dispute in 1984 in the metal industry, the unions won a reduction in basic working hours from 40 to 38.5 hours per week. In exchange, however, the employers won the right to vary working hours locally to suit their production schedules. Thus, under the 1984 agreement, there had to be an *average* of 38.5 hours per week, but this could include some workers say on 35 hours, with others on 40 hours.

Elsewhere in Europe, employers have been seeking to use technological change as a means of achieving greater flexibility in the broader labour market, as well as at the micro level. In the 1984 national wage negotiations in France, the French Employers' Federation sought to trade off a reduction in working hours for greater labour market flexibility. In 1987, the British Engineering Employers' Federation made a similar proposal. These employer initiatives were rejected by the unions in both countries. None the less, employers are increasingly making such proposals, which, against a background of continuing technological change, are of growing importance.

Conclusion

This chapter has introduced the main issues which will emerge in the chapters that follow, in terms of some key concepts and several analytical approaches. Technological change will continue to be a major issue for students and practitioners of industrial relations and HRM. Many of the older industrial societies are experiencing difficulties competing with the newly industrialized countries, which are making extensive use of new technology and have less institutionalized labour markets and less independent union power. The microelectronic revolution is also having a severe effect on the employment prospects of particular groups within the labour force who lack the education and skills to take advantage of new job opportunities. The unpredictable rate of change has made it difficult for governments to anticipate and adapt to the new circumstances. Moreover, many contemporary governments shy away from such planning, following an ideological preference for market forces (Dror, 1986).

In general, employers have been reluctant to involve their employees or unions in making fundamental decisions about technological change on the grounds that such decisions are management prerogatives. In some countries, legislation has established basic rights for employees and their unions to be consulted about the proposed introduction of new technologies. A combination of collective agreements and legislation has also been used to provide minimum compensation for workers who lose their jobs. Nevertheless, the combined effects of economic restructuring and declining levels of unionization in many countries have reduced the degree of influence wielded by unions on technological change and other issues.

Can traditional forms of collective bargining deal effectively with complex issues such as the introduction of new technology? In their pursuit of a more flexible labour market, employers and governments in many countries are seeking to move away from centralized bargaining systems towards more decentralized and enterprise-based approaches. This has been combined, in some cases, with employer-initiated schemes that encourage greater employee involvement in decision-making, albeit the degree of involvement is invariably rather limited.

Many employers have used new technologies not only to reduce costs and increase their competitiveness, but also to achieve a greater degree of flexibility in production processes and the organization of work. Such employers seek to use new technologies and to adjust the quantity, quality and pay of their labour force to match levels of demand, but generally offer little or no scope for employees to exert collective influence on such decisions. If unions are to maintain their relevance, they will need to develop alternative strategies on technological change and to mobilize the support of the workforce. Furthermore, they may increasingly resort to the political arena, to demand that governments legislate to protect the interests of employees who feel threatened by the introduction of new technologies.

Acknowledgements

We are grateful to several colleagues for helpful comments on an earlier draft of this chapter, including Oliver Clarke, Chris Leggett, Mick Marchington and Ed Snape.

References

ACTU/TDC (1987), *Australia Reconstructed: ACTU/TDC Mission to Western Europe – A Report by the Mission Members to the Australian Council of Trade Unions and the Trade Development Council* (Canberra: Australian Government Publishing Service).

Atkinson, J. (1985), 'Flexibility: planning for an uncertain future', *Manpower Policy and Practice* (Journal of the Institute of Manpower Studies), vol. 1 (Summer), pp. 25–30.

Bain, G. S. and Clegg, H. A. (1974), 'A strategy of industrial relations research in Great Britain', *British Journal of Industrial Relations*, vol. 12, no. 1 (March), pp. 91–113.

Bamber, G. J. (1988), 'Unions and new technology', in R. Hyman and W. Streeck (eds), *New Technology and Industrial Relations* (Oxford: Blackwell), pp. 204–19.

Bamber, G. J. and Lansbury, R. D. (1988), 'Management strategy and new technology', *Journal of Management Studies*, vol. 25, no. 3 (May), pp. 197–216.

Batstone, E., Gourlay, S., Levie, H. and Moore, R. (1987), *New Technology and the Process of Labour Regulation* (Oxford: Oxford University Press).

Beer, M., Spector, B., Lawrence, P. R., Mills, D. Q. and Walton, R. E.

(eds) (1985), *Human Resource Management: A General Manager's Perspective – Text and Cases* (New York: Free Press).
Blackburn, P., Coombs, R. and Green, K. (1985), *Technology, Economic Growth and the Labour Process* (London: Macmillan).
Blyton, P. (1985), *Changes in Working Time: An International Review* (London: Croom Helm).
Braverman, H. (1974), *Labor and Monopoly Capital: The Degradation of Work in the Twentieth Century* (New York: Monthly Review Press).
Bray, M., and Taylor, V. (1986), *Managing Labour?* (Sydney: McGraw-Hill).
Brown, R. K. (1967), 'Research and consultancy in industrial enterprises', *Sociology*, vol. 1, no. 1, pp. 33–60.
Burns, T. and Stalker, G. M. (1961), *The Management of Innovation* (London: Tavistock).
Child, J. (1984), *Organization: A Guide to Problems and Practice* (London: Harper & Row, 2nd edn).
CITCA (1980), *Technological Change in Australia, Volume 1, Technological Change and Its Consequences*, Report of the Committee of Inquiry into Technological Change in Australia (Canberra: Australian Government Publishing Service).
Cockburn, C. (1986), 'Women and technology: opportunity is not enough', in K. Purcell *et al.* (eds) (1986), pp. 173–87.
Commons, J. R. (1910), *A Documentary History of American Industrial Society* (Cleveland, Ohio: Clark).
Commonwealth Secretariat (1985), *Technological Change: Enhancing the Benefits*, Vol. II (London: Report of a Commonwealth Working Group).
Dalton, M. (1959), *Men Who Manage* (New York: Wiley).
Davis, E. M. and Lansbury, R. D. (eds) (1986), *Democracy and Control in the Work Place* (Melbourne: Longman Cheshire).
Dodgson, M., and Martin, R. (1987), 'Trade union policies on new technology: facing the challenge of the 1980s', *New Technology, Work and Employment*, vol. 2, no. 1 (Spring), pp. 9–18.
Doeringer, P. and Piore, M. (1971), *Internal Labor Markets and Manpower Analysis* (Lexington, Mass.: Heath).
Dror, D. (1986), 'Industrial relations implications of government policies towards technological change', paper presented to the Seventh World Congress of the IIRA (Geneva: International Industrial Relations Association).
Dunkley, G. (1984), 'Can Australia learn from Austria about incomes policies?', *Journal of Industrial Relations*, vol. 27, no. 3, pp. 365–84.
Dunlop, J. T. (1958), *Industrial Relations Systems* (Carbondale, Ill.: Southern Illinois University Press).
Edwards, P. K. (1987), *Managing the Factory: A Survey of General Managers* (Oxford: Blackwell).
EITB (1983), *Insight: A Review of the Programme to Encourage More Girls to become Professional Engineers* (Watford: Engineering Industry Training Board).
Evans, J. (1985), 'A consultant's note on new technology agreements', in Commonwealth Secretariat (1985), pp. 92–6.

Flanders, A. (1965), *Industrial Relations – What is Wrong with the System?* (London: Faber).

Francis, A. and Willman, P. (1980), 'Microprocessors: impact and response', *Personal Review*, vol. 9, no. 2 (Spring), pp. 9–16.

Gill, C. (1985), Editorial of a special issue on the impact of new technology on work and employment, *Industrial Relations Journal*, vol. 16, no. 2, pp. 5–8.

Gladstone, A. *et al.* (eds) (1988), *Current Issues in Labour Relations: An International Perspective* (Berlin: de Gruyter).

Goldsmith, W. and Clutterbuck, D. (1984), *The Winning Streak: Britain's Top Companies Reveal their Formulas for Success* (London: Weidenfeld & Nicholson).

Gospel, H. F. (1974), 'Employers' organizations: their growth and function in the British system of industrial relations', PhD thesis, University of London.

Guest, D. E. (1987), 'Human resource management and industrial relations', *Journal of Management Studies*, vol. 24, no. 5 (September), pp. 503–21.

Heneman, H. G., Schwab, D. P., Fossum, J. A. and Dyer, L. D. (1986), *Personnel/Human Resource Management* (Homewood, Ill.: Irwin).

Hince, K. and Williams, A. (eds) (1987), *Contemporary Industrial Relations in Australia and New Zealand: Literature Surveys*, Proceedings of the Biennial Conference of the Association of Industrial Relations Academics of Australia and New Zealand (Wellington: Association of Industrial Relations Academics of Australia and New Zealand, and the Industrial Relations Centre, Victoria University).

Hyman, R. (1975), *Industrial Relations: A Marxist Introduction* (London: Macmillan).

Hyman, R. (1987), 'Strategy or structure? Capital, labour and control', *Work, Employment and Society*, vol. 1, no. 1 (March), pp. 25–55.

Industrial Relations Services (1988), 'Is numerical flexibility on the increase?' *Industrial Relations Review and Report*, no. 410, pp. 12–13.

Inkson, K., Henshall, B., Marsh, N. and Ellis, G. (1986), *Theory K: The Key to Excellence in New Zealand Management* (Auckland: Bateman).

Institute of Manpower Studies (1986), *Changing Working Patterns: How Companies Achieve Flexibility to Meet New Needs* (London: National Economic Development Office).

Kelly, J. E. (1982), *Scientific Management: Job Redesign and Work Performance* (London: Academic Press).

Knights, D., Willmott, H. and Collinson, D. (eds) (1985), *Job Redesign: Critical Perspectives on the Labour Process* (Aldershot: Gower).

Kochan, T. A. (1980), *Collective Bargaining and Industrial Relations: From Theory to Policy and Practice* (Homewood, Ill.: Irwin).

Kochan, T. A., Katz, H. C. and McKersie, R. B. (1987), *The Transformation of American Industrial Relations* (New York: Basic Books).

Kuwahara, Y. (1988), 'New technology in the context of structural change', in A. Gladstone *et al.* (1988).

Lansbury, R. D. (1985), 'The Accord between the unions and the government in Australia: a new experiment in industrial relations?', *Labour and Society*, vol. 10, no. 2, pp. 223–35.

Limerick, D., Cunnington, B. and Trevor-Roberts, B. (1984), *Frontiers of Excellence* (Brisbane: Australian Institute of Management Queensland).

Littler, C. (1987), 'Labour process literature: a review 1974–1986', in K. Hince and A. Williams (1987), pp. 57–100.

McGregor, D. (1960), *The Human Side of Enterprise* (New York: McGraw Hill).

MacInnes, J. (1987), 'The question of flexibility', Research Paper no. 5, Department of Social and Economic Research (Glasgow: University of Glasgow).

McKersie, R. and Hunter, L. (1973), *Pay, Productivity and Collective Bargaining* (London: Macmillan).

McLaughlin, D. B. (1979), *The Impact of Labor Unions on the Rate and Direction of Technological Innovation* (Washington: National Technical Information Service PB 295 084).

Margerison, C. F. (1969), 'What do we mean by industrial relations? A behavioural science approach', *British Journal of Industrial Relations*, vol. 7, no. 2 (July), pp. 273–86.

Martin, R. (1981), *New Technology and Industrial Relations in Fleet Street* (Oxford: Oxford University Press).

Martin, R. and Wallace, J. (1985), *Working Women in Recession: Employment, Redundancy and Unemployment* (Oxford: Oxford University Press).

Marx, K. and Engels, F. (1968), *Selected Works* (London: Lawrence & Wishart).

Miller, P. (1987), 'Strategic industrial relations and human resource management – distinction, definition and recognition', *Journal of Management Studies*, vol. 24, no. 4 (July), pp. 347–61.

Mills, C. Wright (1959), *The Sociological Imagination* (New York: Oxford University Press).

Niland, J. and Turner, D. (1985), *Control, Consensus or Chaos? Managers and Industrial Relations Reform* (Sydney: Allen & Unwin).

Northcott, J., with Rogers, P., Knetsch, W. and de Lestapis, B. (1985), *Microelectronics in Industry, An International Comparison: Britain, Germany, France* (London: Policy Studies Institute).

Palmer, G. (1983), *British Industrial Relations* (London: Allen & Unwin).

Parsons, T. and Smelser, N. J. (1956), *Economy and Society: A Study in the Integration of Economy and Social Theory* (London: Routledge & Kegan Paul).

Peters, T. J. (1987), *Thriving on Chaos: Handbook for a Management Revolution* (New York: Alfred Knopf).

Peters, T. J. and Waterman, R. H. (1982), *In Search of Excellence: Lessons from America's Best-Run Companies* (New York: Harper & Row).

Pettigrew, A. (1985), *The Awakening Giant: Continuity and Change in Imperial Chemical Industries* (Oxford: Blackwell).

Plowman, D. H. (1986), 'Compulsory arbitration and national employer co-ordination 1890–1980', PhD thesis, Flinders University of South Australia.

Pollert, A. (1987), *The 'Flexible Firm': A Model in Search of Reality (or A*

Policy in Search of a Practice)? Warwick Papers in Industrial Relations no. 19 (Coventry: University of Warwick).

Purcell, J. (1983), 'The management of industrial relations in the modern corporation: an agenda for research', *British Journal of Industrial Relations*, vol. 21, no. 1, pp. 1–16.

Purcell, K., Wood, S., Waton, A. and Allen, S. (eds) (1986), *The Changing Experience of Employment: Restructuring and Recession* (London: Macmillan).

Roberts, I., Sawbridge, D. and Bamber, G. J. (1987), 'Employee relations in small and medium-sized enterprises', in B. Towers (ed.), *A Handbook of Industrial Relations Practice: Practice and Law in the Employer Relationship* (London: Kogan Page), pp. 199–218.

Roethlisberger, F. J. and Dickson, W. J. (1939), *Management and the Worker* (Cambridge, Mass.: Harvard University Press).

Rojot, J. (1988), 'Employers' responses to technological change', in A. Gladstone *et al.* (eds) (1988).

Rose, M. (1975), *Industrial Behaviour: Theoretical Development since Taylor* (Harmondsworth: Penguin).

Schwartz, R. Cowan (1983), *More Work for Mother* (New York: Basic Books).

Sisson, K. F. (1987), *The Management of Collective Bargaining: An International Comparison* (Oxford: Blackwell).

Slichter, S. H., Healy, J. J. and Livernash, R. (1960), *The Impact of Collective Bargaining on Management* (Washington DC: The Brookings Institution.

Sparrow, P. R. and Pettigrew, A. M. (1987), 'Strategic human resource management in the UK computer supplier industry', Working Paper (Coventry: Centre for Corporate Strategy and Change, University of Warwick).

SPRU (1982), *Micro-electronics and Women's Employment in Britain*, A Report to the Department of Employment and the Manpower Services Commission (Brighton: Science Policy Research Unit, University of Sussex).

Stoneman, P. (1983), *The Economic Analysis of Technological Change* (Oxford: Oxford University Press).

Storey, J. (1983), 'After Japan/after Braverman: a consideration of management control, management science and social science', Occasional Paper 3 (Nottingham: Trent Business School).

Taylor, F. W. (1964), *Scientific Management* (New York: Harper & Row).

Thompson, P. (1983), *The Nature of Work: An Introduction to Debates on the Labour Process* (London: Macmillan).

Walton, R. E. (1985), 'From control to commitment in the work place', *Harvard Business Review*, vol. 64, no. 2, pp. 76–84.

Webb, S. and Webb, B., (1897), *Industrial Democracy* (London: Longman).

Williams, R. and Steward, F. (1985), 'New technology agreements: an assessment', *Industrial Relations Journal*, vol. 16, no. 3, pp. 58–73.

Wilpert, B. and Sorge, A. (eds) (1984), *International Perspectives on Organizational Democracy* (London: Wiley).

Windmuller, J. P. (1984), 'Empoyers associations in comparative perspective: organization, structure, administration', in J. P. Windmuller and A. Gladstone (eds), *Employers Associations and Industrial Relations: A Comparative Study* (Oxford: Oxford University Press) pp. 1–23.

Wood, S. (ed.) (1982), *The Degradation of Work: Skill, Deskilling and the Labour Process* (London: Hutchinson).

II

From Industrial Relations towards Human Resource Management

New Technology: International Perspectives on Human Resources and Industrial Relations, Unwin Hyman, London.

CHAPTER TWO

Technological Change: American Unions and Employers in a New Era

EVERETT M. KASSALOW

The problem of handling technological change in collective bargaining is an old one for unions and employers. However, this chapter concentrates on some of the newer trends in the response of unions and employers to technological change. The chapter first sketches the impact of the new technology on jobs, employment and work, and the general reaction of US unions. It then turns to specific changes in collective bargaining which have resulted from this new wave of technological change.

Viewing the impact of recent and prospective technological change upon the US economy and the labour market, the principal US labour confederation, the American Federation of Labor–Congress of Industrial Organizations (AFL–CIO), has concluded that 'The United States – indeed every industrialized nation – is undergoing a scientific, technological, economic revolution every bit as significant as the industrial revolution of the nineteenth century'. The AFL–CIO has established a new standing committee, one of whose tasks is to help remodel its policies and outlook to meet the challenge of this revolution (AFL–CIO, 1985, p. 6).

This new wave of technological change is having a powerful influence on the world of employment and work. In combination with other economic forces, it continues to reduce the share of employment devoted to goods production, while expanding the service sector. This translates into more white-collar employees and a declining proportion of blue collars (or manual workers). In manufacturing, for example, the share of manual operatives fell from 80 per cent in 1960 to 68 per cent in 1982. The white-collar manufacturing force rose from 20 per cent to 32 per cent.

As a result of technological and related change, among the white-collar groups in manufacturing the employment prospects for engineers and technicians appear to be particularly strong. Indeed, for technicians the outlook seems outstanding. One forecast suggests that as computers take over more operations in factories and 'equipment interfaces . . . solve some of the problems of applications engineering', sooner or later there may be 'some substitution of technician jobs for engineering jobs'. It concludes that technicians 'are the new skilled workers of the economy' (Office of Technology Assessment, 1984, p. 122).

Beyond manufacturing, forecasters see a continuing growth in the share of the service sector in the US economy. Goods production employment has fallen steadily in post-war America to around 25 per cent of overall employment, and the combined effects of technology and shifts in consumer taste promise to extend this trend.

The nature of work itself is changing under the impact of some of the new technology. As one writer recently put it, earlier technological change 'saw machines replacing manual labour and human manipulations', with the worker shifting roles to 'an emphasis on controlling the apparatus to perform its function'. However, 'the new era is typified by artificial intelligence built around the computer', which is replacing many human operations 'by permitting an infinite number of functions to be carried on with no direct human intervention' (Fischer, 1985, p. 1).

All of this has great repercussions on labour and management attitudes and relations. However, we must recognize that it does not mean that overnight, or even in a decade, millions of employees will be transformed into high-tech, computer specialists of one type or another. A recent report of the US Bureau of Labor Statistics (BLS), for instance, projects on the one hand that computer programmers, computer systems analysts, data processing equipment repairers and computer operators will be among the fastest-growing occupations in the next decade; but in *absolute* numbers more mundane service occupations like those of cashier, janitor, truck driver, waiter and waitress will each add almost twice as many jobs as almost any of these high-tech positions (see Table 2.1).

Table 2.1 *Occupations with largest and fastest projected employment growth, USA, 1984–95*

Occupation	*Employment growth ('000s)*	*% growth 1984–95*
Largest job growth 1984–95		
Cashiers	556	29.8
Registered nurses	452	32.8
Janitors and cleaners	443	15.1
Truck drivers	428	17.2
Waiters and waitresses	424	26.1
Wholesale trade sales persons	369	29.6
Nursing aides, orderlies, etc.	348	28.9
Sales persons, retail	343	12.6
Fastest job growth 1984–95		
Paralegal personnel	51	97.5
Computer programmers	245	71.7
Computer systems analysts (EDP)	212	68.7
Medical assistants	79	62.0
Data processing equipment repairers	28	56.2
Electrical & electronic engineers	206	52.8
Electrical & electronic technicians & engineers	202	50.7
Computer operators	111	46.7

Source: US Bureau of Labor Statistics, *Monthly Labor Review*, November 1985.

The prospect for the growth of an enormous number of low-paid service workers deeply troubles the AFL–CIO. It fears that computers and robots will take over 'more and more functions in the workforce' and there is the likelihood of the creation of a 'two-tier workforce'. This would be a job structure of relatively 'few executives, scientists, engineers, professionals and managers', paid high salaries at the top. At the bottom would be a mass of 'low-paid workers . . . [doing] simple low-skill jobs, dull, routine, high-turnover jobs . . . in a poor work environment'. In between will be fewer and fewer well-paid 'skilled, semi-skilled and craft production and maintenance jobs', which traditionally have offered 'opportunity and mobility' to the masses of employees who begin in 'entry level jobs' (AFL–CIO, 1983, p. 7). All of this is further complicated by the fact that most of the private service jobs (which hold the prospect of greatest employment expansion in the years ahead) are poorly unionized and often poorly paid.

This fear of a two-tier workforce is not shared by all economists. One BLS survey, for instance, concludes that while 'some trends in the industrial and occupational structure of employment could cause a degree of earnings bipolarization', a variety of factors influence the 'occupational structure' and 'earnings of workers in specific occupations', and an analysis of 'available data' indicates no 'bipolarization over the 1973–82 period'. Furthermore, the BLS argues, according to its 'projections of employment by occupation, bipolarization is not likely to occur between 1982 and 1995' (see Rosenthal, 1985; also Levitan and Carlson, 1984, and Stanback, 1983[1]).

From an industrial relations viewpoint it does seem that the occupations in which US unions have their greatest strength are those where employment prospects are weak, while those where unions tend to be weak are projected for strong growth. Thus, in 1980 unionism was about 40 per cent among operatives (this group includes semi-skilled workers in manufacturing and elsewhere, as well as truck drivers), and 33 per cent among labourers, while the unionization rates were only 22.7 per cent for professionals and technicals and 16 per cent for clericals, the more rapidly growing occupations (BLS, 1980; Adams, 1985). The AFL–CIO, then, has recently begun to respond more forcefully and directly to the organizing challenge posed by the technological and occupational shifts of recent decades.[2]

Technological Change: a Possible Threat to Unionism

It is useful to remind students and practitioners outside the USA that, unlike the case in many countries and notably in most of Western Europe (where collective agreements are negotiated on an industry-wide level, either for a large region or the whole country), in the USA the collective agreement is usually at a company or plant level. When, therefore, new technology helps spawn an entirely new plant, it is quite possible this new plant may operate on a non-union basis, and pose a threat to other unionized operations. Most US employers strongly resist unionization when they open new business establishments. Indeed, some US businesses have a clear-cut policy of seeking alternative dual sourcing, non-unionized plants, that is, a non-union alternative to an already unionized plant. A few unions in basic metal production (including steel and aluminium) and in automobiles have succeeded in inserting provisions into their collective agreements with large companies to make it easy for these unions to gain recognition at new plants of these companies, but these are very exceptional cases. For example, as the electronics industry has expanded, the rate of unionization has declined, as most of the industry's companies have succeeded in defeating union efforts to gain recognition at new plants.

Even within establishments where unions are already recognized, management may take the position when a major technological change occurs that the resulting new jobs are not covered by the existing collective agreement, and seek to staff them on a non-union basis. The Communication Workers of America (CWA) reports such a case when certain skilled operations were computerized at a plant of the American Telephone and Telegraph Co. (AT&T). The company sought to remove some part of the jobs from the unit represented by the union by describing them as 'a management control function'. It also refused to train existing members of the union's 'bargaining unit, thus depriving the unit and the unionised employees of both knowledge and work' (Kennedy *et al.*, 1982, pp. 67–8). The union, however, expressed a strong grievance on this issue and eventually won its case at arbitration.[3]

The threat that technology can, and often does, pose to a union's very existence in the USA must be kept in mind, as we sketch below some of the specific problems and developments that technological change has brought to collective bargaining in the USA in recent years. It certainly colours the union response to technological change.

Factors Influencing Union Attitudes toward Technological Change

There is a long-standing conventional wisdom with regard to the attitude of American unions toward technological change. It has usually been contended that US unions do not resist technological change, but generally prefer to negotiate on its consequences and for a share of its benefits. Beyond this, it is held that, where a company is expanding employment, a union is more likely to be immediately receptive to technological change. If competition is severe, a union may have no alternative but to accept technological change promptly to help its firm survive. Craft unions, it has been argued, were more likely to resist technological change in the past, for fear that the resulting new organization of work would reduce or eliminate the need for their particular skills. On the other hand, it has been argued that for industrial unions 'technological changes affect such a small fraction of their membership' and, indeed, may help other parts of it that they are 'likely to pursue a policy of adjustment to technological change' rather than resist it (Slichter *et al.*, 1962, p. 345).

While this conventional wisdom about industrial unions has prevailed for a long time, new developments and problems call for this wisdom to be modified. In recent years some ingrained union positions have confronted certain needs of new technology, as well as the problem of growing foreign competition.

The New Technology and Work Organization: the Industrial Relations and Human Resources Context

Some of the new technology introduced into older, well-unionized industries has collided with long-established job practices and wage classifications. Long before unionism was established in most major US industries and factories, management, in keeping with engineering and scientific management practices devised by Taylor and others, had subdivided tasks, with a minimum of scope and responsibility left to workers. Related to these highly subdivided jobs were job classifications and wages. This seemed to be the essence of successful, modern mass production. (Whether it ever truly was, can be debated elsewhere!)

When industrial unions came on the scene in the 1930s and 1940s, they were neither able (nor strong enough) nor, perhaps, very keen to overthrow these arrangements. (The unions, however, criticized and helped reduce some of the pace of the Tayloristic system in many plants and industries.) For the most part they built walls of protection around these many job and wage classifications, controlling access to them by seniority and other rules, negotiating rates for each job.

In the 1980s, in part as a result of the introduction of new technology, managers often find these tight job boundaries constraining and less useful for maximum utilization of new technology. Additionally, they often find need for greater input and initiative from employees if the technology is to work well. (There is also a realization, perhaps, that the Tayloristic methods were never truly the best way to utilize human resources in production.) Of course, not all the pressure for change comes from new technology. It is impossible to separate these pressures from those stemming from new – for many US companies – organization insights into management excellence (as mentioned in Chapter 1). As they seek more flexible utilization of human resources, however, employers may come up against the protections and controls that unions have built into the old system to safeguard employees. Unions and their members are frequently suspicious that proposals for more flexible deployment of workers will lead to the 'speed-up' or 'stretch-out' of the past, or to lay-offs and unemployment.

In a new joint venture by General Motors (GM) and Toyota in a California plant – formerly owned by GM and formerly covered by a collective agreement with the United Automobile Workers (UAW) – just such an issue took months to resolve. Toyota, which had the direct operating managerial responsibility, at first refused to recognize the UAW at the reopened establishment; but it became evident that the company's greatest interest was in obtaining flexibility of deployment of the workforce, which it enjoyed in its Japanese plants.

This issue was resolved when, in return for recognition, the UAW accepted a collective agreement that included only four separate classifications, three of which were for maintenance, with only one production job classification. This contrasts with typical practice at US auto plants where there may be as many as 100 separate production worker classifications. While local union leaders at the California plant were at first cautious and uneasy about this new agreement, subsequent reports suggested they were working to the mutual satisfaction of the union and management (*Daily Labor Report*, 3 October 1985).

In planning an entirely new small car, Saturn, for future production, GM went beyond this step, and enlisted the UAW's cooperation even in its technical drafting stages. Before the plant for this new car was under construction, GM and UAW agreed that UAW's members would 'be the primary source for recruitment' at the eventual 6,000 member workforce. 'Permanent job security', except in the case of 'unforeseen or catastrophic events or severe economic conditions', is to be guaranteed to these employees, who will be on a salaried basis (quite distinct from UAW employees elsewhere in GM who typically are on an hourly basis). There will be one production classification and three–four skilled classifications, which would assure the company of great flexibility in deploying the workforce on what is expected to be state-of-the-art technology. The union is to be a 'full partner' in all decision-making, and wide autonomy and control is planned for workers on the shopfloor (*Daily Labor Report*, 29 July 1985).

Some opposition to the Saturn agreement has been expressed by groups within the union, which fear excessive concessions have been made to management in controlling and deploying the workforce. Right-wing critics outside the industry charge that the agreement is, in effect, a closed shop, one that violates employees' rights to choose or reject being represented by a union, once the plant is fully under way.[4]

It is, in any event, mutually agreed by GM and the UAW that the Saturn agreement is separate from the remainder of the company's car operations, which are largely covered by a separate master agreement with the UAW. (Indeed to launch the Saturn project GM set up a new separate corporation.) But it is difficult to believe that, if the new methods of production and manning on which Saturn and the California GM–Toyota plants are based prove successful, they will not spill over into the industry generally.

In fact, modification of the old job and classification schemes has been occurring on a piecemeal basis in a number of individual GM and Ford plants and in other industries. On the other hand, when the Chrysler Company sought formal, sweeping changes in its job classification system in negotiations in 1985, it was turned down; although the union did agree to a 'pilot programme' under which classifications would be reduced in a few plants in return for certain concessions and protections from the company.

The process of change does seem to be continuing inexorably, not only as regards technology, but also as regards union–management practices on which it impacts. In a renovated plant of the LTV Steel Co. in Cleveland, the new rust-proof steel electro-galvanizing line, by agreement between company and union, will 'change work practices from customs that have prevailed [in the steel industry] since the 1930s . . .'. The changes are so important that one source feels that these new arrangements, under which steelworkers 'will largely manage themselves' and earn salaries instead of wages, could 'serve as a model for much needed work reforms throughout the beleaguered industry'. Under the new plan, workers will be 'divided into four skill levels instead of rigid job classes', and will move from job to job. Workers will also have a major voice in hiring and firing (*Business Week*, 23 December 1985).

In separate contract negotiations in 1987 between the UAW, Ford and GM, the parties made statements in favour of the more flexible work arrangements. Separate contract negotiations between the steelworkers' union and most of the major steel companies in 1986 also tended to include provisions conceding greater flexibility to management in deploying the workforce.

Instances of major change in work rules are also occurring in other companies – unionized and non-unionized. But the new, more flexible type of work arrangements are far from being the rule in industry. Moreover, it is still far from clear that most traditional, authoritarian-style managements are prepared to share responsibility on any large scale with the workforce. Resistance to these new styles and forms is often especially keen among middle and lower managers, who feel threatened by such changes.

As for the workforce, there is as yet no clear picture. Some past studies seemed to indicate that employees prefer jobs with greater variety and responsibility.[5] But one recent student (Weiss, 1985) finds that earlier empirical studies that argued workers prefer 'enriched' jobs overlooked the self-selection process involved among employees who volunteered for such enriched jobs. He adds: 'It is not surprising that . . . workers who ask to be reassigned to more complex jobs prefer the jobs they requested.' After studying some 2,900 semi-skilled electronics workers, Weiss insists that there is a positive correlation between higher quit rates (his measure of dissatisfaction in this context) and those employees who were randomly assigned to more 'complex' jobs. He concludes: 'The evidence . . . suggests that if job enrichment takes the form of increasing the complexity of semi-skilled production jobs (job enlargement), the job satisfaction of workers is likely to fall.' This research counters those who have been enthusiastically promoting job reorganization as all things to all people. However, since Weiss's research is limited to one firm, and his sole criterion for job satisfaction or dissatisfaction seems to be the quit rate, perhaps we should not yet make any sweeping claims for the research.

Ranged against the resistances to job change and reorganization are the threats of tough foreign competition and much of the new technology. With regard to the latter, it does appear that, as old-style mass production gives way to more specialized production, including forms of computerized automation, the need for greater input and control by workers is likely to force new work arrangements in many plants and offices. These developments help account for managements' growing interest in establishing quality circles in the US (see Chapter 6 in this book).

Union–Management Committees for Cooperation on Technology

Managements sense that greater input from employees is essential. In many companies, more formal arrangements have been established for consultation with the union prior to the installation of new technology. Pressure for such consultation also comes from some unions, for defensive reasons.

The 1980 collective agreement between the CWA and AT&T established a new joint Technology Change Committee. The agreement states:

> The Company and Union recognize that technological changes in equipment, organization, or methods of operation have a tendency to affect job security and the nature of the work to be performed. The parties, therefore, will attempt to diminish the detrimental effects of any such technological change by creating a joint committee to be known as the Technology Change Committee to oversee problems and recommend solutions of problems in this area . . . (AT&T and CWA, 1980).

The agreement adds that the company will notify the union 'at least six months' in advance of major technological changes. Discussions would then ensue on what the impact on employees could be and what alternatives could be offered to them, such as moving to another job in the same or other localities, termination allowance, early retirement, as well as company training for other assignments (AT&T and CWA, 1980, p. 31).

Somewhat similar language calling for consultation on technological change is incorporated in the separate master agreements between GM, Ford and the UAW. Union officials suggest that no dramatic improvements have flowed from these new consultation procedures; but officials of both unions (CWA and UAW) do agree that, as the years pass, the meetings under these clauses are increasingly helpful.

Of course many employers have long consulted informally with their unions when major technological change is contemplated. But the negotiation of formal arrangements in several major firms may mark an important change to the structure of industrial relations – especially if it is placed in the context of new departures like Saturn and the LTV mill described above, where the unions (and employees) are being consulted from the start about the plant layout, the installation of the machinery, and so on.

Advance Notice on Technological Change and Plant Closings

More routine in character have been union–management agreement clauses assuring unions of advance notice of impending technological change, or of plant closings. Surveys seem to indicate that the numbers of such clauses in collective agreements are increasing (though only a minority of agreements yet include them), probably as a result of the heightened sensitivity of unions to technological change.

Typical of the collective agreement clauses providing the union notice of technological change is the following:

> The Company shall notify the union before the introduction of any technological change . . . and shall arrange to discuss with the union the effect of such change on employees covered by this Agreement.[6]

An example of a contract clause providing notice prior to a company's closing a whole or major part of a plant is the following:

> The Company shall give notice in writing to the union of the closing of a plant or department at least six months prior to such closing.[7]

Not satisfied with what can be accomplished only through collective bargaining, the union movement is also pushing for the enactment of federal legislation to help regulate plant closings.

Unions Reach for Greater Voice over Investment Decisions

Related to the changes in technology and the process of rationalization going on in much of American industry have been the efforts of a few unions to gain some influence over companies' investment decisions.

Both the United Food and Commercial Workers (UFCW) and the United Steelworkers have been confronted with declining companies in the meat-packing and basic steel industries. As plants have been closed in whole or in part, the unions have had to make wage or other concessions to these companies to help them survive. In return for concessions in its agreement with the Armour (meat-packing) Company, in addition to obtaining a moratorium on plant shutdowns, the UFCW also gained the right to receive a copy of the company's 'capital investment plan for the next five years', and the company had 'to reveal its actual expenditures each year' (*Daily Labor Report*, 29 September 1982, p. 10). In its 1983 agreement with leading basic steel companies the steelworkers' union received a pledge from the companies to 'apply any savings' made as a result of the union's economic concessions to 'the needs of the existing facilities covered by' the collective agreements, 'such as capital equipment needed to modernize' or 'to preserve the working capital needs of such plants'. The steel companies are forbidden from investing in other (non-steel) segments of their business, and they must 'provide annually adequate information to the Union' on the savings made and related capital expenditures.

These are rather new areas into which unions have pushed the collective bargaining process. It is not yet clear how far-reaching their consequences may be. However, many US companies are providing a much greater flow of information to their employees and unions than in the past. In itself this is likely to have important consequences for industrial relations.

Technological Change and Union–Management Approaches to Training

Coping with the new technology (as well as with other forces such as foreign competition) seems to be leading unions and employers into new training programmes. Craft unions in the USA have long traditions of participating in training programmes designed to prepare the workforce for their industries. There are many examples of joint (between unions and employers) apprenticeship programmes in the skilled trades in US industrial history. But, until recent years, most major industrial unions did not participate to any great extent with their employers in matters of training and retraining (except where they, too, were involved in joint apprenticeship programmes to train skilled maintenance employees). Generally, in big industry, training was the province of the employer. Several industrial unions have, however, recently begun to change their positions.

As technological change has accelerated, and as its impact has spread, a number of unions – craft and industrial – have moved to new roles. The Graphic Arts International Union, a craft union resulting from the merger of previously independent printing unions, took the initiative, some years ago, to establish a series of training centres around the country. In these centres members of the Graphic Arts Union (subsequently known as the Graphic Communications International Union) have the opportunity to be trained on the newest printing technology (often obtained with the assistance of employers who share the union's interest in upgrading the skills of their employees).

But the newest changes involve the industrial unions. These unions are looking for ways and means of upgrading the skills of their members to match the jobs associated with the new technology. In other cases they see training as a means of helping employees displaced by technology (and other forces) to find new jobs.

Several years ago, the CWA negotiated programmes in their collective agreement with AT&T which, recognizing the 'environment of fast-paced technological' exchange, provide not only for job-specific training for employees, but also for more generic training to assist in workers' personal career development, and to fill 'job vacancies anticipated by the company'.

The collective agreement between Ford and the UAW signed in 1982 and then further strengthened in their 1984 agreement establishes a multi-million dollar Employee Development and Training Program. This took the form of a separate, jointly established new corporation, financed by Ford. The purpose of this new corporation is to assist workers laid off for economic reasons, as well as following technological change. The programme is jointly governed through a National Development Training Center. Personal counselling, basic literary and communication skills (where necessary), computer training, targeted training for specific occupations and professions (often provided by outside professionals – paid for out of these funds), etc., are all part of this large effort. The Center is also developing wide-ranging college and university opportunities, which 'will provide tailored college-level business programmes to meet' the career needs of employees.[8] Similar agreements have been negotiated between the UAW and GM. In 1986, CWA and AT&T followed this same route and established a separate new corporation (the Alliance for Employee Development and Training) under joint management.

In all of these cases the emphasis is on employee career training for jobs outside their immediate employer, as well as within it. While other companies and unions have not necessarily taken similar steps to establish separate new training corporations, greater emphasis on training and collective bargaining agreements is more and more common in the USA.

Technological Change: New Income and Job Protection Plans

Over several decades unions and employers have worked out a variety of programmes to afford some protection to employees displaced by advancing technology (and other economic factors). These include: the right to transfer to other jobs (including, in some cases, jobs in another location of the same company, and in these instances collective agreements often provide some help from the employer with moving expenses); severance pay when termination is final; supplementary insurance payments (especially in the steel, auto, rubber, agricultural machinery and glass-making industries); early retirement, etc. In one or two industries (especially in parts of longshoring), unions and employers have negotiated to establish a special fund financed by employer payments to handle displaced employees. In a small number of companies, unions have established the principle, in collective bargaining agreements, that no one is to be laid off as a result of technological change, with attrition reducing the work-force as improved technology reduces the firm's manpower needs.

By no means all US collective agreements contain all these provisions, and some contain few or even none of these. But they illustrate the ways in which unions and employers have tried to deal with the displacement problem.

Of recent interest is the special 'job bank' established in the 1984 collective agreements between the GM and Ford corporations and the UAW. This is designed to protect workers against job losses owing to technology, outsourcing (contracting out) of production, negotiated productivity improvements, or the movement of work owing to transfer or consolidation of work in the company (usually to a more productive facility).[9] Lay-offs caused by a reduction in production volume are not covered under this programme.

Any employee who has one year or more seniority (length of service) who would be laid off as a result of any of these causes was protected for the life of the 1984–7 agreement, and through the next agreement, which normally would expire in 1990. Displaced employees first exercise their seniority 'bumping' rights, but those still displaced after this are placed in an 'Employee Development Bank'. In that bank they receive their regular pay. They can be assigned by a joint UAW–GM Job Security Committee to: a training programme; as 'a replacement to facilitate the training of another worker'; a job at another GM plant; a job outside the union–management unit, including non-traditional jobs (for example community work); etc. Relocation allowances are 'available for permanent transfers'. Employees in the bank remain on the payroll and regularly report to work until reassigned. Funding for the programme was set at a maximum of around 1 billion US dollars.

One critic of the programmes argued, 'In essence, GM has paid a billion for an unlimited license to automate and outsource'.[10] By 1987, these job security provisions were further reinforced by agreements providing that there were to be no lay-offs in the companies except for serious cyclical shifts in the auto markets.

New Technology and Employee Health, and Personal Security Problems in Collective Bargaining

The introduction of some automated equipment in offices and plants has provoked union concern that new devices may imperil employees' health. Particular anxiety has been expressed about the greater stress experienced by secretaries and other people who spend long periods before video display terminals (VDTs).

Several unions have formulated programmes to protect employees from any hazards stemming from new advanced equipment in the workplace. These call for transferring pregnant employees from hazardous jobs involving prolonged work on VDTs, better protection against low-frequency radiation, periodic eye examinations, payment for optical equipment prescribed for work on VDTs, no use of VDTs during the final work hour to allow employees' to adjust to normal light, etc. (BNA, 1984, pp. 34–5).

A few unions, especially in the white-collar field, have succeeded in negotiating agreements embodying these kinds of protection for employees. The Service Employees Union gained such an agreement with one office of the Equitable Life Insurance Co. in 1984. It included 'extra break time', as well as 'the right to transfer to non-VDT work if they are pregnant' for VDT operators. The agreement also calls for safety equipment such as 'glare-reduction devices, detachable keyboards', etc. (*Wall Street Journal*, November 1984).

One can anticipate a gradual growth of these kinds of provision in collective agreements to deal with parts of the new technology, although there is as yet no widespread agreement on the health effects of VDTs and other similar devices.

Finally, there is some growing concern about the threat that some of the new technology presents to the individual rights of the workers. The use of remote control monitoring of workers and their performance from centralized locations has been protested by the CWA. In a similar vein the International Union of Electronic Workers has warned its local unions to take measures to 'prohibit the surveillance of individual workers by television cameras', adding that 'cameras connected to robots to help perform their work must be limited to that function' (Straw and Foged, 1983, p. 166).

The foregoing are relatively new bargaining areas for US unions but, as in the case of safety and health issues, one can anticipate increased bargaining demands and activity in the years ahead as the new technology is used more widely.

Conclusions

New technological advances are already having a strong impact upon the US industrial relations system, and the outlook is for more change and impact. Some serious questions remain about the broad income and employment consequences of this impact, especially in the years immediately ahead. These large questions aside, within the tradition of union–employer relationships there is some evidence that the kinds of recent initiatives described above, if generalized, could yield a framework in which labour and management, with some help from government, can cope with the great technological changes taking place. The displacing impact of increasing world competition, however, will continue to be a threat to employee job security in some industries. Moreover, employees are likely to experience greater effects of displacement in some sectors of the private economy where collective bargaining is not established (given that less than 20 per cent of all private-sector employees in the USA are covered by collective bargaining agreements).

Notes

1 Levitan and Carlson (1984) are critical of the AFL–CIO conclusions on the prospects of a two-tier labour force, although Stanback (1983) supports the view that new technology may create a large pool of low-level service jobs.
2 At its October 1985 Convention AFL–CIO delegates gave their support to a series of new proposals for membership-building that have been advanced by the AFL–CIO's Committee on the Evolution of Work. See *Daily Labor Report* (Bureau of National Affairs, Washington, DC), 1 November 1985, pp. A9–10. The AFL–CIO has also proposed a wide-ranging series of government measures to help deal with the great structural changes in the economy (see AFL–CIO, 1983; 1985).
3 Other cases, where new technological work was taken out of an existing union–management agreement covering most of a plant, are described by a staff member of the International Machinists Union in Kennedy *et al.* (1982), pp. 124–9.
4 On opposition to the Saturn agreement within the UAW, see: *New York Times*, 28 October 1985. On right-wing opposition, see complaints of the National Right to Work Foundation in *Daily Labor Report*, 9 August 1985.
5 For example, Locke and Schweiger (1979) conclude that such employee participation 'usually leads to higher job satisfaction'.
6 From the agreement between the International Union of Electrical Radio and Machine Workers and the Ingersoll-Rand Co. (this union recently changed its name to the International Union of Electronic Workers). This is quoted in Murphy (1981), p. 6.
7 Agreements sometimes add that such notices can be waived when the closing is due to 'causes beyond the control of the employer'. See BLS (1981), pp. 9–10.
8 This description is taken from a series of pamphlets and reports issued by Ford–UAW on the Program, as well as from interviews with some UAW staff officials who are part of the new Center. General Motors and UAW are operating a similar Program.
9 The description here is based primarily on the *UAW–GM Report*, reproduced in *Daily Labor Report*, 27 September 1984. For analyses of the 1984 auto contracts, see H. Young, special assistant to the President of the UAW, and E. J. Savoie, Director, Labor Relations Planning and Employment, Ford Motor Co., in the *Labor Law Journal*, August 1985.
10 Harley Shaiken (formerly of Massachusetts Institute of Technology) quoted in *Wall Street Journal*, 24 September 1984.

References

Adams, L. (1985), 'Changing employment patterns of organized workers', *Monthly Labor Review*, February.

AFL–CIO Committee on the Evolution of Work (1983), *The Future of Work* (Washington DC: AFL–CIO).

AFL–CIO Committee on the Evolution of Work (1985), *The Changing Situation of Workers and their Unions* (Washington DC: AFL–CIO).

AT&T and CWA (1980), *Memorandum of Understanding on Technological Change*, August.

BLS (1980), *Earnings and Other Characteristics of Organized Workers*, Bulletin 2105, Bureau of Labor Statistics (Washington DC: US Government Printing Office), May.

BLS (1981), *Major Collective Bargaining Agreements: Plant Movement, Interplant Transfer and Relocation Allowances*, Bureau of Labor Statistics (Washington DC: US Government Printing Office).

BNA (1984), *VDTs in the Workplace: A Study of Effects on Employment* (Washington DC: Bureau of National Affairs).

Fischer, B. (1985), 'Technology's impact on the labor force', Address to Point Park College, October.

Kennedy, D., Craypo, C. and Lehman, M. (1982), *Labor and Technology: Union Response to Changing Environments* (Pittsburg: Pennsylvania State University Press).

Levitan, S. and Carlson, P. (1984), *The Eroding Middle Class: A New Idea?* (Washington DC: Center for Policy Studies).

Locke, E. A. and Schweiger, D. M. (1979), 'Participation in decision-making: one more look', *Research in Organizational Behavior*, vol. 1, 1979 (New York: JAI Press).

Murphy, K. (1981), *Technological Change Clauses in Collective Bargaining Agreements* (Washington DC: Department of Professional Employees, AFL–CIO).

Office of Technology Assessment (1984), *Computerized Manufacturing Automation, Employment, Education and the Workplace* (Washington DC: US Government Printing Office).

Rosenthal, N. H. (1985), 'The shrinking middle class: myth or reality', *Monthly Labor Review*, March.

Slichter, S. H., Healy, J. J. and Livernash, E. R. (1960), *The Impact of Collective Bargaining on Management* (Washington DC: The Brookings Institution).

Stanback, T. (1983), 'Work force trends', in *National Academy of Engineering Symposium on the Long Term Impact of Technology on Employment and Unemployment* (Washington DC: National Academy Press, June).

Straw, R. and Foged, L. (1983), 'Technology and employment in telecommunications', *The Annals*, November.

Weiss, A. (1985), 'The effect of job complexity on job satisfaction: Evidence from turnover and absenteeism', *Report* No. 1597 (Cambridge, Mass.: National Bureau of Economic Research).

New Technology: International Perspectives on Human Resources and Industrial Relations, Unwin Hyman, London.

CHAPTER THREE

Collective Bargaining and New Technology: Some Preliminary Propositions

THOMAS A. KOCHAN and BOAZ TAMIR

This chapter presents preliminary propositions on the effects of microelectronic technologies on collective bargaining and goes on to explore the ability of collective bargaining to accommodate technological changes to the interests of the parties to employment relationships. Examples are drawn from US experiences, but it is argued that a full model and an adequate testing of the propositions requires comparative data from countries with diverse industrial relations institutions and traditions.

The purpose of this chapter is to sketch preliminary propositions about the effects that innovations in microelectronic technologies will have on the institutional structures and processes of collective bargaining, and the ability of collective bargaining to accommodate the interests of the parties who have a stake in the outcomes of technological change. While the focus of our analysis will be primarily on collective bargaining and industrial relations in the USA, a number of the propositions apply to other industrial relations systems in which unions rely on North American and British styles of collective bargaining as the primary mode of worker influence over decisions involving the introduction of new technology.

Indeed, full empirical testing of the responsiveness of collective bargaining to the challenges posed by new technologies will require comparative data from countries with very different industrial relations structures, processes and institutional traditions. This is because we see the North American traditions of job-control unionism at the workplace and managerial rights at the strategic level of organizational decision-making as posing significant barriers to the effective implementation and use of new technology. We also see the potential for protracted conflict in US industrial relations over the future of unions and their roles in society, in strategic managerial decision-making, in collective bargaining and in workplace relations. Thus, a central proposition running through all of our analysis is that those industrial relations systems that are less wedded to job-control unionism can more easily accommodate an expansion of union participation in decision-making to strategic levels of management, and those that are not diverted by basic power conflicts over labour's role are more likely to accommodate new technologies more easily and use them more fully to the benefit of the different parties involved.

In the sections that follow we will outline the theoretical framework we are currently developing and which we hope to use to test these very general propositions. However, we are in a very early stage of our research on the effects of new technologies on industrial relations and human resource management processes and outcomes. This chapter should therefore be read as only a preliminary effort to outline our theoretical perspective. The model will undoubtedly be modified as more empirical evidence becomes available.

Technology as an Interactive Variable

Another key proposition guiding the analysis to follow is that the availability of new technologies increases the range of choices open to decision-makers in designing employment relationships. As others (Walton, 1982; Pava, 1985; Salzman, 1985; Zuboff, 1985) have persuasively argued, the introduction of new technologies serves as an opportunity for decision-makers to 'unfreeze' existing employment practices and arrangements in ways that will fundamentally alter the nature of the employment contract (Osterman, 1985). Therefore, we propose that the effects of new technology cannot be studied in isolation from the current institutional arrangements governing employment practices. It is the interactions between (1) the changes the parties make in existing human resource management or industrial relations practices and (2) decisions about new technology that will determine how the interests of employers, workers, unions and the broader society will be affected when new technology is introduced.

While new technologies are not expected to have a deterministic effect on skills, work organization and other industrial relations outcomes, the choices that determine the net effects of technology tend to be made at earlier stages of the decision-making process than collective bargaining can reach effectively, particularly as it is traditionally structured in the USA. Thus, if workers and their unions are to be effective in influencing these choices and their results, significant changes in the structure and process of union–management relations will be needed. If this proposition is correct it implies that the traditional North American principle for collective bargaining – namely, that it is management's job to make the basic strategic managerial decisions (e.g. to determine the design of new technologies) and it is the union's role to negotiate over the impacts of these decisions – will no longer be an effective means for representing workers or accommodating the interests of employers on this issue. Worker interests will not be given sufficient weight in strategic management decisions regarding new technology. As a result, workers and their unions will be less supportive of technological change during its implementation and neither workers nor employers will achieve the full potential benefits of new technologies. Therefore, those collective bargaining and industrial relations systems or relationships that provide a role for employee representatives at earlier stages of the planning and decision-making process are expected to produce both a smoother adaptation to new technologies and a better accommodation of the interests that workers, employers and society bring to these decisions.

Thus, two broad sets of empirical questions need to be

addressed in future research to test these arguments: (1) under what conditions do the institutional structures and processes of collective bargaining and industrial relations adapt in ways that allow unions to influence technological decisions at earlier stages of the decision process than has traditionally been the case, and (2) how do the results differ in situations where unions are gaining access to earlier stages of decision-making from cases where traditional collective bargaining arrangements continue to serve as the central mechanisms for worker voice?

The General Model

The general model that we are using to guide our analysis argues that new technology will interact with other changes in external markets and the business strategies of employers to affect various aspects of the institutional structure of industrial relations and the outcomes of interest to the parties to employment relationships. The model starts by focusing on the key characteristics of the market environment that are expected to interact with and influence employers' use of new technology. It then suggests that the business strategies that employers use to respond to changing markets will influence their goals for technology and will moderate the effects new technology has on the institutional aspects of industrial relations. The institutional aspects of industrial relations are conceptualized here within the three-tiered framework developed in our research on the changing nature of US industrial relations (Kochan, McKersie and Katz, 1987). Of special interest here will be how new technology affects the workplace level of industrial relations as it modifies the organization of work and affects individual employee participation, mobility, motivation and trust. At the collective bargaining level of industrial relations the central questions centre on the effects of new technology on employment security, compensation systems and training policies. At the strategic level the central questions involve the role of worker representatives in the design and implementation of new technology.

The effects of new technology on the goals of the parties to employment relationships are expected to depend on how these institutional aspects of industrial relations are handled. The broad goals considered here span the employers' objective of improving economic performance, workers' concerns for employment expansion and rising incomes, and societal concerns for economic growth and equitable distribution of incomes. Moreover, since we expect that the *direct* effects of new technology are to displace labour, we see the quality of the adjustment policies as an additional outcome of interest in evaluating the effectiveness of collective bargaining and industrial relations systems in managing technological change. We will now elaborate on the more specific propositions linking the various stages of the model.

Markets, Technology and Business Strategies

Our view of how new technologies will interact with changing markets and business strategy choices that result draws heavily on our recent work on strategic choices in industrial relations and on the arguments of Piore and Sabel (1985). These works lead us to suggest that (1) growing internationalization of competition, (2) shortening of business life cycles, and (3) increasing segmentation of markets and market niches all heighten the pressures for technological change. Together these forces exert strong downward pressures on labour costs and increase the need for flexibility in the use of technology and labour in order to adapt quickly to changing market conditions and opportunities.

These market pressures are not expected, however, to produce a deterministic response from employers. Rather they induce employers to reassess their business strategies and to choose whether to adapt by attempting to (1) compete on the basis of low labour costs and high volumes, or (2) search out market niches and competitive strategies that stress high product quality, technological superiority, or in some other way support a high wage/high productivity employment relationship. The type of strategic business response employers follow will influence the goals that they set for the use of new technology and this in turn will influence the consequences new technology has for industrial relations practices and outcomes. The key choice is between strategies that attempt to rely on labour cost minimization or those that seek a competitive advantage through means that can support a high wage/high productivity employment relationship.

There is a growing belief that in markets characterized by global competition, open access to markets, few restrictions on international trade and ease of technology transfer, it will be difficult for firms in the USA or in other advanced industrialized countries to depend on a strategy of being the low labour cost competitor. However, where this strategy is followed we can expect increased labour–management conflict and the expansion of employment conditions found in secondary labour markets – high turnover, narrow jobs, few opportunities for training and advancement, reliance on part-time or contract workers, and managerial styles that stress tight managerial control over workplace decisions. Many of the firms that attempt to follow this strategy ultimately will lose competitive position to lower labour cost producers in developing countries.

We believe that labour cost minimization strategies tend to be a common initial response by employers as business units or products move to more mature stages of their life cycles and, therefore, some firms will choose this strategy. In these situations new technology will be used to eliminate as much labour content as possible, to reduce skill levels of the residual labour left in the process, and to strengthen managerial controls over the work process. In the event that this becomes the predominant strategic response to the use of new technology, we can expect greater incomes inequality, less employment security, and strong efforts on the part of employers to limit worker and union participation in decisions regarding new technology.

Firms that adapt to changing markets by searching for competitive strategies that emphasize new product or service development capabilities, technological superiority and/or high product or service quality will pose a different set of challenges to employment relationships and industrial relations practices. While the direct effect of new technology will also lower labour content in these firms, the changes in industrial relations practices in firms following this strategy are likely to be quite different from those discussed above. The primary reason is that these firms will place a high priority on achieving a high degree of teamwork, cooperation and commitment, and flexibility in the utilization of human resources. We can best outline the types of changes that new technology is likely to bring about in firms following these strategies by utilizing the three-tiered framework for analysing industrial relations issues that we have introduced elsewhere (Kochan, McKersie and Katz, 1987).

Workplace Impacts

There seems to be a broad consensus emerging among those studying the introduction of new technology in both office and factory settings that the primary effects of new technology are to increase the need for teamwork, the ability to analyse problems and to understand the interdependencies among different segments of the production or service delivery systems. Several examples from cases we are currently studying will illustrate this point and clarify some of the difficulties these changes pose for industrial relations systems that have traditionally followed a tight job-control model of union–management relations.

In most of the new plants opened in the auto industry and in those plants that have had major infusions of new technology, management has sought to reduce the number of job classifications, organize work around work teams rather than individual jobs, reduce the reliance on seniority in promotions and job assignments, redesign the compensation system to pay people for their knowledge or skills attained rather than on the basis of their specific job assignments, and decentralize some of the tasks and duties traditionally performed by first-line supervisors to the rank-and-file workers (Katz, 1985).

In another case we have studied, new plant design teams have incorporated hourly workers and had them work alongside design engineers in order to reduce the time required to bring the new plant into operation and to engender greater acceptance for the new work systems and rules that would be used in the plant.

Perhaps the clearest case that illustrates the effects new technology along with new concepts in human resource management have on work systems can be seen in the design of the new Saturn division of General Motors (GM). The Saturn division was established to build a small car on a competitive basis in the USA. The process and the substantive results of the new plant design are unique given the traditions of US industrial relations practice. Union representatives participated in the design team thereby giving them access to the full range of technical and financial information available to their managerial and technical colleagues.

The design of the human resources and industrial relations system that emerged from this joint process calls for:

1 extensive employee participation at all levels of the new organization, from the workplace to the business unit to the top level management staff committee, and even to the GM strategic advisory committee for the Saturn division;
2 acceptance of the principle of consensus decision-making as the mode of operation;
3 a flexible work organization system with only three to five job classifications;
4 a wage payment system that provides for performance incentives and bonuses;
5 an all salaried compensation system;
6 guaranteed employment for 80 per cent of the workforce; and
7 automatic recognition of the union as representative of the blue-collar employees in the new plant.

In many ways, this case stands out as the exception to the general pattern of traditional collective bargaining. It thereby demonstrates the *potential* role of collective bargaining in the design of and adaptation to both new technologies and new principles of work organization. However, the vast majority of bargaining relationships do not provide workers or their union representatives with a voice in decision-making at these early stages of the process (see Chapter 8 in this book).

As the above examples suggest, the introduction of new technology interacts with new principles of human resource management and work organization to alter dramatically a number of traditional industrial relations practices, many of which are becoming central topics of negotiations in bargaining relationships. We can summarize the central effects that technology is expected to have as follows.

First, there is strong pressure to broaden narrow jobs and reduce the number of job classifications so as to increase flexibility in job assignments. Second, greater emphasis is put on team forms of work organization rather than individual job assignments. Along with this is a growing interest within manufacturing organizations to experiment with pay-for-knowledge compensation systems to again facilitate training, teamwork, and diffusion of understanding of different tasks within generic work clusters or groups.

Third, efforts to decentralize and internalize some of the tasks traditionally performed by first-line supervisors are found in those settings where quality circles or other forms of employee participation have expanded to incorporate various work organization issues (see Chapter 6 in this book). Work assignments, routine maintenance, peer discipline, certification of skill levels, and in some cases recommendations for promotion are becoming part of the responsibilities of the work groups in the most advanced settings.

All of the above serve to weaken and challenge the job-control traditions of American unionism. While we have no way of estimating the extent to which these practices are diffusing across bargaining relationships, it is clear that managements attempt to introduce some or all of these new practices in many instances as part of the process of introducing new technology. Thus, those bargaining relationships that are deeply wedded to job-control union practices have the most difficulty adapting to these new, more flexible work systems.

Unions facing employer efforts to introduce these changes can be expected to resist them initially because they strike at the heart of the established roles and sources of power held by unions at the workplace. Employers in turn may respond to the opportunities that new technology offers for weakening unions or avoiding unionization of new worksites in a manner similar to the way the majority of American employers have utilized innovations in behavioural science to avoid unions through more direct communications and participation. If this emerges as the dominant employer strategy and union response, the use of new technology will be caught up in the larger power struggles and conflicts between American labour and management.

An alternative response of labour and management is to see the introduction of new technology and its attendant changes in workplace practices and roles as an opportunity for union leaders to adopt new roles and for the parties to establish new institutional structures and processes for worker participation and representation. But this approach inevitably means broadening and strengthening the role of unions and breaking with the traditions of US collective bargaining by involving worker representatives in strategic decision-making at earlier stages than is required by law. This approach is only likely to be followed, therefore, in situations where unions are already strong and secure in the employment relationship, and management sees few options for successfully introducing new technologies without the support of the unions with which it deals. The experience of Saturn and the United Auto Workers (UAW) serves as the visible case in point for this approach in the USA. Yet it also currently stands out as the exceptional case in US collective bargaining and industrial relations.

Changes for Collective Bargaining

It should be clear from the above discussion that we see technology interacting with changes in the environment, business strategies and human resource practices to put pressure on unions and employers to expand collective bargaining and integrate it with changing practices at the workplace and the strategic levels of industrial relations. Beyond this general point, however, a number of more specific issues will play prominent roles in collective bargaining over new technology. Three of these will serve as particular subjects in our research: (1) employment security bargaining, (2) wage payment systems, and (3) training.

The willingness and ability of firms to cope with the employment consequences of technological change have traditionally been a key determinant in the degree of resistance to or acceptance of technological change by workers and their unions (Levinson *et al.*, 1971). Where firms have introduced new technology in an environment of expanding market opportunities and have been able to avoid major labour displacement or to offer adjustment assistance to those adversely affected, collective bargaining has been generally successful in producing negotiated solutions (Somers, Cushman and Weinberg, 1963). There is no reason to expect this to be any different as current technological change occurs. Indeed, we expect to see not only an increase in negotiations over such traditional employment adjustment strategies as advance notice, retraining, severance pay, early retirement incentives, etc., but innovations as well on topics such as employment stabilization guarantees or commitments, joint training funds and jointly administered training programmes, and employment forecasting and planning.

Intertwined with bargaining over employment planning and adjustment strategies will be a host of compensation design issues. Again, as in past waves of technological change, the issue of how the parties share the economic gains derived from new technology will be a central topic at the bargaining table. This is particularly likely to be the case in settings where, for other reasons, unions are not able to 'take wages out of competition' through negotiation of a standard wage covering all competitors in the product market. Thus we are likely to see more frequent resort to profit sharing, gains sharing and employee stock ownership plans, and other ways of sharing both the risks and the benefits of investments in new technology. At a more specific job level, important negotiations will occur over the *criteria* that will be used to attach wages to specific jobs or specific skills. If microelectronic technologies reduce the emphasis on motor skills and physical dexterity, while increasing the analytical requirements and interpersonal skills, traditional job evaluation models will need revision. Moreover, in settings where team forms of work organization emerge, the traditional wage systems of paying people for their specific job assignment will continue to be transformed into systems that pay people for skills attained. This will remain an area of experimentation worth following, as new technologies and work systems mature.

In a 1982 speech to the dedication of a new UAW–Ford Motor Company joint training programme, John T. Dunlop described training as 'one of the untapped, unworked areas of labor–management relationships' (Savoie, 1985). This is likely to change dramatically in those bargaining relationships subject to the infusion of significant amounts of new technology, especially in settings where new technology is being used to upgrade the quality of the products or services and the flexibility and analytical capabilities of the workforce. Training is less likely to feature prominently in management's bargaining agenda in settings where (1) management is attempting to use new technology to minimize labour costs, or (2) management is attempting to use new technology to weaken or shrink the union by allocating new jobs to non-bargaining unit employees. Where management is following these cost minimization and/or control-driven strategies, training issues will be subsumed in the larger collective bargaining conflicts over worker security and union survival. Where the analytical requirements of jobs are upgraded by new technology, however, training is likely to become one of the central issues in collective bargaining.

Two well-known examples of the expanding role of collective bargaining into training issues illustrate the directions that bargaining is likely to take. Both situations are ones in which strong unions are present and employers recognize the need to upgrade the skills of the workforce to make the new technology achieve its potential. Both situations also illustrate how effective training strategies require union leaders and management industrial relations/human resource professionals to be involved in strategic decisions regarding the design and use of new technologies at earlier stages of the decision process than is traditional.

The Communication Workers of America (CWA), American Telephone and Telegraph (AT&T) and the various regional companies that were part of the Bell System prior to divestiture have established a series of training advisory boards (TABs) to plan and administer various training efforts aimed at both providing new skills needed for those who will work with new technology and providing marketable skills for those likely to be displaced by new technology. These TABs, and the 36 million US dollars allocated to fund these programmes, were negotiated as part of the 1982 collective bargaining agreement between CWA and AT&T. Since the TABs have been set up, AT&T has been divided up into a number of separate and independent companies, and much of the telecommunications industry in which AT&T previously operated has been deregulated or otherwise become subject to more intense competition.

A recent review of the status of training activities across the new organizations suggested that the commitment to and degree of investment in training varies considerably (Straw, 1985). We would expect that training will diffuse the fastest and be given the greatest support by both labour and management in situations where (1) unions and employers are sharing information on new technology and integrating human resource management concerns into early stages of strategic decision-making on new technology, and (2) collective bargaining is used to support and extend the funding, joint planning and joint administration of training activities. In short, the way that training activities are addressed at the level of collective bargaining will depend on whether unions and employers take a joint, consultative approach to new technology at the strategic level of industrial relations activities, or whether management seeks for strategic and power-bargaining reasons to limit union access to information and consultation in early stages of decision-making over new technology.

The second illustrative case involves the UAW, Ford and GM. In 1982 negotiations both Ford and GM agreed to establish national joint development and training programmes (the specific names of these joint efforts vary across the two companies; however their general structures and objectives are quite similar). Originally these efforts were funded at the level of 5 cents per work hour contribution. In 1984 negotiations the funding levels were doubled and some special additional funds were allocated for safety and health training (Savoie, 1985). At Ford these contributions translate into approximately 35–40 million US dollars for 1984. Because of its larger workforce, the annual funding level at GM is likely to be about 200 million US dollars per year. The joint efforts support a wide variety of career counselling, college courses, general skills building, union leadership training, and retraining for laid-off workers. In principle, these funds are to supplement, not substitute for, company funds that support the training required to adapt the current and future workforce to the needs of new technology as it is invested.

Aside from craft union apprenticeship programmes, the UAW and Ford and GM training efforts represent the most advanced form of *jointly* controlled and administered training efforts ever to come out of US collective bargaining. Whether this joint approach diffuses to other collective bargaining settings in the future is likely to depend again on whether such a strong joint process is consistent with the goals that management has for new technology and the nature of the labour–management relationship at the strategic levels of industrial relations.

Conclusions

As noted at the outset, this chapter is only a preliminary report on our efforts to begin to conceptualize the role that new technology will play in the US collective bargaining system. In developing propositions we seek both to understand how new technology will interact with other factors in the environment and in the organizational contexts of the bargaining relationship to modify institutional structures and patterns of bargaining, and to assess the effectiveness of collective bargaining in adapting to new technology and in translating new technology into outcomes that benefit or at least accommodate the interests of workers, employers and the larger society. Our underlying argument is that, for the US collective bargaining system to cope with new technology effectively, it will require fundamental changes from traditional practices. Unions will need to play a more influential role at the strategic level of business decision-making and modify many of the job-control traditions associated with collective bargaining relationships at the workplace.

This will not be an easy or smooth adaptation process. The propositions under development and tentatively presented here are designed to understand the diversity of processes and outcomes that can be expected. In our future research we hope to provide the empirical data needed to test these propositions in the USA and in other national settings.

Acknowledgement

Partial support for this research was provided by the MIT Auto Project and the MIT Management of the 1990s Project. The views expressed are solely those of the authors.

References

Katz, H. C. (1985), *Shifting Gears* (Cambridge, MA: MIT Press).

Kochan, T. A., McKersie, R. B. and Katz, H. C. (1987), *Strategic Choices in Industrial Relations* (New York: Basic Books).

Levinson, H., Rehmus, C. M., Goldberg, J. P. and Kahn, M. L. (1971), *Collective Bargaining and Technological Change in American Transportation* (Evanston, Ill.: The Transportation Center).

Osterman, P. (1985), 'Technology and white collar employment: A research strategy', Paper presented at the Winter Meetings of the Industrial Relations Research Association.

Pava, C. (1985), 'Managing new information technology: design or default', in R. E. Walton and P. R. Lawrence (eds), *Human Resource Management: Trends and Challenges* (Boston: Harvard Business School Press), pp. 69–102.

Piore, M. J. and Sabel, C. (1985), *The Second Industrial Divide* (New York: Basic Books).

Salzman, H. (1985), 'The new Merlins or Taylor's automation? The impact of computer technology on skills and workplace organization', Boston University Center for Applied Social Science *Working Paper*, 85–5, May.

Savoie, E. J. (1985), 'Current developments and future agenda in union–management cooperation in training and retraining of workers', *Labor Law Journal*, August, pp. 535–47.

Somers, G. G., Cushman, E. L. and Weinberg, N. (eds) (1963), *Adjusting to Technological Change* (New York: Harper & Row).

Straw, R. J. (1985), 'Training for employment security and personal growth: the CWA agenda', Paper presented at the Twentieth Atlantic Economic Conference, Washington, DC, 1 September.

Walton, R. E. (1982), 'Social choice in the development of advanced information technology', *Human Relations*, vol. 35, pp. 1073–84.

Zuboff, S. (1985), 'Technologies that informate: implications for human resource management', in R. E. Walton and P. R. Lawrence (eds), *Human Resource Management: Trends and Challenges* (Boston: Harvard Business School Press), pp. 103–39.

III

Towards Industrial Democracy and Employee Involvement

CHAPTER FOUR

Co-determination and Technological Change in the German Automobile Industry

GREG J. BAMBER and RUSSELL D. LANSBURY

Industrial democracy was one of the major issues of the 1970s. The introduction of new technology is one of the main concerns of the 1980s. This chapter sheds light on both issues. It shows how co-determination has influenced managerial behaviour. Although the postwar consensus about industrial relations in Germany is increasingly questioned, the chapter concludes that there is still an underlying consensus and that car manufacturers in the English-speaking countries have some important lessons to learn from their German counterparts.

The impact of technological change on industrial relations emerged as an increasingly important issue in advanced market economies during the mid-1970s. The consequences of technological change for employees and management differ according to the social, economic and political context in different countries (Sorge *et al.*, 1983). Factors that influence the way in which new technologies are introduced depend, *inter alia*, on the organizational strength of unions, the legal rights to participate in managerial decision-making and the relationships between the main industrial relations parties – employers, unions and governments. Most of these factors reflect the economic situation and relative power of the parties. The way in which new technologies are introduced also varies between different industrial sectors, styles of management and types of union (Bamber, 1988). Although the legal framework is important, it is imperative to examine how the parties actually behave within a particular context; legal rights provide opportunities for action, but can also limit the range of alternatives available to workers' representatives. Hence, while unions may have access to particular information about proposed technological changes, they may not be able to participate in the design or selection of the technologies.

This chapter explores some aspects of industrial relations and technological change in three West German[1] car manufacturing firms. By focusing on such a specific context, we can begin to illustrate how co-determination operates in practice. Such a focus is justifiable, because the West German industrial relations institutions are much admired overseas and its motor industry has been one of the most successful in the Western world.

The Political and Economic Context

Following the Second World War, there was an 'economic miracle' in West Germany. In the post-war reconstruction, it enjoyed rapid economic growth, low unemployment, political stability and an apparently high degree of consensus in the industrial relations arena.

There was some controversy about the notions of industrial democracy that were introduced in the 1970s to increase rights of co-determination for employees and their unions in decisions about the workplace. The consensus was further challenged in the late 1970s, as unemployment rose faster than in most other Western countries. Unemployment in Germany was negligible in 1970 (0.6 per cent), but had risen to almost 8 per cent by 1985 (Bamber and Lansbury, 1987, Table A.5). To confront this growing social problem, the unions increasingly campaigned for a reduction in working hours. This campaign precipitated major industrial disputes in the steel industry in 1978–9 and in the metal and printing industries in 1984. Moreover, in 1982, the Social Democratic Party lost office, having been in the federal government since 1966 (albeit in coalition for part of this period). Against this background, the post-1982 Christian Democrat (Kohl) government aimed to constrain unions' rights to strike and to modify the famous institutions of co-determination (*Mitbestimmung*). In spite of these aims, the unions were seeking a greater influence on decision-making. Their emphasis extended from narrow economic issues to wider qualitative issues, concerning investment policy, health and safety, work organization and new technology.

Industrial Relations and Co-determination

By contrast with the English-speaking and the Latin countries, most union members in West Germany belong to an *industrial* union with a centralized organization. On average, Germany loses fewer working days in industrial disputes than the English-speaking countries. In West Germany, negotiations between unions' and employers' representatives are generally conducted at industry-wide and regional levels, though some collective agreements cover single enterprises. At the plant or workplace level, negotiations are conducted between the senior managers and works council representatives. The whole system of co-determination builds on the premise that the management and workers' representatives accept some degree of joint responsibility for industrial relations, at three levels: at the plant level for human resourcing practices and the organization of the labour process; at the board of directors level for longer-term strategic planning; and at the regional and national levels of the unions and employers' associations for the regulation of pay and hours of work. The regional level is becoming increasingly important (Weiss, 1986).[2]

Works councils (*Betriebsrat*) are the main instrument for implementing co-determination. Some employers initiated works councils voluntarily in the nineteenth century. Works councils were legally enshrined in the 1920s, but their legal rights have been enlarged during the post-war years, for example, by the Works Constitution Act 1972 and the Co-determination Act 1976. Works councils are elected by all employees in an undertaking regardless of their union affiliation. However, there are separate elections for wage-earners and salaried staff, as illustrated in Figure 4.1. There are works councils at the plant level, and in multi-plant companies at the central corporate level. Although works councillors do not have to be union members, they usually hold union positions themselves or cooperate closely with union officers. Works councils cannot call a strike, but they have the right to take legal action against employers for alleged breaches of

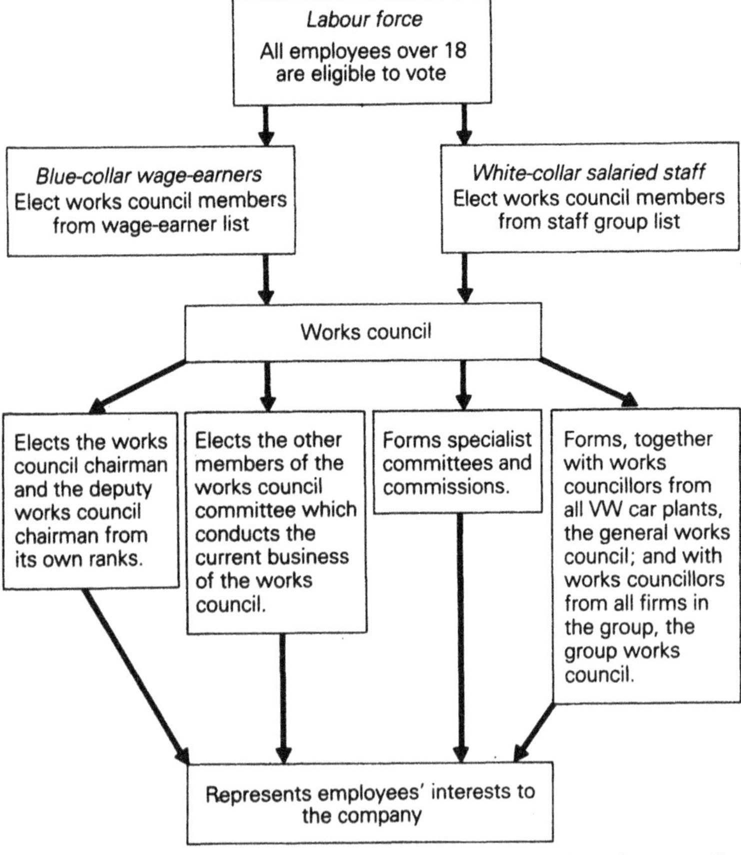

Figure 4.1 *The system of election to the VW general works council*
Source: Adapted from VW General Works Council (1981), p. 24.

contractual or legal rights. There are a variety of other rights accorded to works councils, for instance in regard to information disclosure, consultation and co-determination.

Another important aspect of co-determination is associated with the institution of two-tier company boards. The lower, management board (*Vorstand*) runs the firm, designs long-term policy and controls most decisions. However, the major decisions are formally endorsed by the upper, supervisory board (*Aufsichtsrat*). The latter generally meets only four times per year, so cannot interfere directly in management. Nevertheless, it appoints the top managers and monitors the firm's accounts. Some German observers argue that supervisory boards should also *advise* management as well as *monitor* it (*Financial Times*, 4 May 1988).

Supervisory boards include employee representatives. Since 1951 in the coal and steel (*Montan*) industries there has been parity of employee and shareholder directors in the supervisory boards. In addition, the employee directors usually initiate the appointment to the management board of the Labour Director, who plays a very important role. Outside the *Montan* industries, in firms with more than 2,000 employees, there has been a weaker form of parity since 1976. The main car manufacturers all fall into this category. There are at least two vital differences between the co-determination arrangements in this category and those in the *Montan* industries. First, in any impasse the chairperson (who is nominated by the shareholders) has the decisive casting vote. Second, one employee representative on the supervisory board must be nominated by the senior managerial employees (cf. Bamber, 1986, p. 6).

The composition of the supervisory board of a typical car manufacturer is illustrated in Figure 4.2. This shows that the ten employees' representatives include four different groups: union representatives, wage-earners and salaried staff, as well as a managerial employee. Although most decisions are made by consensus, if a vote is necessary the managerial representative, in particular, may not necessarily vote with the other employees, but may align with the shareholders. As one works council puts it, the managerial representative 'is the permanent victim of a conflict of interest' (VW General Works Council, 1981). Therefore, the employee side generally has less institutionalized power in the

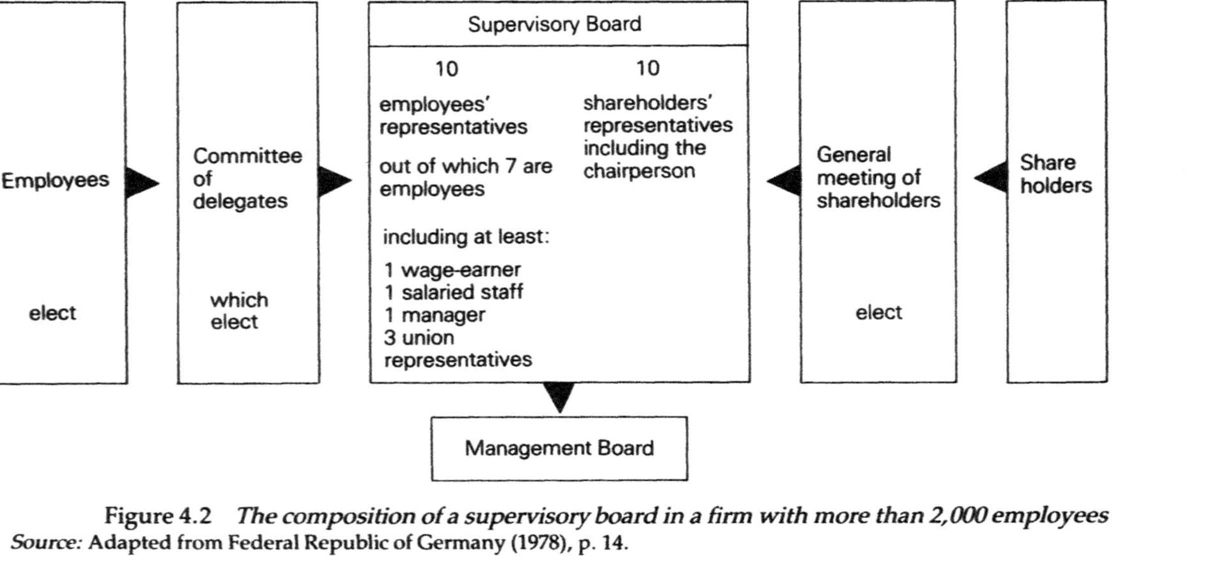

Figure 4.2 *The composition of a supervisory board in a firm with more than 2,000 employees*

Source: Adapted from Federal Republic of Germany (1978), p. 14.

supervisory boards of car manufacturers, in comparison with those of the *Montan* coal and steel firms.

Technological Change

Against such a background, how have the industrial relations parties coped with issues raised by the introduction of new technology? Under section 90 of the Works Constitution Act 1972, management is obliged to keep the works council informed about the process of technological innovation. This process, however, may extend over a long period of time; therefore, there is some controversy about the stage at which the council should be informed: when management first contemplates a new idea, when the final decision is taken, or after implementation on the shopfloor has proved feasible? If introducing flexible manufacturing for example, a firm may experiment with different types of industrial automation before a final decision is taken. However, even after a particular solution has been approved by top management, difficulties in implementing the new technology may lead to a change of the decision.

The 1972 Act is ambiguous on these matters. On the one hand, decisions about the selection and implementation of technological change remain a managerial prerogative; the works council has to be informed, but it cannot prevent management from introducing new technology. On the other hand, management is required to negotiate with the works council about any social or industrial relations consequences of technological change, such as provisions for any workers who lose their jobs, or the establishment of new wage structures. Hence rights of co-determination apply not to managerial decisions about innovation *per se*, but only to those *consequences* that directly affect the workplace.

In most German firms, it is managerial custom and practice to inform the works council *after* the final decision has been taken to introduce new technologies. At that stage, of course, there is only a limited range of options available to the works council. It can negotiate about the social and economic repercussions for employees, but this involves accepting any adverse consequences, even though the works council has not participated in the decisions that led to these outcomes. However, many works councils are attempting to extend their influence to the whole innovation process. If a works council can gain information in the early stages of decision-making, it may be able to persuade management to take other issues into account and to experiment with different technical solutions to particular problems.

The unions and works councils already have a great deal of experience of technological change. There was considerable technical innovation in West German industry in the 1960s and 1970s. None the less, throughout most of this period, the context was one of economic growth, with a high demand for labour. Thousands of foreign 'guest-workers' were imported into Germany. By contrast, in the early 1980s, with much higher unemployment, it was increasingly questioned whether the current industrial relations institutions were still as appropriate for coping with the challenge of the 'microelectronic revolution', as they were in the earlier period of more rapid economic growth.

To examine the extent to which employees are able to influence the decisions of management, it is necessary to study how co-determination operates *in practice*. Although the distinction between managerial prerogatives and co-determination rights is legally defined, the accommodation between these competing principles is determined by the power and influence of the parties. As the economic and political context changes with major innovations, the relative power relationship between management and the works council may be renegotiated.

Car Manufacturing

There has been a high degree of technological change in recent years in the car industry, especially with the introduction of advanced manufacturing systems involving robotics and other microelectronic devices. There has also been a state of crisis in this industry, as the slump in demand due to the world economic recession created excess capacity. In Western Europe, in the 1980s, there was an excess capacity of 2.5 million cars. Furthermore, the German manufacturers, like their counterparts elsewhere in Europe and overseas, also faced intense competition from Japanese producers. In 1985, 10.7 million cars were sold in Western Europe, but 1.4 million of them were imported from

Japan – an increase of nearly 200 per cent from this source in one decade (*Financial Times*, 4 February 1986).

During the 1960s, the West German car industry consistently enjoyed growth rates well above the national average. Its growth was fuelled by exporting, but this subsequently became more difficult as the D-Mark rose in value against other currencies. By the 1980s, German labour costs were the highest in the world.

The German car industry is highly unionized, with about 90 per cent of its blue-collar workers belonging to the Metal Workers' Union (IG Metall), the biggest union in the world, with about 2.7 million members. The unions have exercised considerable influence over the industry through the collective bargaining process, at national and regional levels, as well as through the employee representatives on the works councils and the supervisory boards. However, market fluctuations in the industry have threatened stable employment and led to cuts in the number employed by some firms during the 1974–5 and 1982–3 economic recessions. These cuts were generally not achieved by compulsory redundancies, but rather by voluntary means, through offers of separation payments and early retirement, and by banning recruitment.

Even though all of the car manufacturers are subject to the same labour laws, they have handled issues arising from economic and structural changes differently. To some extent, this reflects their differing economic performances and markets. As shown in Table 4.1, the luxury car makers (Group I) BMW and Daimler Benz have had a remarkably constant growth pattern; during the 1965–82 period, their production seemed hardly to suffer in the business cycle troughs. These companies produced more cars in almost every year than they did the year before. By contrast, the high-volume family car makers (Group II) experienced serious cyclical troughs and even decline during the 1970s. Ford-Werke, Opel (General Motors), Audi and VW all experienced severe problems during this period (Windolf, 1985).

A company's financial situation provides opportunities or constraints for those who determine its human resource and industrial relations policies and practices. Neither Daimler Benz nor BMW have declared any workers redundant compulsorily since 1965; both companies have ameliorated the impact of technological changes relatively easily, as they were increasing

Table 4.1 *Index of production of passenger cars for the six largest German car manufacturers, 1965–1982*

	Company	*1965*	*-66*	*-67*	*-68*	*-69*	*-70*	*-71*	*-72*	*-73*	*-74*	*-75*	*-76*	*-77*	*-78*	*-79*	*-80*	*-81*	*-82*
Group I	BMW	100 (93.5)	105	107	116	149	170	175	195	210	198	233	286	305	334	351	353	361	388
	Daimler Benz	100 (174.0)	110	115	124	148	161	163	186	191	195	201	217	235	232	249	252	258	268
	Audi (VW)	100 (144.1)	119	98	137	184	220	196	208	284	185	142	167	221	205	224	198	216	212
	Ford	100 (316.4)	92	61	66	95	129	151	138	144	90	131	154	172	172	173	133	154	164
Group II	Opel (General Motors)	100 (615.7)	105	88	105	128	132	135	142	141	94	106	149	150	155	156	128	132	155
	VW	100 (1,363.2)	102	80	106	112	111	119	101	100	86	77	90	94	99	96	90	84	82

Notes: 1965 = 100
Figures in brackets give absolute number of passenger cars in 100,000s for 1965.

Source: Windolf, P. (1985), 'Industrial robots in the German automobile industry', in W. Streeck (ed.), *Industrial Relations and Technological Change in the British, Italian and German Automobile Industry: Three Case Studies* (Berlin: International Institute of Management).

output. The other companies have declared redundancies. However, they have not laid off their workers at will. Indeed, under section 110 of the Works Council Act 1972, management must negotiate with the works council before cutting its payroll and must establish a social plan that covers matters such as redundancy pay. At VW, for example, the works council has pressed the company to establish a policy of employment security. In practice this policy encourages labour hoarding during times of recession (instead of dismissals) and even restrictions on output (delayed delivery) in peak times (instead of recruitment). Hence, during 1980–82 when production at VW fell by 9 per cent, employment remained fairly stable. As the works council does not have to cope with threats of dismissals, it can concentrate on other issues such as the improvement of working conditions, training and reskilling.

Comparative studies between the German and American automobile industries show that, typically, the Germans react to changes in output by adjusting the total number of hours worked, while the Americans react by adjusting the total number of workers employed. These differences reflect the differing legal contexts of human resource management (HRM) and industrial relations in each country (Altshuler *et al.*, 1984). The restrictions on unilateral action by management are greater in West Germany, as are the costs of making employees redundant. There is less legal regulation of the employment relationship in the USA. Thus, US employers have greater flexibility and it is cheaper and easier for them to declare redundancies.

In West Germany, however, the 'secondary labour force' of guest-workers has also been used as an economic buffer against market fluctuations. The proportion of guest-workers varies from less than 10 per cent to almost 50 per cent between the various German car plants. Although guest-workers have the same employment protection rights as the 'primary labour force' of Germans, in practice guest-workers may have less power to enforce these rights. As unemployment increased in West Germany, some guest-workers went back to their native homes; a few have received financial compensation for so doing, either from their employer or from the government. Thus, in 1975, foreign workers constituted 9.4 per cent of the German workforce; by 1985, they constituted only 7.2 per cent (Streeck, 1987, Table

IV). In earlier years, employers (especially Ford-Werke) tended to award fixed-term contracts to foreign workers. This meant that when the contract came to an end the employment relationship was automatically terminated. By the 1980s, however, works councils increasingly refused to agree to such contracts, so they became less prevalent.

Case Studies

The following short case studies are of Daimler Benz, Volkswagen (VW) and Ford-Werke. We interviewed managers, union representatives and members of the works councils. We also studied background documents and information from other sources. We focused on technological changes and some associated HRM and industrial relations issues.

These firms' shares of the German car market in 1984 were (with 1985 shares in brackets): Daimler Benz – 9.8 per cent (11.5 per cent); VW – 27.9 per cent (28.6 per cent); Ford-Werke – 12.3 per cent (10.7 per cent) (*Financial Times*, 20 February 1986). Although each of the three firms has quite different histories and structures, they do have some management characteristics in common. Strategic decisions about the introduction of new technology are generally made at their corporate headquarters, which for VW and Daimler Benz are in West Germany and for Ford are overseas. In each of these three firms, a central works council negotiates agreements that are applied across the whole firm. Corporate HRM policies about job structures and information to be made available to the works council did not vary greatly between the three companies. The application of policies, however, varied considerably between plants within each company. The variations reflected the different traditions, products, local conditions and the practices of management and works council representatives in particular locations. Such local and inter-plant variations often seem to be glossed over in accounts of industrial relations in Germany.

Daimler Benz

Daimler Benz is the largest German-owned private sector industrial firm (in terms of sales). It makes trucks, buses and

Mercedes Benz cars, and claims to have invented the motor car in 1885. A century later, its long-term strategy was to diversify away from reliance on vehicles and into other high-tech industries. It has taken over such other firms as MTU, the engine manufacturer; Dornier, the aerospace firm; and the AEG electrical company. According to one observer, Daimler Benz is one of the 'top ten' firms in the world.[3] As a highly profitable company, Daimler Benz has been a leader in terms of pay and conditions in the industry. In view of its success, Daimler Benz has been used by the unions as a 'target' for industrial action to establish new standards; for this reason, Daimler Benz featured prominently in the unions' 1984 campaign for shorter working hours. Senior management said that in recent years IG Metall had deliberately aimed to influence the works councils in this company to encourage a more 'political' attitude on all economic issues affecting Daimler Benz. This was particularly the case following the defeat of the federal Social Democratic government in 1982. Some managers blamed IG Metall for employee representatives on the supervisory board refusing to ratify the election of several new board members in recent years, including the Daimler Benz chairman.

IG Metall, however, has had its own problems at Daimler Benz. At the Stuttgart (Untertürkheim) plant, several candidates representing the Green Party have defeated Social Democratic Party candidates in the works council elections. Further, in the campaign for a shorter working week during 1984, a local IG Metall representative in the nearby Sindelfingen plant defied the national leadership and led his members out on strike before it had been officially proclaimed, apparently to force the hand of IG Metall in the campaign.

In general, Daimler Benz seeks works council views and is willing to amend its proposals if necessary. Management and works council representatives regularly negotiate on issues associated with technological change. For instance, the management discussed the arrangements for new transfer lines with the works council at the planning stage; the company subsequently agreed to give employees more training and guaranteed that their performance would not be monitored on an individual basis.

There was some overt conflict over new technology at the Daimler Benz plant in Mannheim, when workers were asked to register their work times on a computer. The works council objected on the grounds that this would involve undue surveillance over employees in the plant. An arbitration panel discussed the issue and recommended that new rules governing the use of computers should be formulated. Subsequently, management had to account for the use made of data collected on workers' performance levels and only certain uses were permitted.

Although the 1972 Act requires companies to disclose information to their works councils before changes are introduced, Daimler Benz did not feel obligated to co-determine issues involving management rights. Thus, even if the works council disagreed with a decision, the company could still proceed with its intended course of action. Daimler Benz managers complained that the works council wished to extend the scope of co-determination to cover all decisions. Although the company did not seek to eliminate co-determination, it did want to limit its scope to particular issues. Management argued that, though many issues such as pensions were not subject to co-determination, they were already discussed with the works council, so no extension of scope was necessary. Management aimed to retain as much flexibility as possible, to operate as it wished. The company was concerned not to fall behind the Swedes and Japanese in the introduction of new technologies, which were necessary for corporate survival in a highly competitive environment.

Volkswagen (VW)

VW is the youngest of the three firms, having been established in the 1930s. Unlike Daimler Benz, in the mid-1980s VW was reducing its degree of diversity, by, for example, selling its office equipment subsidiary to Olivetti. On the other hand, VW assembled cars in other countries to a much greater extent than Daimler Benz. VW is a high-volume producer of family cars. However, in recent years, it has generally aimed to move 'up market', especially by 'cross-fertilizing' product and process ideas from its specialist subsidiary, Audi. In the mid-1980s, VW held the largest market share for cars in Europe as a whole, as well as in West Germany. VW employs more people in its car plants than the other two firms. In 1985 its Wolfsburg plant employed just over 61,000 people, which makes it the biggest single plant in the Western world. VW differs from the other German car manufacturers in that it is a quasi public sector enterprise: until 1988, it was 40 per cent owned by the Lower Saxony *Land* and the federal governments. Accordingly, each of these governments had two shareholders' representatives on VW's supervisory board. (In 1988 the federal government sold its shareholding, so was no longer eligible to nominate such representatives.)

In the 1970s, VW was severely affected by the economic recessions in Europe and by tough competition from the Japanese, especially in its American market. Its production fluctuated (see Table 4.1) and declined considerably during the 1970s, not least because VW was too dependent on the famous Beetle model for too long. Consequently, VW faced setbacks with some of its overseas ventures; for instance, Nissan took over its Australian plant and VW had to reduce the size of its Brazilian subsidiary, which it subsequently merged with Ford of Brazil. In Germany, following the first oil shock and the slump in sales of its old Beetle model, in 1974 VW cut its workforce by 14,300 (Streeck, 1984a, p. 61), though it had to compensate those people who had contracts of employment. Nevertheless, by 1985 VW's employment had increased again, to an all-time high level.

The VW works council is under more of a direct influence from IG Metall than its counterparts in other companies; 87 per cent of VW's 237 works councillors belong to IG Metall. The chairman of IG Metall is also deputy chairman of the VW supervisory board, while a former IG Metall official is the Labour Director responsible for human resources, industrial and social affairs within the corporation. IG Metall has never had a strike at VW, not even during the 1984 shorter working week dispute, as VW had already agreed to cut working hours.[4] Nevertheless, there have been significant differences between the works council and VW management. In the early 1980s, for instance, management met strong resistance from the works council when VW tried to introduce new 'leadership principles' to be applied in the workplace; the works council feared that this innovation might reduce the influence of the union at the plant level. Nevertheless, the leadership principles agreement was eventually signed in 1983. On the other hand, works council members complained that they had not succeeded in agreeing formal contracts with VW about technological change, since the company would not concede co-determination rights over this issue. The works council was primarily concerned about how new technology should be introduced and managed, rather than whether it should be installed. In fact, VW uses robots to a greater extent than most other car manufacturers.

VW management pays considerable attention to scientific management techniques. Such techniques do not appear to be strongly contested by the VW works council or unions.[5] Yet, there are frequent negotiations between the company and a works council subcommittee about the standards set by the industrial engineers for assembly-line activities. Moreover, the works council has insisted that the management take 'humanization' principles into account when VW determines new investments and designs new jobs or work measurement activities. With the support of the works council, VW has also established some pilot projects that use semi-autonomous work groups. IG Metall has been successful in coordinating the activities of works councils at VW and other car makers to enlarge the work-cycle time and the number of work-breaks. IG Metall has signed a contract with VW that specifies more and longer work-breaks than in the other automobile manufacturers. This separate contract was possible because VW does not belong to the employers' association (*Gesamtmetall*) that negotiates with IG Metall on behalf of most of the industry. In this respect, VW has greater autonomy in its HRM and industrial relations policy than the other firms.

Ford-Werke

Ford-Werke is another high-volume producer of family cars. However, its performance has fluctuated. In the early 1980s, its profitability fell and it declared some redundancies. In 1985, its market share was slightly less than Daimler Benz, even though the latter is a producer of luxury and specialist vehicles. Ford-Werke claims to be an independent company, but the majority of its shares are held by the Ford Motor Company, USA, which pioneered the mass production of automobiles early in the twentieth century.[6] Internationally, Ford is much the largest of the three firms; it is the second largest car manufacturer in the world (after General Motors). The individual national Ford companies in Europe are coordinated by Ford of Europe, which has its headquarters in Britain. This overseas dimension influences decision-making in Ford-Werke, and, in turn, its HRM/industrial relations policy and practices. Nevertheless, Ford-Werke must adhere to the same laws that apply to VW and Daimler Benz. Therefore, Ford-Werke's formal structure of works councils and co-determination is similar to that of the other German car makers.

In Britain, Ford management often portrays the German workers as much more productive and cooperative than their British counterparts (Beynon, 1984). The manual workers' unions in Britain, for example, would not cooperate with Ford's post-1979 international corporate policy to promote employee involvement (EI). This policy aimed to achieve better quality and higher productivity by fostering participation by employees in decisions that affect them in the workplace. Ford has implemented EI in the USA and other countries, including Australia, to win employee acceptance of various changes in technology and other matters that facilitate improvements in product quality and sales. Both in North America and in Australia, Ford has persuaded the main union to cooperate with EI (on EI in North America, see Chapter 6 in this book). However, it was not only the British unions that were suspicious about EI. The HRM and industrial relations policies which originate from Ford's American parent and its European HQ in Britain are not always easily transplanted to West Germany. In Ford-Werke, the works councillors' doubts about EI were similar to those of the British shop stewards. In Britain and Germany there was concern that the EI policy could be used to undermine either the shop steward, or the works council role, in the workplace. This concern was particularly strong in plants where mistrust and poor relationships between management and the workforce led to suspicions about Ford's motives, especially when the memories of recent lay-offs were still fresh in the minds of workers. At Cologne it took the company almost two years to persuade the works council to provisionally accept the EI policy.

There was a similar experience with the introduction of Quality Circles (QCs), which the works council initially opposed. Negotiations between Ford-Werke and the works council then led to an experiment: a one-year trial period, after which the works council agreed to a limited programme of Quality Circles within the company. The works council restricted the objectives of these QC circles to the improvement of the *quality*, rather than the *quantity*, of work performed. Together with the management, the works council established joint steering committees with the authority to decide where Quality Circles could be installed and the uses for which they could be employed.

Ford has also taken some initiatives, however, to involve employees more directly in some fringe areas of decision-making that, hitherto, were the sole prerogative of management. For example, a large group of employees working on the development of the new Granada model were asked for suggestions about new model designs a year before production was due to begin. Following some of these suggestions, Ford did change both the product design and the methods used for its assembly. Furthermore, before workers were required to work on the new model, they were given extensive training in new production methods and transferred gradually to their new jobs. Because of the co-determination laws, Ford-Werke was less able to 'hire and fire' than its sister companies in Britain and the USA.

Conclusions

The German companies that we studied were all seeking to maximize the use of new technologies. They also aimed to pre-empt the outbreak of disputes about new technology by engaging in advance consultation.[7] However, their managers saw much change at workplace level as routine, which would be accompanied by *informal* consultation at the workplace. Works councils have no general right to co-determine the introduction of new technology, so managers did not always consult works councils *formally* before introducing changes. Works councils tried to insist that management consulted them about major changes. Nevertheless, several works council members claimed that the information that they received from management often came too late for them to influence the fundamental decisions and that the information was often too complicated, so required considerable technical expertise to analyse it. Works councils and unions may also be uncertain about how to deal with technological change because the long-term costs and benefits are difficult to forecast.

We infer from these three cases that co-determination has not induced a profound shift in power from capital to labour, but it does influence managerial behaviour. As the co-determination laws were strengthened in the 1970s, managers were constrained to devote more time and resources to the process of consultation. Managers were also obliged to pay more attention than before to the issues of workers' skills, qualifications and their quality of working life. As one manager put it: 'When introducing new technology, ten years ago the engineers would simply look in the catalogues at the technical data. Now they take ergonomics into serious consideration, otherwise they know that the personnel specialists and the works councils will oppose such new technology.'[8]

One consequence of co-determination has been to lengthen the planning horizons for technological change and to heighten the priority given by managers to 'the human resource implications'. This has increased the role and status of personnel managers in German industry. Within the corporate hierarchy, technical specialists are now obliged to involve the HRM specialists before finalizing plans for technological change.

To cope with the co-determination procedures, many works councils have built up their own organizations, especially at the central corporate level. The central works councils have offices, office equipment, secretaries and other facilities including their own professional assistants. Some critics hold that West German co-determination has fully incorporated the workers' representatives into management. Our observations do not support this view. We found a high degree of political consciousness and independence from management among the works councillors and worker directors we interviewed. Most managers seemed to pay serious attention to the views of such worker representatives. These views were bolstered by their strong links with their union.

British shop stewards also tend to be politically conscious and independent of management. They have far fewer resources, however, and a decreasing proportion of managers seem to pay serious attention to their views. Furthermore, the few worker directors that exist seem to be personally isolated from their unions and from collective bargaining (Brannen *et al.*, 1976; Towers *et al.*, 1986). If anything, perhaps incorporation of such worker directors is more likely in Britain than in Germany.

In another contrast with Britain, union goals in Germany are generally pursued peacefully through the institutions of co-determination, rather than by engaging in industrial action. As

Korpi argues (in relation to Sweden) such collective behaviour does not necessarily reflect union weakness, but may reflect strength (Korpi, 1978). Often, the unions in Sweden and Germany may be able to win concessions without resorting to strikes.

Despite the increase in unemployment during the 1980s and in spite of several major industrial disputes, it would be premature to write the obituary of the post-war industrial consensus in Germany. Although the industrial democracy tide has ebbed in the 1980s, there are still more opportunities for German workers to participate in managerial decisions than is the case for their counterparts say in Australia, New Zealand, Britain or North America.[9] In recent years, compared with their German rivals, the car manufacturers in these other countries have been less successful in the market-place, have placed less emphasis on human resource planning, training and consultation, and have experienced more industrial disputes. Therefore, the car manufacturers in these English-speaking countries still have some important lessons to learn from their German counterparts.

Acknowledgements

The authors thank Professor Friedrich Fuerstenberg and his erstwhile colleagues at the Ruhr Universität Bochum, for providing such a good base for the conduct of this study in 1984. They appreciated the kind cooperation of Daimler Benz, Ford-Werke, Volkswagen and IG Metall. They also thank several colleagues for helpful comments on an earlier draft, including: Peter Kaim-Caudle, Osman Durrani, Otto Jacobi, Doug Miller, Horst Minte, Ed Snape, Wolfgang Streeck, Siegi Steininger, Peter Wickens and Paul Windolf. An earlier version of this chapter was published in *New Technology, Work and Employment*, vol. 1, no. 2, 1986; its publishers, Basil Blackwell, kindly gave permission for this version to be included in this book.

Notes

1 Throughout this chapter the terms German, Germany and West Germany all refer to the Federal Republic of Germany.

2 On the German context more generally, see Miller, 1978; Clark *et al.* (1980); Marsh *et al.* (1981); Fuerstenberg (1983); Fuerstenberg and Steininger (1984); Bunn (1984); Gourevitch *et al.* (1984); Fuerstenberg (1987); Streeck (1987); Price and Steininger (1987); Weiss (1988).
3 *Financial Times,* 1 August 1984; the others in 'the top ten' (not in order of merit) were: Club Méditerranée, Deere & Co., Electrolux, Hewlett-Packard, Honda, IBM, Marks & Spencer, Mars, Olivetti.
4 Although not formally subject to the 1984 strike, VW still had to stop production for five weeks because of a shortage of components. One common tactic of the German unions is to strike only in one district (*Tarifgebeit*), e.g. in Nordwürttemberg–Nordbaden, the home of Daimler Benz and Bosch, the important component maker.
5 VW learned such managerial techniques from the Ford Motor Company which helped establish VW. Apparently, Henry Ford visited the Wolfsburg plant with Adolf Hitler in the late 1930s to admire the way in which his concepts had been applied by VW. There is a substantial literature from the labour-process school on scientific management, Taylorism and Fordism – for instance, see Braverman (1974); Littler (1982); Wood (1982); Blackburn *et al.* (1985).
6 There are many publications on the motor industry in general and, it seems, on the Ford Motor Company in particular; see, for instance, Nevins and Hill (1984); Lacey (1986); Halberstam (1986).
7 Streeck *et al.* were unable to find a single example of strikes over the introduction of robots in the German car industry in the early 1980s, see Streeck (1984a).
8 From an interview conducted by the authors in the West German car industry.
9 See, for example, the papers by Fuerstenberg, Davis and Lansbury, Bamber and Snape, and Strauss in Davis and Lansbury (1986).

References

Altshuler, A. *et al.* (1984), *The Future of the Automobile: The Report of MIT's International Automobile Program* (London: Allen & Unwin).
Bamber, G. J. (1986), *Militant Managers? Managerial Unionism and Industrial Relations* (Aldershot: Gower).
Bamber, G. J. (1988), 'Unions and technological change', in A. Gladstone *et al.* (eds), *Current Issues in Labour Relations: An International Perspective* (Berlin: de Gruyter).
Bamber, G. J. and Lansbury, R. D. (eds) (1987), *International and Comparative Industrial Relations* (London: Allen & Unwin).
Beynon, H. (1984), *Working for Ford,* 2nd edn (Harmondsworth: Penguin).
Blackburn, P. *et al.* (1985), *Technology, Economic Growth and the Labour Process* (London: Macmillan).
Brannen, P. *et al.* (1976), *The Worker Directors* (London: Hutchinson).

Braverman, H. (1974), *Labor and Monopoly Capital* (New York: Monthly Review Press).

Bunn, R. F. (1984), 'Employers' associations in the Federal Republic of Germany', in J. P. Windmuller and A. Gladstone (eds), *Employers' Associations and Industrial Relations: A Comparative Study* (Oxford: Clarendon), pp. 169–201.

Clark, J. *et al.* (1980), *Trade Unions, National Politics and Economic Management: A Comparative Study of the TUC and DGB* (London: Anglo-German Foundation).

Davis, E. M. and Lansbury, R. D. (eds) (1986), *Democracy and Control in the Workplace* (Melbourne: Longman Cheshire).

Federal Republic of Germany (1978), *Co-determination in the Federal Republic of Germany* (translations of the Acts of 1952, 1972 and 1976) (Bonn: The Federal Ministry of Labour and Social Affairs).

Fuerstenberg, F. (1983), 'Technological change and industrial relations in West Germany', *Bulletin of Comparative Labour Relations*, vol. 12, pp. 121–37.

Fuerstenberg, F. (1987), 'Industrial relations in the Federal Republic of Germany', in G. J. Bamber and R. D. Lansbury (eds), *International and Comparative Industrial Relations* (London, Sydney and Boston: Allen & Unwin).

Fuerstenberg, F. and Steininger, S. (1984), *Qualification Aspects of Robotisation: Report of an Empirical Study for the OECD* (Bochum: mimeo, Ruhr Universität Bochum).

Gourevitch, P. *et al.* (1984), *Unions and Economic Crisis: Britain, West Germany and Sweden* (London: Allen & Unwin).

Halberstam, D. (1986), *The Reckoning* (New York: William Morrow).

Korpi, W. (1978), *The Working Class in Welfare Capitalism: Work, Unions and Politics in Sweden* (London: Routledge & Kegan Paul).

Lacey, R. (1986), *Ford: The Man and the Machine* (London: Heinemann).

Littler, C. (1982), *The Development of the Labour Process in Capitalist Societies* (London: Heinemann).

Marsh, A. *et al.* (1981), *Workplace Relations in the Engineering Industry in the UK and the Federal Republic of Germany* (London: Anglo-German Foundation).

Miller, D. (1978), 'Trade union workplace representation in the Federal Republic of Germany', *British Journal of Industrial Relations*, vol. 16, no. 3, pp. 335–54.

Nevins, A. and Hill, F. E. (1984), *Ford: Decline and Rebirth, 1933–1962* (New York: Scribner's).

Price, R. J. and Steininger, S. (1987), 'Trade unions and new technology in West Germany', *New Technology, Work and Employment*, vol. 2, no. 2, pp. 100–11.

Sorge, A. *et al.* (1983), *Microelectronics and Manpower in Manufacturing: Applications of Computer Numerical Control in Great Britain and West Germany* (Berlin/Aldershot: International Institute of Management/Gower).

Streeck, W. (1984a), *Industrial Relations in West Germany: A Case Study of the Car Industry* (London: Heinemann).

Streeck, W. (1984b), 'Industrial change and industrial relations in the motor industry: An international view', *University of Warwick Public Lecture* (23 October).
Streeck, W. (1987), 'Industrial relations in West Germany: Agenda for change', *Discussion Paper,* Wissenschaftszentrum Berlin für Sozialforschung.
Towers, B. *et al.* (1986), *Worker Directors in Private Industry in Britain* (London: Department of Employment Research Paper).
VW General Works Council (1981), *Co-determination in the Volkswagenwerk AG* (Wolfsburg: documentation issued by the VW General Works Council).
Weiss, M. (1988), 'Institutional forms of workers' participation with special reference to the Federal Republic of Germany', in A. Gladstone *et al.* (eds), *Current Issues in Labour Relations: An International Perspective* (Berlin: de Gruyter).
Windolf, P. (1985), 'Industrial robots in the German automobile industry: New technology in the context of industrial relations', in W. Streeck (ed.), *Industrial Relations and Technological Change in the British, Italian, and German Automobile Industry: Three Case Studies* (Berlin: International Institute of Management).
Wood, S. (ed.) (1982), *The Degradation of Work: Skill, Deskilling and the Labour Process* (London: Hutchinson).

New Technology: International Perspectives on Human Resources and Industrial Relations, Unwin Hyman, London.

CHAPTER FIVE

Worker Participation in Decisions on Technological Change in Australia

EDWARD M. DAVIS and RUSSELL D. LANSBURY

In recent years, Australian unions have campaigned for the right to be informed and consulted about decisions to implement new technology. In a landmark case in 1984, such a right was granted by the Australian Conciliation and Arbitration Commission to workers covered by federal (national) awards. However, workers' rights come into force only after *management has decided on change. Some unions have negotiated agreements with employers which extend workers' rights in the face of new technology. Many unions, however, lack the resources to play a major role in decision-making even where they have achieved the right to do so. This has inhibited the achievement of greater industrial democracy in Australia.*

Several developments have fuelled momentum towards increased industrial democracy in Australia, particularly with regard to technological change. Following judgements of the Arbitration Commission in 1984, workers covered by federal (national) awards have been granted the right to be informed and consulted about decisions to implement new technology. In addition, several unions have negotiated agreements with employers that extend employee and union rights in the face of new technology. This chapter examines the factors that have encouraged greater industrial democracy and draws attention to employee and union involvement in decisions on technological change. Finally, factors limiting the practice of greater industrial democracy are examined.

Since the term 'industrial democracy' has had varied and conflicting interpretations, we first define its meaning. Industrial democracy is the significant involvement of workers, for the most part through their unions, in the important decisions that affect their worklife. Factors that will determine the level of industrial democracy include the influence that workers and their representatives wield, the importance of the matters over which they have influence (and correspondingly the importance of those matters over which they have little or no influence) and the proportion and accountability of the workers involved in consultative processes (Davis and Lansbury, 1986).

Towards Increased Industrial Democracy

Four factors are identified as influencing the level of industrial democracy. These are the declared commitment of the federal Labor Party government, led by Bob Hawke, to industrial democracy; the economic circumstances in the mid-1980s; decisions of the High Court and the Arbitration Commission; and the growing determination of at least some unions to achieve greater influence over the critical decisions that affect their members' worklife.

The Political Context

The Hawke government was first elected in 1983. Its predecessor, a conservative coalition government led by Malcolm Fraser, had proffered little effective support for industrial democracy. Although at least two ministers indicated that they favoured the development of more participative styles of management

(Pritchard, 1977), their interest bore little fruit. Indeed, it would have been surprising if the Fraser government had acted to stimulate industrial democracy, since this was generally believed to increase union power and reduce managerial power. Persistent themes throughout the Fraser government's term of office were that unions were too powerful and that measures should be taken to curb rather than promote their influence.

By contrast the Hawke government came to office with a firm commitment to encourage more consultative and cooperative styles of management in both the public and private sectors. This was detailed in the *Statement of Accord* negotiated between the Australian Labor Party (ALP) when still in opposition and the Australian Council of Trade Unions (ACTU) (Lansbury, 1985). The Accord included the general statement that 'continuous consultation and cooperation between the parties involved' would be a feature of government policy. On more specific matters, the Accord committed the government to consult with unions over taxation reform, rights for employees to be notified and consulted about employer proposals for technological change, and the achievement of better industrial relations in the public sector. Elsewhere, the Accord stated that the government would seek the cooperation of unions and employers with a review of Australian industrial relations, and before the introduction of new industrial legislation. It also declared that 'consultation is a key factor in bringing about change in industry. This consultation will be extended to industry, company and workplace levels' (ALP/ACTU, 1983).

The Prime Minister and the Minister for Employment and Industrial Relations reiterated the government's concern for industrial democracy at a well-attended seminar on Industrial Democracy and Employee Participation held in Melbourne in mid-1984. The Prime Minister drew attention to the operation of tripartite consultative processes foreshadowed in the Accord, such as the Economic Planning Advisory Council and the Advisory Committee on Prices and Incomes. On this basis, he claimed that 'industrial democracy at the macro, or national, level' had been established (DEIR, 1985). Employers at the enterprise level were encouraged to follow the government's lead and, in particular, to share appropriate information with employees and the unions representing them, and to involve employees and unions in the discussion and analysis of policy. None the less, employers were told that they must accept the responsibility for making the final decisions in their enterprises.

The government has taken steps to honour its commitment. The Melbourne seminar launched *Guidelines on Information Sharing*, drafted by the tripartite National Labour Consultative Council (NLCC). These encouraged employers to share information with employees and their unions as a pre-condition for greater industrial democracy (NLCC, 1984). In addition, the government has made grants available to employers and unions in the public and private sector to assist in the implementation of more participative management styles. Relevant research has also been subsidized: between 1984 and 1986, approximately 2 million Australian dollars were made available. Grants were used to raise awareness among employees and managers of the issues involved, to encourage the development of more consultative structures, and to provide appropriate training.

Perhaps the most obvious reflection of the government's interest has been the changes introduced in the federal public sector. A policy paper, *Reforming the Australian Public Service*, stated that:

> A more participative approach to management will improve decision-making by ensuring full opportunities for the staff who will be affected to make their views known and to have them properly considered. An administration more responsive to the needs of staff will enjoy improved morale and performance, while at the same time enriching the working lives of men and women who are part of the Government's workforce. (Stanton, 1984)

The areas tackled have included work organization, financial and staff planning, occupational health and safety, and the introduction of new technologies. In addition, and as detailed in the Public Sector Reform Act 1984, each department and prescribed authority has been required to develop and implement an 'industrial democracy plan'. The Hawke government also commissioned a Policy Discussion Paper on industrial democracy, which was released in 1986. It proposed measures to encourage the introduction of industrial democracy but cautioned against prescriptive legislation in this area. Instead, the paper recommended that the government consider a variety of 'facilitative measures', including financial incentives (such as taxation benefits) to organizations that introduced approved forms of industrial democracy. It also urged the provision of education and training, and advice and assistance to employers and unions to encourage initiatives at the enterprise level. Such measures fell well short of union demands for 'framework legislation' that would compel employers to undertake more extensive actions to introduce industrial democracy within the workplace (DEIR, 1986).

Economic Recovery (1983–5) and Decline (1985–7)

Significant interest had been shown in industrial democracy in the first half of the 1970s. Remnants of this lingered in South Australia, at least until the holding of an international conference on industrial democracy in 1978. Thereafter, in this state as elsewhere, discussion ebbed. A factor often cited as responsible was the deterioration in economic circumstances. This was reflected in the annual movement of consumer prices and in levels of unemployment. In the mid-1970s inflation rose steeply to approximately 15 per cent and remained relatively high until 1984. Similarly, the proportion of the labour force unemployed rose in the mid-1970s; it peaked at 9.8 per cent in 1983. It was generally assumed that the economic problems facing workers and their employers crowded out explicit concern for industrial democracy. For workers and unions, priorities were the defence of jobs and real living standards; management therefore was under less pressure to implement more participative styles of management.

The ALP–ACTU Accord committed the government to implement a more expansionary economic policy. Government fiscal and monetary policy in 1983 and 1984 was designed to promote economic growth, while incomes policy restrained inflation. The immediate outcome, aided by factors such as the breaking of a lengthy drought in the rural heartland and strong growth in the US economy, was a startling recovery with growth of gross domestic product (GDP) at 10.1 per cent for the financial year 1983–4. On a calendar year basis, GDP growth of approximately 5 per cent per annum was achieved in 1983, 1984 and 1985.

Inflation was reduced from 10.1 per cent in 1983 to 4.0 per cent in 1984. Subsequently, however, it rose and fluctuated between 7 per cent and 10 per cent (1985–7). The expansionary policy early in the Hawke government's term led to an increase in employment and a significant fall in unemployment. The latter has been around 8 per cent for much of the period. Arguably, the existence of more favourable economic conditions provided fertile soil for the growth of industrial democracy. But other problems intervened, including: a stubborn deficit on the balance of payments, high interest rates, extraordinary volatility in the exchange value of the Australian dollar, and the persistence of higher inflation than experienced by major trading partners.

Few commentators expect that economic growth will quickly return to the levels achieved between 1983 and 1985 and there are fears of increased unemployment. But a factor that distinguishes the mid-1980s from the mid-1970s is a greater, though still rather limited, commitment of government to industrial democracy. In addition, the difficult economic circumstances have focused attention on the need for more participative and cooperative styles of management. As discussed in the ACTU-Trade Development Council (TDC) report, *Australia Reconstructed*, industrial democracy is regarded as a means to improve organizational efficiency, productivity and hence competitiveness. The report emphasized that industrial democracy, together with greater attention to the implementation of appropriate technologies, improved forms of work organization and higher levels of training, should be 'harnessed as a force in production' (ACTU/TDC, 1987, p. 138).

High Court and Commission Decisions

Dr J. E. Isaac, a former Deputy President of the federal Arbitration Commission, has argued that the practice of conciliation and arbitration federally and within the states has tended to restrict industrial democracy (Isaac, 1980). It has commonly buttressed the notion of managerial prerogative and thereby limited the opportunities for workers and their unions to be involved in the planning and organization of work. Isaac has commented that the federal Arbitration Commission has held a narrow view of the sorts of matters over which it should adjudicate. In this respect it has been influenced by the High Court. Isaac quotes a former Chief Justice, Sir Garfield Barwick, who stated that the management of an enterprise should not be a subject matter for industrial dispute. Since the Arbitration Commission is permitted by the Constitution to be involved only in the prevention and settlement of *industrial disputes*, it has not generally been able to make rulings about the process of management.

In 1983, however, in the Social Welfare Union Case, the High Court's decision indicated that it was ready to take a broader view of what constituted an 'industrial dispute' (Smith, 1985). A major implication has been that matters previously regarded as managerial prerogative might now be determined by the Commission. This impression was reinforced in the High Court's decision in late 1984 to uphold a ruling of the Victorian Industrial Relations Commission. The Victorian Commission had been challenged on its decision to ratify the insertion of a clause in the Commercial Clerks' Award requiring extensive consultation between employers and employees *before* the introduction of technological change in the workplace. The new clause required employers to notify the Federated Clerks' Union and employees of any decision to begin feasibility studies on technological change, to consult with the union and employees during the feasibility study and to advise these groups as soon as any decision was made. Further, the employer was also obliged to consult on the issue of alternative proposals. One judge commented in his summing up that the workers' claim

> is a demand to be treated as more than wage-hands – to be treated as men and women who should be informed about decisions which might materially affect their future, and to be consulted on them. It is a demand . . . to be treated with respect and dignity. (*Employee Participation News*, no. 3, 1984)

Other decisions have also been important. Most notably a Full Bench of the federal Arbitration Commission heard a lengthy test case on the issue of job protection. The ACTU, supported by the Hawke government, sought the establishment of rights for employees to be notified and consulted by employers about the proposed introduction of technological change. In its Termination, Change and Redundancy Decision (1984), the Commission granted rights in the award for workers to receive information and be consulted by employers over their plans for technological change and organizational restructuring. The decision, which preceded the High Court's ruling on the Commercial Clerks' Award, was hailed as a landmark in Australian industrial relations. Taken together with the ruling of the High Court, it has suggested an erosion of managerial prerogative (Deery, 1986).

It should be noted, however, that under the Termination, Change and Redundancy Decision the rights to information and to consultation come into force only *after* management has decided on change. By this stage there may be little scope for workers to influence the decision itself. Furthermore, the rights granted do not extend to decision-making powers, but simply require management to give notice and engage in consultation about change. Finally, the extent to which the award changes can be used to increase worker and union influence depends upon the response of these bodies. If unions make good use of the information and enter the consultative process with well-argued proposals, then the rights granted by the Commission may well yield benefits.

The Review of Australian Industrial Relations, chaired by Keith Hancock, also gave strong support to broadening the jurisdiction of the Arbitration Commission (Committee of Review, 1985). It argued that government should legislate to remove 'artificial limitations' on the ability of the federal tribunal to deal with workplace matters. It also encouraged employers to provide relevant information to, and consult with, employees and the unions representing them and to pursue industrial democracy. Such behaviour was believed to be particularly appropriate in the case of proposals for technological change (Lansbury and Davis, 1985). To the extent that the federal government implements the Hancock recommendations, further impetus will be given to the momentum for industrial democracy. A Bill on these matters was tabled in federal parliament in May 1987, but then withdrawn before the 1987 federal election. It was tabled again in 1988.

Union Pressure

Unions have long sought to influence management decision-making. But, for the most part, union efforts have been restricted to issues connected with wages and conditions. During the 1970s many unions indicated a desire to participate in a broader range of issues. This, among other things, encouraged debate and the formulation of an explicit ACTU policy on industrial democracy at its 1977 biennial congress. This has been revised at subsequent congresses (Davis, 1986). Current ACTU policy declares that democracy in the workplace is a fundamental democratic right which should be enshrined in legislation, that it should be channelled through unions, that education courses are desirable to prepare members for increased participation in decision-making, and that both participative and representative forms of industrial democracy are acceptable. No single model is envisaged. The point is made that the implementation of industrial democracy will lead to a more equal distribution of power within the enterprise; traditional patterns of ownership, organization and control will inevitably be challenged.

Two developments are of particular interest. First, ACTU officials have argued that the Accord represents a blueprint for industrial democracy. It is seen to encourage greater worker participation, through unions, in the determination of the critical matters affecting worklife. Further, this participation takes place at national, industry, enterprise and workplace levels. Second, unions have been encouraged to play an active part in the drive for industrial democracy. Following policy revisions made at the 1985 congress, they are urged to draw up claims that identify those issues of greatest importance to workers (such as employment security, work organization, technological change, and occupational health and safety) and then to seek rights to information, to consultation and to decision-making influence on these matters. In other words, unions have been encouraged to negotiate on industrial democracy, just as they have conducted negotiations on wages and conditions.

The growth of explicit interest in industrial democracy at national level has been reflected in the policies and experience of several unions. Two prominent examples are the Administrative and Clerical Officers' Association (ACOA), which covers clerical staff within the federal public service, and the Amalgamated Metal Workers' Union (AMWU), which covers maintenance and other metal workers.

The ACOA has welcomed government interest in the development of more participative management styles. But it has insisted that government policy on industrial democracy will not be translated into practice unless union workplace representatives are given the time, training and facilities to prepare for joint consultative meetings. To date, the ACOA's impression is that the establishment of consultative councils has increased the flow of information to union members. In addition, the union, through consultation and negotiation, has been able to exercise a greater influence over a broader range of matters than formerly.

Problems have, however, been encountered. First, so many initiatives for union–management consultation have flourished that the union has not been able to offer an adequate response. It has lacked the resources to train and assist its members to assume a more participative role in management. Second, in many sections of the public sector, management has shown little willingness to consult with worker representatives and has been reluctant to provide information, resources and facilities to union representatives (Robson, 1986).

Industrial democracy has been on the AMWU's agenda since the mid-1970s (Ruskin, 1986). For most full-time officials and active shop stewards, it has meant the pursuit of greater rights and influence within the workplace. The blueprint for this was set out in the AMWU's Shop Stewards' Charter which listed union claims for rights to information, to facilities and to influence within the workplace (Davis, 1980). The term 'industrial democracy' was regarded with some suspicion by many within the union. This was on two counts. First, many stewards reported that managements were reorganizing methods of work in ways that often increased workers' influence over the immediate aspects of their job. Workers were exhorted to support the revised approach on the basis that it was 'industrial democracy'. Stewards objected to the fact that they had not been consulted about the reorganization, they pointed to the limited nature of decision-making opportunities granted to workers, and were generally cynical of management intentions to implement industrial democracy. Second, many full-time officials and stewards felt uncomfortable with the orientation to consensus that appeared, according to conventional wisdom, to be an ingredient in industrial democracy. This did not sit easily with the union's traditional emphasis on militant struggle for improved wages and conditions (Sweeney, 1976).

Current AMWU approaches to industrial democracy emphasize the importance of negotiations over increased rights for workers; the Shop Stewards' Charter remains the appropriate vehicle for workplace democracy. But, in line with sentiments expressed in the Accord, union officials have appeared less reserved about entering into more consultative and cooperative arrangements with employers. An example of this was the joint statement of metal unions and employers which concluded a forum on Jobs and Industry in 1983. The forum focused on the sharing of information, a joint approach to tackling the problems and a sharing of the benefits. Underlying this change of emphasis has been the view that management can no longer be left to managers. The crisis of manufacturing is too severe. The union must therefore play an active role in planning the future of the industry, and this inevitably propels it beyond past strategies based on union *reaction* to management decisions.

Technological Change

The issue of worker participation in decisions on technological change generated relatively little debate among industrial relations specialists before the mid-1970s. This was despite the fact that important new technologies had been introduced, for example on the waterfront, and in banking and insurance. The absence of debate was due in large measure to the ease with which new technologies were accommodated. For instance, although containerization resulted in a large reduction in employment on the waterfront, workers were placated with generous redundancy settlements. In the finance industry, technological change stimulated rather than depressed the demand for labour.

From the mid-1970s, however, worker and union concern about new technologies increased. First, it became apparent that technological change was occurring at a more rapid rate and on a broader scale. The implementation of change was evidently not confined to mining and manufacturing, but, particularly through the use of microelectronic technology, was affecting the large services sector. Second, it was clear that new technologies often wrought major changes in employment (and prospects for future employment), employer demand for skills, the organization and supervision of work, relativities in wages and conditions, and occupational health and safety. Third, all this was occurring within an increasingly unstable economic context with higher unemployment.

The thrust of ACTU policy, mirrored in the policies of many of its affiliates, was not that new technologies should be opposed. The ACTU recognized that they could make a significant contribution to improving the competitiveness of Australian industry, raising standards of living and ameliorating working conditions. The ACTU's emphasis was that workers and unions should be involved in decisions on whether new technologies should be introduced, what sort of technologies should be considered and how they should be implemented. The ACTU argued that worker and union participation should be guaranteed through appropriate changes to awards and through legislation. This view was put to the Committee of Inquiry into Technological Change in Australia (CITCA), which was established by the Fraser government and which published its report in 1980.

Employers and their associations have been rather less fearful about the alleged ill-effects accompanying technological change. Employers have argued that the implementation of technological change is crucial to the ability of Australian industry to compete in both domestic and overseas markets. Where industry keeps abreast of change, benefits can be anticipated in the form of increased employment, improved productivity and real income, and the removal of repetitive, unhealthy and unpleasant work tasks. Therefore, governments are requested to encourage research into the implementation of technological change; they are asked to remove restrictions that hamper the introduction of change; and they are asked to establish programmes to provide appropriate education and training for workers. But while employers recognize the importance of informing and consulting with workers on matters connected with technological change, they have urged the government not to impose particular structures for these purposes. Rather, the provision of information and the practice of consultation should be left to develop in each organization as appropriate.

The Hancock Committee paid some attention to industrial relations and technological change, though this did not feature strongly in its Report. Two researchers, commissioned by the

Committee, pointed out that employers are generally unwilling to see any erosion of their power to make decisions; that they are sceptical of the benefits to be gained from worker participation; and that they fear that union power may well be increased. None the less, the Hancock Report urged employers to give greater emphasis to consultation and participation, and to put less store on managerial prerogative. The anticipated outcome was both better and more readily accepted decisions (Lansbury and Davis, 1985).

The case of Telecom Australia, one of Australia's largest employers, is of interest. In 1977, Telecom management proposed to introduce new computer-controlled technology that would have the effect of centralizing the work of engineers. The Australian Telecommunications Employees' Association (ATEA), which represented these workers, objected that there had been minimal consultation with the union over this plan and articulated members' fears for their jobs, career opportunities and job satisfaction (Musumeci, 1985). The ATEA's objection was not to the technology chosen by management, but to their plans to reorganize the workforce.

Telecom refused to adopt the ATEA's counter-proposals and a strike ensued. The Arbitration Commissioner who heard the matter determined that the alternative system proposed should be allowed to operate for a trial period, and then be evaluated. The criteria for judgement were efficiency of operation, standard of service, job satisfaction, career opportunities, maintenance of technical standards, retention of expertise, and the public interest. The trials, and further Commission hearings, paved the way for a technology agreement between Telecom and relevant unions. Importantly, the agreement specified the principles to be applied in the process of technological change. These included joint management–union consideration of proposals for change (including those submitted by unions) *before* a firm decision had been made, and employer provision of information and resources to unions to enable them to make accurate assessments of the implications of the employer's proposals.

Limits to Industrial Democracy

This chapter has pointed to a momentum for industrial democracy and greater worker participation in decisions on technological change. But there are significant obstacles. First, many employers and their organizations have stated that they will resist moves towards industrial democracy, since these involve an erosion of managerial prerogatives. The Confederation of Australian Industry (CAI) sees industrial democracy as 'radical social change involving an abrogation of property and ownership rights' (Noakes 1985). Employers cannot be expected to welcome this. Their preference is for 'employee participation', which inculcates a sense of worker involvement in decision-making without interfering with management's right to make decisions. In addition, employers seek direct, task-centred participation rather than the setting-up of consultative structures, and participation on a voluntary basis rather than that imposed by legislation.

In a similar vein, the Business Council of Australia (BCA) has argued for employee participation and opposed industrial democracy. The distinction drawn by the BCA is that employee participation occurs within a framework of managerial prerogatives; industrial democracy seeks the redistribution of power to workers and unions and challenges the framework itself. Moreover, employee participation applies to the workplace. By contrast, industrial democracy includes demands for union influence at the enterprise, industry and national level as well. It is therefore much more threatening to employers.

Further concerns of the BCA are that industrial democracy will be channelled through unions; this will increase union power and disenfranchise the significant proportion of workers who are not union members. The BCA argues that the focus on worker and union rights at the heart of demands for industrial democracy will be a source of conflict between unions and management. Where rights are achieved, these will build in rigidities and costs, to the detriment of the enterprise. The way forward therefore lies with management strategies that encourage greater employee involvement in work and that ensure that the enterprise is flexible and able to adapt in the face of a changing economic and technological context.

A second major obstacle arises out of the paucity of union resources. Many unions do not have the ability to become more involved in deciding the complex issues facing management, because there are too many unions, which are generally underfunded. At the last count, there were 323 unions representing 3.2

million members. Only ten unions had 80,000 or more members; 154 unions each had fewer than 1,000 members. Inevitably, union resources are spread more thinly than if a smaller number of unions covered the same population of members. The problem is compounded by the relatively low dues that are charged. For instance, members' fees in Swedish and West German unions are two to three times higher than those of their Australian counterparts (Beyme, 1980). Unions in those countries have established major educational and research facilities, which have been integral to worker and union involvement in decision-making.

Australian unions are aware of this handicap. Officials in the ACOA, the ATEA and the AMWU have drawn attention to the need for greater resources and the need to dedicate these resources to the education and training of members, to equip members with the skills and confidence to be more involved in management. They also call for more research facilities to enable them to draw up their own proposals, for example about new technologies.

There are no easy solutions, although several measures might assist in the medium term. First, as advocated by the Hancock Report, federal legislation to facilitate union amalgamations may diminish the number of unions, with remaining unions being larger and better resourced. Second, union decisions to increase the rate of dues will prove of direct benefit. This could be more easily accomplished if unions paid heed to ACTU policy, endorsed at the 1987 congress, that all unions should charge, at minimum, 1.25 per cent of the All Industry Group average weekly wage. Third, unions have benefited from government industrial democracy grants. Fourth, a lesson from the experience in Telecom is that unions should negotiate over industrial democracy and that a principal claim on employers should be the provision of training and facilities to enable worker representatives to be more effectively involved in the process of management.

Conclusion

Workers' participation in decisions on technological change has been affected by wider moves towards greater levels of industrial democracy. Government support, a more facilitative legal context, and a growth in union interest have laid the basis for greater worker participation. With regard to decisions on technological change, unions made headway through the Termination, Change and Redundancy Decision, which granted workers and unions rights to information and to consultation on this and other matters. While important, the decision should be seen in perspective. Management is under no obligation to share its decision-making prerogative. More generally, there remains some determined resistance on the part of many employers to the implementation of more worker participation, and many unions lack the resources to play a greater role in management decision-making. These factors inhibit the achievement of greater industrial democracy in Australia.

References

ACTU (1982), *Consolidation of ACTU Policy Decisions, 1951–1982* (Melbourne: Australian Council of Trade Unions).

ACTU/TDC (1987), *Australia Reconstructed* (Canberra: Australian Government Publishing Service).

ALP/ACTU (1983), *Statement of Accord* (Melbourne: Australian Council Trade Unions).

Beyme, K. V. (1980), *Challenge to Power* (London: Sage).

Committee of Inquiry into Technological Change in Australia (CITCA) (1980), *Technological Change in Australia*, vols I–III (Canberra: Australian Government Publishing Service).

Committee of Review into Australian Industrial Relations Law and Systems (1985), Chairman: K. Hancock, *Report*, Vols I–III (Canberra: Australian Government Publishing Service).

Davis, E. M. (1980), 'Decision-making in the Amalgamated Metal Workers and Shipwrights Union', in G. W. Ford, J. M. Hearn and R. D. Lansbury (eds), *Australian Labour Relations: Readings*, 3rd edn (Melbourne: Macmillan), pp. 124–48.

Davis, E. M. (1986), 'Unions and industrial democracy', in Davis and Lansbury (eds) (1986), pp. 133–45.

Davis, E. M. and Lansbury, R. D. (eds) (1986), *Democracy and Control in the Workplace* (Melbourne: Longman Cheshire).

DEIR (1985), *Proceedings of a Seminar on Industrial Democracy and Employee Participation* (Canberra: Department of Employment and Industrial Relations/Australian Government Publishing Service).

DEIR (1986), *Industrial Democracy and Employee Participation: A Policy Discussion Paper* (Canberra: Department of Employment and Industrial Relations/Australian Government Publishing Service).

Deery, S. J. (1986), 'New technology, union rights and management prerogatives: The Australian experience', *Labour and Society*, vol. 11, no. 1, pp. 67–81.

Isaac, J. E. (1980), 'Industrial democracy in the context of conciliation and arbitration', in R. D. Lansbury (ed.), *Democracy in the Workplace* (Melbourne: Longman Cheshire), pp. 34–53.

Lansbury, R. D. (1985), 'The accord between the unions and government in Australia: A new experiment in industrial relations?', *Labour and Society*, vol. 19, no. 2, pp. 223–34.

Lansbury, R. D. and Davis, E. M. (1985), 'The Hancock Report and industrial democracy', *Journal of Industrial Relations*, vol. 27, no. 4, pp. 544–54.

Musumeci, M. (1985), 'Industrial democracy and technological change: A union view of the telecom experience', in Department of Employment and Industrial Relations, *Proceedings of a Seminar on Industrial Democracy and Employee Participation* (Canberra: Australian Government Publishing Service), pp. 165–7.

National Labour Consultative Council (NLCC) (1984), *Guidelines on Information Sharing* (Canberra: Australian Government Publishing Service).

Noakes, B. (1985), 'An Employer Perspective of Industrial Democracy', in Department of Employment and Industrial Relations, *Proceedings of a Seminar on Industrial Democracy and Employee Participation* (Canberra: Australian Government Publishing Service), pp. 19–24.

Pritchard, R. L. (ed.) (1977), *Industrial Democracy in Australia* (Sydney: CCH Australia), pp. 179–212.

Robson, P. (1986), 'Public service reform and industrial relations', in *Proceedings of a Conference on Industrial Relations in the Public Sector* (Canberra: Centre for Continuing Education, Australian National University).

Ruskin, N. (1986), 'Union policy on industrial democracy: The AMWU', in Davis and Lansbury (eds) (1986), pp. 76–191.

Smith, G. F. (1985), 'The High Court and industrial relations in the 1980s', *Australian Bulletin of Labour*, vol. 11, no. 2, pp. 82–101.

Stanton, M. (1984), 'Industrial democracy in the Australian public service', *Canberra Bulletin of Public Administration*, vol. 11, no. 3, pp. 160–73.

Sweeney, S. (1976), 'Pluralism and worker participation: An Australian perspective', *Australian Bulletin of Labour*, vol. 2, no. 2, pp. 30–47.

CHAPTER SIX

Employee Involvement Programmes and Worker Perceptions of New Technology in North America

ANIL VERMA and WILFRED ZERBE

*Employee involvement (EI) can affect worker perceptions of new technology in two ways. First, it can increase worker acceptance of new technology by legitimating the need to introduce new technology. Second, worker participation in on-the-job decisions can lead to perceptions of greater participation in technology issues. Results of a survey of employees in three high technology firms in the USA showed that EI programmes increase worker acceptance of the need to introduce new technology. Worker perceptions of participation in decisions can be represented by two factors characterizing more immediate (*proximal*) job aspects, and less immediate (*distal*) aspects. EI appears to increase the immediacy of decisions involving technology. In this way workers appear to compensate for increases in acceptance of technology at the strategic level with an increased desire for participation at the workplace level.*

This chapter examines the link between two important developments in recent years: direct employee participation in decision-making and the introduction of new technology. Employee-involvement (EI) programmes such as quality circles (QCs) and autonomous work groups have been introduced in organizations in many parts of the world (Wilpert and Sorge, 1984). Many of these participative structures are designed to provide direct worker participation in decisions affecting workers' jobs. In North America most such programmes generally provide for worker inputs into decisions about quality, process and output, but rarely into decisions relating to the introduction and use of new technology in their jobs. It is reasonable to assume, however, that workers may desire direct participation in technology decisions. If such participation is to be extended to this important area, it is important to understand workers' perceptions of new technology and related concerns.

Despite a wide-ranging and diverse literature on technology, examination of worker perceptions has not received much attention from researchers. We attempt to fill this gap by examining worker perceptions of participation in technology decisions. First, we consider how workers perceive participation in technology decisions in relation to participation in other areas of the job. Second, we explore how the presence of EI programmes may be altering perceptions of the need to participate in technology decisions. Given that EI programmes emphasize worker identification with organizational needs (Verma and McKersie, 1987), it is possible that workers in an EI programme begin to identify more strongly with organizational goals of upgrading technology, which may in turn lead to greater acceptance of new technology. Further, as workers adapt to participation in decision-making in some areas, they may become more inclined to participate in technology decisions. Thus, EI programmes may be heightening workers' awareness of technology and also enhancing their wish to participate in technology decisions. This chapter uses data from employee attitude surveys in three organizations to address these two questions.

Conceptual Framework

In the social sciences in North America much of the research on technology has focused on its impact on jobs, organizational structure and organizational processes such as the locus of power and influence (for a review see Fry, 1982, and Rousseau, 1983). Although all these studies treat technology as an independent or determining variable, rather than as a dependent variable, they do provide a foundation on which to develop a conceptual model of how workers perceive technology.

One school of researchers has emphasized the negative impact of technology on workers. This approach is well-articulated by Braverman (1974), who suggests that technology may be employed in a manner so as to deskill jobs and increase the amount of control that managers exercise over workers. Other scholars have either modified this view, or presented an opposite view in which technology's negative effects are either small, or are outweighed by its positive effects on workers (Harvard University, 1970; Shepard, 1971, 1977; Form and McMillen, 1983). If the overall effect of technology has been positive in the aggregate experience of workers, we may expect workers to perceive technology in favourable terms (cf. Chapter 11 in this book). For example, in a study of employees in an office environment, it was found that workers generally agreed that computers helped workers in their jobs and disagreed that computers would remove responsibility and decision-making from workers and deskill their jobs (Gutek, Bikson and Mankin, 1984). In another national (USA) sample of 2,655 respondents, it was found that 78 per cent of workers without any experience of technological change perceived technology as a 'friend' (Form and McMillen, 1983). Among workers who had experienced technological change, a still higher proportion (81 per cent) of workers perceived technology as a 'friend'. Fewer than 6 per cent of the workers perceived technology as a 'foe', with the rest perceiving it as 'friend and foe'.

In this study, we explore how workers perceive technology in relation to other issues. We do this at the strategic level and at the level of the workplace. At the strategic level, workers may accept the role of technology in maintaining a successful organization. To that extent, workers will perceive the introduction and use of new technology as a necessary organizational goal similar to other strategic goals, such as improving productivity and maintaining competitiveness in the market. Adoption of new technology can thus be perceived as a strategic response to ensure organizational survival.

If workers perceive technology as a necessary organizational goal at the strategic level, how do they perceive it at the workplace level? It may be argued that the pace of technological change has raised a number of concerns in the minds of workers. For example, some jobs are lost or altered by technological change. A number of researchers have outlined these and other negative effects of technology (Meissner, 1969; Davis and Taylor, 1976; Edwards, 1979). There is an apparent conflict between accepting the strategic need to upgrade technology, and the possible negative impact on jobs. One way in which workers can reconcile this conflict is by acquiring a feeling of control on the job through participation in decision-making (Locke and Schweiger, 1979). Workers' desire for participation in technology decisions should therefore be examined as an indicator of how workers relate to technology at the workplace level.

Desire for participation in decisions concerning technology must be examined in relation to desired participation in other job areas. The 1977 Quality of Employment Survey asked workers if they would like to have a 'say' in a number of job areas. Respondents on the whole appeared to want more 'say' in some areas of the job, such as safety and work methods, and appeared less interested in areas such as hiring and lay-off decisions (Quinn and Staines, 1979). In another study, more workers appeared interested in participating in decisions relating to issues such as work method and quality than in personnel and business decisions (e.g. hiring, management salaries, selection of supervisor, plant expansion, investment plans) (Kochan, Katz and Mower, 1984). Both of these studies suggest that some issues are of greater concern to the worker than others. However, lower priority cannot be interpreted as an indication that some areas are of no significance to workers. These priorities indicate, in our view, an ordering by workers of decision areas that they can relate to and comprehend well enough to participate in decision-making. Thus, decision areas such as work methods and quality are not only higher on the priority list for workers, but they are also closer to the worker in terms of his or her sphere of operation. Based on this notion of distance from the worker's sphere of operation, we can construct a continuum on which decision areas close to the worker may be called 'proximal' and those at a greater distance 'distal'.

The conflict between worker self-interest at the workplace level, on the one hand, and acceptance of technology as a strategic organizational goal, on the other hand, can be placed on this proximal-distal continuum. We propose that one way in which workers can resolve or reduce this conflict is by placing technology closer to proximal decision areas. This allows the worker to accept the legitimacy of new technology at the workplace level. Essentially, the worker takes the position, 'technology is important both to the organization and to me and I want to be involved in such decisions'.

The introduction of direct worker participation in decision-making may affect perceptions of technology in a number of ways. EI programmes usually provide for participation in more proximal areas such as work methods, quality and output, but rarely provide for worker inputs into decisions concerning technology. Such EI programmes, in general, attempt to socialize workers into greater identification with the strategic goals of the organization (Verma and McKersie, 1987). It may, therefore, be expected that EI programmes will further enhance worker acceptance of organizational goals (Erez, Earley and Hulin, 1985) and further push workers' perceptions of technology towards those of proximal job aspects. In this way workers compensate for any increase in acceptance of technology at the strategic level with an increased desire for participation at the workplace level.

Research Method

Employees at three firms were surveyed with respect to their perceptions of aspects of their jobs, including the use of new technology. At each firm EI programme participants and non-participants were surveyed.

The EI programmes at the three firms surveyed were similar to quality circles (QCs). Workers in a group of eight to twelve meet once a week to identify problems relating to quality, work methods, waste, output, etc. The group then develops suggestions for improvements, with the help of staff experts. Many suggestions are implemented by management, though they have no obligation to do so. Membership in the programme is voluntary. Since all these programmes are relatively new (one–

three years old), only a minority (10–25 per cent) of workers were participating in these programmes at the time of the survey.

The Firms

Firm One manufactures high-technology engineering products in a number of US locations. This firm is a leader in its industry despite tough competition, and has a positive financial outlook. Labour–management relations are traditionally 'arms-length' but good. The survey was carried out in a plant situated in the Northwest of the USA, which employed some 10,000 workers. Survey respondents were chosen randomly from both participants and non-participants at the plant. The survey was administered to a total of 577 employees in the plant, of which 253 (44 per cent) were members of a QC at the time of the survey and 324 (56 per cent) were non-participants. Non-participants were further divided into those who indicated that they would volunteer for participation in a QC if given the opportunity to do so, and those who would not.

Firm Two is a large high-technology manufacturing and data-processing company. The survey setting was in the Northeast of the USA, at a complex employing about 4,000 workers. The survey was conducted in 1982, about twenty months after the introduction of the EI programme. The survey was administered to 387 employees, of which 218 (56 per cent) were participants in the EI programme. Of the non-participants, 113 indicated that they would volunteer to participate, 36 that they would not, and 20 did not answer the question.

Firm Three is a large US communication services firm. The survey was conducted in the early stages of the employee involvement programme, less than a year after it was introduced. The survey was administered to 171 employees; 31 indicated that they were participants in the EI programme.

Measures of Participation in Decision-Making

Employees at all three firms were asked about the extent of participation they felt they should have in decisions concerning twelve job aspects. The twelve aspects were:

1. when the work day begins and ends (labelled for analysis purposes HOURS);
2. the use of new technology on the job (TECHNOLOGY);
3. the way the work is done (METHODS);
4. the level of quality of the work (QUALITY);
5. who should be fired if appropriate (FIRE);
6. how fast the work should be done (RATE);
7. who should be hired (HIRE);
8. how much work people should do in a day (QUOTA);
9. handling of complaints or grievances (COMPLAINTS);
10. who should do what job (ASSIGN);
11. who gets promoted (PROMOTE); and
12. the selection of a supervisor (SUPERVISOR).

Employees indicated their desired participation on a four-point scale from 'no say' to 'a lot of say'.

Measures of Strategic Goals

In Firm One, three items were used to assess worker identification with strategic goals. Respondents were asked how much they agreed with the statements:

- 'There is a need to improve productivity if the company is to survive as a business';
- 'Competition from the market is getting tougher all the time'; and
- 'Productivity can be increased and we can be competitive only if workers and managers all pitch in'.

Measures of Perceptions of Technology

In Firm One, four additional items were used to assess perceptions of technology. Respondents were asked how much they agreed with the statements:

- 'Technology in the plant must be upgraded'; and
- 'I have a better understanding of the need to upgrade technology since QCs started'.

Respondents were also asked to rate how much say they thought they actually had in the use of new technology in their jobs, and the extent to which their participation in the use of new technology on their jobs had increased since QCs started.

Results

Perceptions of Technology

The way in which employees perceive the need to upgrade technology was assessed at Firm One by examining how it related to measures of strategic goals. A strong relationship was found. The item 'technology in the plant must be upgraded' was significantly correlated with items reflecting the need to improve productivity ($r = .42, p < .01$), the need for managers and workers to contribute ($r = .38, p < .01$), and increasing market competition ($r = .43, p < .01$). Overall these four items had high internal consistency (Cronbach's Alpha = .77). (Such statistical terms are explained in the Glossary at the end of this chapter.) Workers therefore see the need to upgrade technology as highly related to strategic company goals.

The perception of technology in relation to other job aspects was also examined. The ratings of desired participation in decisions concerning the twelve job aspects described above were factor analysed. A separate principal components factor analysis was performed for each firm. Two factors were chosen to represent the relations between job aspects at each firm. For Firms One and Two, a minimum eigen-value criterion was applied; for Firm Three, a Scree test indicated two factors. Varimax rotation was applied to the factors.

Overall the same two factors were uncovered at each firm. The first factor is best represented by the items reflecting participation in decisions concerning the methods used to perform work, the quality of the work performed, and how fast the work is done. The second factor is best characterized by items reflecting decisions about hiring, firing, promotion and supervision. The first factor thus represents aspects of decisions that are more immediate (or proximate) to employees and the second factor those that are more managerial (or distal) to employees. Table 6.1 presents the factor pattern for each firm. The implications of the factor pattern across

Table 6.1 *Rotated factor loadings of desired participation in job aspects (Firms One, Two and Three)*

	Firm One		*Firm Two*		*Firm Three*	
	Distal	*Proximal*	*Distal*	*Proximal*	*Distal*	*Proximal*
HIRE	.781	.045	.721	.246	.756	.075
PROMOTE	.779	.118	.784	.123	.708	.240
FIRE	.772	.073	.664	.097	.531	.279
SUPERVISION	.706	.111	.752	.167	.678	.164
COMPLAINTS	.636	.230	.570	.205	.500	.389
HOURS	.523	.273	.495	.394	.477	−.008
ASSIGNMENT	.519	.414	.762	.188	.737	.212
RATE	.068	.837	.395	.657	.241	.739
QUALITY	.029	.742	.056	.741	.080	.783
METHODS	.326	.667	.180	.807	.183	.789
QUOTA	.145	.663	.713	.271	.593	.338
TECHNOLOGY	.414	.427	.233	.729	.483	.165

firms strongly support the representation of relations among perceptions of decision-making by the distal and proximal factors.

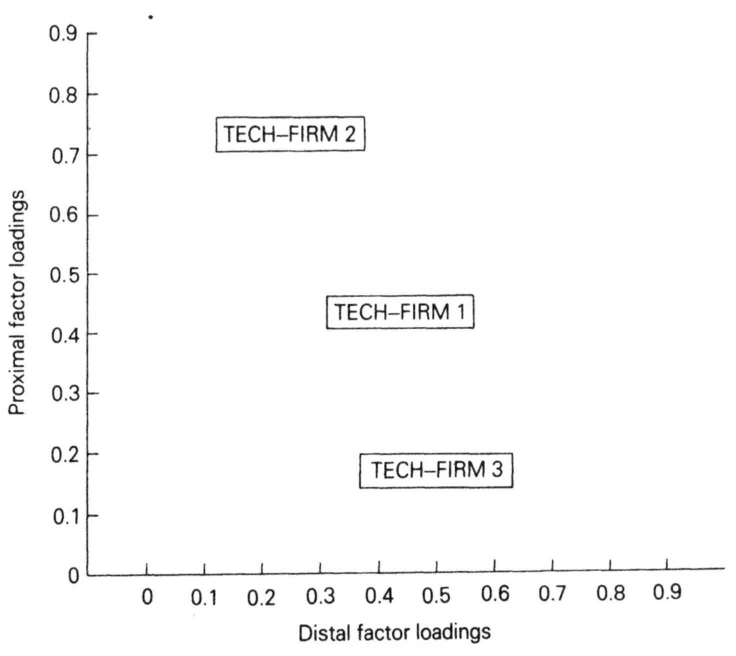

Figure 6.1 *Technology on the proximal–distal map (Firms One, Two and Three)*

Decisions concerning the use of new technology, however, are perceived differently across firms in relation to other aspects. In Firm One, decisions concerning technology load equally on both the distal and proximal factors; technology is perceived as moderate in its immediacy to employees (see Figure 6.1). In contrast, employees at Firm Two perceive technology as more immediate; technology has a high loading on the proximal factor and minor loading on the distal factor. Apparently workers at Firm Two see their participation in decision-making on technology as most like that concerning the methods, rate and quality of their work. At Firm Three technology loads moderately on the distal factor and has a small loading on the proximal factor. Across the three firms, decisions concerning technology are perceived as more closely related to managerial decisions, but this association is not a strong one (see Figure 6.2).

There are numerous possible reasons for differing perceptions of technology in relation to other job aspects across firms. Firms

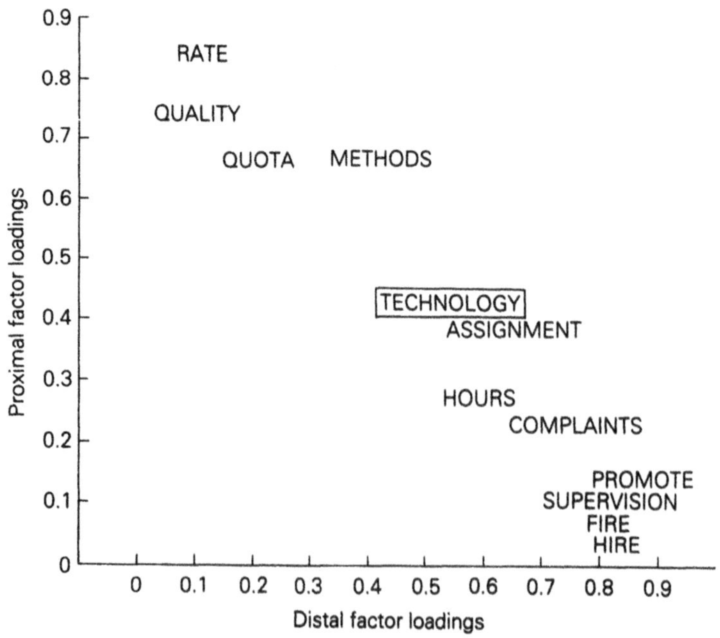

Figure 6.2 *Rotated factor loadings of desired participation in various job areas (Firm One)*

may be more or less reliant on new technology, its introduction may be more or less recent, and more or less stable. Differences between employees may contribute to perceptions. The results shown in Table 6.1 contain all respondents at each firm, some of whom were participants in EI programmes while some were not. In the next section we will consider how participation in EI can affect employee perceptions.

Perceptions of Technology and EI

The effect of EI programmes on workers' perceptions of technology was examined by comparing programme participants, non-participating volunteers and non-volunteers. Two sets of analyses were performed. First, the factor analyses of desired participation in job-aspect decisions reported above were repeated on participants, volunteers and non-volunteers. Second, mean responses of each group of items concerning technology were compared.

When performed separately for participants, volunteers and non-volunteers, the factor pattern reported for all respondents in each firm tends to vary, owing to the diminished sample size. In general, though, the items characteristic of distal aspects mark the first factor and those characteristic of proximal aspects mark the second factor. Of interest is the loading for the item concerning the use of new technology.

Table 6.2 shows the loadings of the technology item on the proximal and distal factors for each group of respondents in each firm. For Firm One the relative loadings of the technology item on the proximal and distal factors were most similar for volunteers and non-volunteers; participants tended to show a diminished loading on the distal factor. In other words, participants in the EI program perceived technology as closer to the proximal items than did non-participants. In the case of Firm Two, all respondents viewed technology as strongly associated with the proximal factors, but participants placed technology closer to the proximal factor than did the volunteers. Participation in the EI programme at Firm Three strongly affected how technology was perceived. Volunteers and non-volunteers saw technology as moderately associated with the distal factor and not at all proximal. EI participants, however, viewed technology as strongly related to proximal aspects and not related to distal aspects.

Table 6.2 *Loadings of desired participation in decisions concerning technology on proximal and distal factors for Firms One, Two and Three*

	N	*Factor*	
		Proximal	*Distal*
Firm One:			
All respondents	563	.427	.414
Participants	250	.486	.299
Volunteers	149	.373	.423
Non-volunteers	158	.496	.524
Firm Two:			
All respondents	364	.729	.234
Participants	209	.729	.218
Volunteers	35	.596	.340
Non-volunteers	106	.747	.232
Firm Three:			
All respondents	167	.166	.483
Participants	30	.761	.142
Volunteers	61	.000	.589
Non-volunteers	38	.145	.567

Comparison of loadings of technology across groups, then, supports the argument that EI programmes shift worker perceptions of technology away from distant aspects, such as promotion and supervision, and toward more immediate aspects like work methods, quality and rate (see Figure 6.3). When perceptions of technology are overall more proximal, as in Firm Two, EI has less effect. Again, variation is evident across firms. Some variation may be attributable to the relative impact of EI programmes. It is likely that their effect is due to both actual participation and informal communication by participants to non-participants. The programme at Firm Three was relatively new, thus lessening its effect on non-participants and increasing its effect on participants.

The impact of participation in EI programmes can also be illustrated by the average scores of items related to technology. Mean differences between participants, volunteers and non-volunteers in Firm One were assessed on five items measuring: perceived need to upgrade technology, desired and actual participation in decisions concerning technology, the perceived impact of QCs on understanding of the need to upgrade

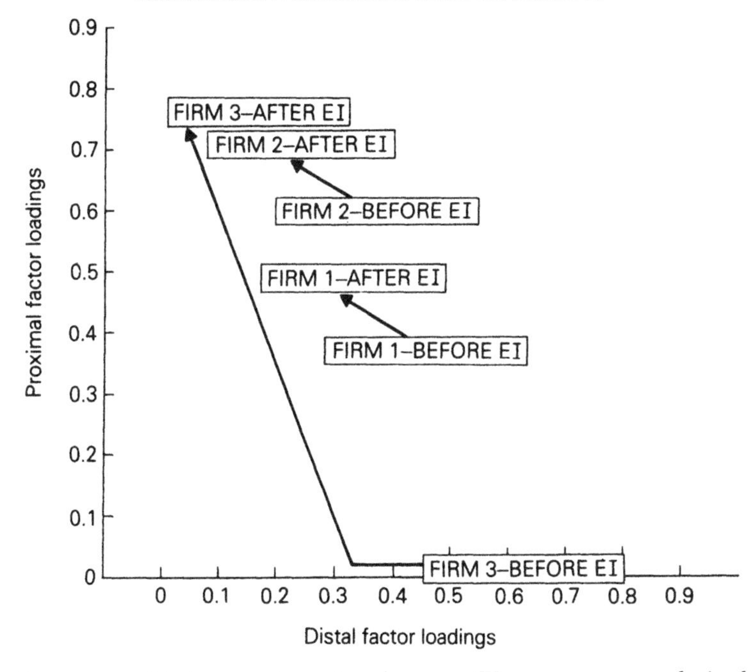

Figure 6.3 *Effect of employee involvement (EI) programme on desired participation in technology decisions*

technology, and participation in the use of technology. In addition mean differences were assessed on three items measuring agreement with strategic company goals. The particular items are shown in Table 6.3.

Comparison of participating employees with those who do not participate should show the effect of participation. However, because employees choose whether or not to participate, it may be that differences in perceptions of technology are the results of self-selection. That is, employees with particular attitudes toward technology and EI programmes are more likely to choose to participate. The fact that not all employees are able to participate, even if they wish to do so, allows us to test this selection hypothesis. If participation *per se* has an impact on perceptions, we should find mean differences between participating employees and those who have not participated but indicate that they would volunteer to do so. A selection effect would be evidenced by differences between such volunteers and non-volunteers.

Table 6.3 *Differences between Firm One participants, volunteers and non-volunteers on measures of strategic goals and participation in decisions concerning technology*

	QC Participants (n = 238)	*Non-participants*		*F*
		Volunteers (n = 145)	*Non-volunteers (n = 146)*	
Technology in the plant must be upgraded	4.40^{ab}	4.24^{a}	4.16^{b}	6.36^{**}
I have a better understanding of the need to upgrade technology since QCs started	3.86^{a}	3.21^{a}	2.87^{a}	57.23^{**}
How much say do you think you *should* have in the use of new technology on your job?	3.97^{a}	4.00^{b}	3.48^{ab}	11.61^{**}
How much say do you think you *actually* have in the use of new technology on your job?	2.27^{a}	1.99^{a}	1.97	3.56^{*}
Since QCs were introduced, has your participation increased in the use of new technology on your job?	3.42^{ab}	3.18^{a}	3.05^{b}	14.17^{**}
There is a need to improve productivity if the company is to survive as a business	4.41^{ab}	4.24^{a}	4.08^{b}	8.67^{**}
Competition from the market is getting tougher all the time	4.48^{ab}	4.27^{a}	4.27^{b}	6.33^{**}
Productivity can be increased and we can be competitive only if workers and managers pitch in	4.60^{ab}	4.43^{a}	4.28^{b}	11.28^{**}

Notes:
* $p < .05$
** $p < .01$
Group item means sharing a superscript (a or b) are significantly different from each other (Student–Newman–Keuls test, pairwise probability of Type I error = .05).
n = sample size.

A multivariate analysis of variance (ANOVA) was performed on the eight items in Table 6.3. The overall F-test was significant ($F = 10.58$, $p < .001$), permitting univariate tests on items. Univariate F-tests were significant for all items, as shown in Table 6.3, indicating mean differences between the three groups. Student–Newman–Keuls multiple range tests were performed on pairs of means for each item to determine whether the differences among groups was attributable to selection or participation.

The results provide strong evidence that participation in EI programmes increases employee perceptions of their participation in and understanding of decisions concerning technology. In only one case was evidence found for a selection effect in the absence of a participation effect: both volunteers and participants reported significantly higher *desired* participation in technology issues than non-volunteers. In contrast, the other seven items showed only an effect of participation or a participation effect above and beyond a difference between volunteers and non-volunteers. Participants perceived more of a need for technology to be upgraded, and reported that their understanding of this need had increased since QCs had started. Similarly, participants reported significantly higher *actual* participation in decisions concerning technology, and that QCs had increased their participation.

The final three items in Table 6.3 show that participants were significantly more likely to espouse strategic company goals than either volunteers or non-volunteers. Participants in EI programmes do not see new technology as less strategically important. This suggests that EI programmes promote worker acceptance of strategic management goals.

Summary and Conclusion

The results of this study suggest that workers recognize and accept the need to upgrade technology at the strategic level. Such acceptance is matched by a desire for participation in decisions relating to the use of technology at the workplace level. Desire for participation in technology decisions is similar to desire for participation in proximal issues such as work methods and quality, and dissimilar to distal issues such as hiring, firing and supervision.

When workers experience participation in decision-making through EI programmes, both their acceptance and the desire for participation is enhanced. This result is particularly significant, given that none of the EI programmes at the three firms included in this study provided for participation in technology decisions. At Firm One, participants in the EI programme also perceived a higher level of actual participation in technology decisions even though such participation was not explicitly provided for in the programme. This suggests that actual participation in certain job aspects has an impact on perceptions of participation in other areas.

EI programmes are playing a major role in enhancing worker acceptance of technology. Such participative programmes can, therefore, play an important role in the successful introduction of and management of new technology. But adoption of EI programmes will require a willingness on the part of management to involve workers in a range of technology-related decisions. As the results of this study suggest, if EI programmes continue to proliferate without increased participation in technology-related decisions, more and more workers will see these programmes as meaningless rhetoric and lose interest. Perhaps it is for such reasons that many North American EI programmes appear, like fads, to wither away (Lawler and Mohrman, 1985).

Glossary of Statistical Terms

ANOVA: analysis of variance tests the difference between group means on one or more independent variables. Univariate ANOVA considers one dependent variable at a time. Multivariate ANOVA considers multiple dependent variables simultaneously.

Cronbach's Alpha (α): an index of reliability, or the extent to which a measure is consistent over persons, time and situations.

Factor analysis: a type of analysis used to discern the underlying dimensions or regularity in phenomena. Its general purpose is to summarize the information contained in a large number of variables into a smaller number of factors. Principal components factor analysis is a particular factor analytic method. The number of factors chosen is a function of two tests: (1) the minimum *eigen-value* criterion, which excludes factors that explain less than the variables they contain; and (2) the *scree test*, which examines the marginal explanatory contribution of including additional factors in a solution.

The European Foundation for the Improvement of Living and Working Conditions has for some years been engaged in a programme of research to evaluate the potential of participatory processes and procedures, in relation to the introduction of new technology. This is not a theoretical research programme, but one that deals with the analysis of real situations within companies, and one that aims at providing positive suggestions for involvement and action by those directly concerned. The structure of the Foundation, a tripartite body bringing together representatives of governments, unions and management within member countries of the European Community (EC), has made it possible to develop the research with the assistance of those involved in the processes of technological change, and to allow them to examine and assess the final results.

So far, the Foundation has carried out three research projects. The first phase consisted of a field-based analysis focused on the emerging phenomenon of collective technology agreements. This project was developed through twenty-one case studies, set out in five national reports and summarized in a consolidated report. The data and experiences brought out in this first phase were then subjected to a second-level analysis by an international group of experts, with a view to producing a resource that would allow the parties concerned to achieve a better understanding of the interrelations between the various salient factors, and thus to direct their activities. This second project has produced a practical and flexible set of guidelines (not a manual, still less a model) for the unions, the employers and the governments involved in the process of technological change. Third, with a view to broadening the framework of observation in the research and providing benchmarks for future action, a major opinion survey is being conducted across the EC. This survey, which will be completed in 1988, covers a sample of more than 10,000 representatives of management and workers in about 2,500 companies affected by major technological changes. Figure 7.1 shows the development of the Foundation's research in this area.

Changing Industrial Relations

Many people have worries and uncertainties about the introduction of new technology. Despite the enormous potential for

F-test: the test of significance most often associated with analysis of variance.

p: the probability that a given result is due to chance alone, also called the level of significance. This is the probability, adopted by the experimenter, of committing a Type I error, or concluding falsely that a real relationship exists.

r or Pearson product moment correlation: a statistical measure of the degree of covariation or linear relationship between two variables.

Student–Newman–Keuls multiple range test: a test of the significance of the difference between pairs of group means.

Varimax rotation: factor analytic solutions can be rotated to improve interpretability. Varimax rotation maximizes the variance between rotated factors.

For further explanation of these terms, the reader is referred to a statistical text such as F. N. Kerlinger, *Foundations of Behavioral Research* (New York: Holt, Rinehart & Winston, 1973); or B. G. Tabachnik and L. S. Fidell, *Using Multivariate Statistics* (New York: Harper & Row, 1983).

Acknowledgement

The authors would like to thank Thomas A. Kochan for making available part of the data used in this study.

References

Brass, D. J. (1985), 'Technology and the structuring of jobs: employee satisfaction, performance and influence', *Organizational Behavior and Human Decision Processes*, vol. 35, pp. 216–40.

Braverman, H. (1974), *Labor and Monopoly Capital: The Degradation of Work in the Twentieth Century* (New York: Monthly Review Press).

Dachler, P. H. and Wilpert, B. (1978), 'Conceptual dimensions and boundaries of participation in organizations: a critical evaluation', *Administrative Science Quarterly*, vol. 23, pp. 1–39.

Davis, E. and Taylor, J. C. (1976), 'Technology, organization, and job structure', in R. Dubin (ed.), *Handbook of Work, Organization, and Society* (Chicago: Rand McNally), pp. 379–420.

Edwards, R. (1979), *Contested Terrain: The Transformation of the Workplace in the Twentieth Century* (New York: Basic Books).

Erez, M., Earley, P. C. and Hulin, C. L. (1985), 'The impact of participation on goal acceptance and performance: a two-step model', *Academy of Management Journal*, vol. 28, pp. 50–66.

Form, W. and McMillen, D. B. (1983), 'Women, men and machines', *Work and Occupations*, vol. 10, pp. 147–78.

Fry, L. W. (1982), 'Technology–structure research: three critical issues', *Academy of Management Journal*, vol. 25, pp. 532–52.

Gutek, B. A., Bikson, T. K. and Mankin, D. (1984), 'Individual and organizational consequences of computer-based office information technology', in S. Oskamp (ed.), *Applied Social Psychology Annual*, vol. 5 (Beverly Hills, Calif.: Sage Publications).

Harvard University Program on Technology and Society (1970), *Technology and Work. Research Review 2* (Cambridge, Mass.: Harvard University Press).

Kochan, T. A., Katz, H. C. and Mower, N. R. (1984), *Worker Participation and American Unions* (Kalamazoo, MI: Upjohn Institute).

Lawler, E. E., III and Mohrman, S. (1985), 'Quality circles after the fad', *Harvard Business Review*, vol. 63.

Locke, E. A. and Schweiger, D. M. (1979), 'Participation in decision-making: one more look', in B. M. Staw (ed.), *Research in Organizational Behavior*, vol. 1 (Greenwich, Conn.: JAI Press).

Meissner, M. (1969), *Technology and the Worker* (San Francisco: Chandler).

Quinn, R. P. and Staines, G. L. (1979), *The 1977 Quality of Employment Survey* (Ann Arbor, MI: Institute of Social Research, University of Michigan).

Rousseau, D. M. (1983), 'Technology in organization: a constructive review and analytic framework', in S. E. Seashore, E. E. Lawler, P. Mirvis and C. Cammann (eds), *Assessing Organizational Change* (New York: Wiley Interscience).

Shepard, J. M. (1977), 'Technology, alienation, and satisfaction', *Annual Review of Sociology*, vol. 3, pp. 1–22.

Shepard, J. M. (1971), *Automation and Alienation* (Cambridge, Mass.: MIT Press).

Verma, A. and McKersie, R. B. (1987), 'Employee involvement: the implications of non-involvement by unions', *Industrial and Labor Relations Review*, vol. 40, pp. 556–68.

Wilpert, B. and Sorge, A. (eds) (1984), *International Yearbook of Organizational Democracy*, vol. II (London: Wiley).

Withey, M., Daft, R. L. and Cooper, W. H. (1983), 'Measures of Perrow's work unit technology: an empirical assessment and a new scale', *Academy of Management Journal*, vol. 36, pp. 45–63.

CHAPTER SEVEN

Technological Participation in Europe: Options and Constraints in Human Resource Management an Industrial Relations

PETER CRESSEY and VITTORIO DI MARTIN

Based on an international programme of research of the E Foundation for the Improvement of Living and Conditions, this chapter examines the changing pa industrial relations in the context of technological c explores the constraints in which the social partners are o the difficulties they face in formulating strategies, and t of uncertainty and defensiveness which often dominat of transition. The authors advocate 'technological par and they analyse the key factors which facilitate c development. They show how the traditional mean vention (e.g. regulatory legislation in support participation) may be inadequate and they discuss ways of enhancing technological participation.

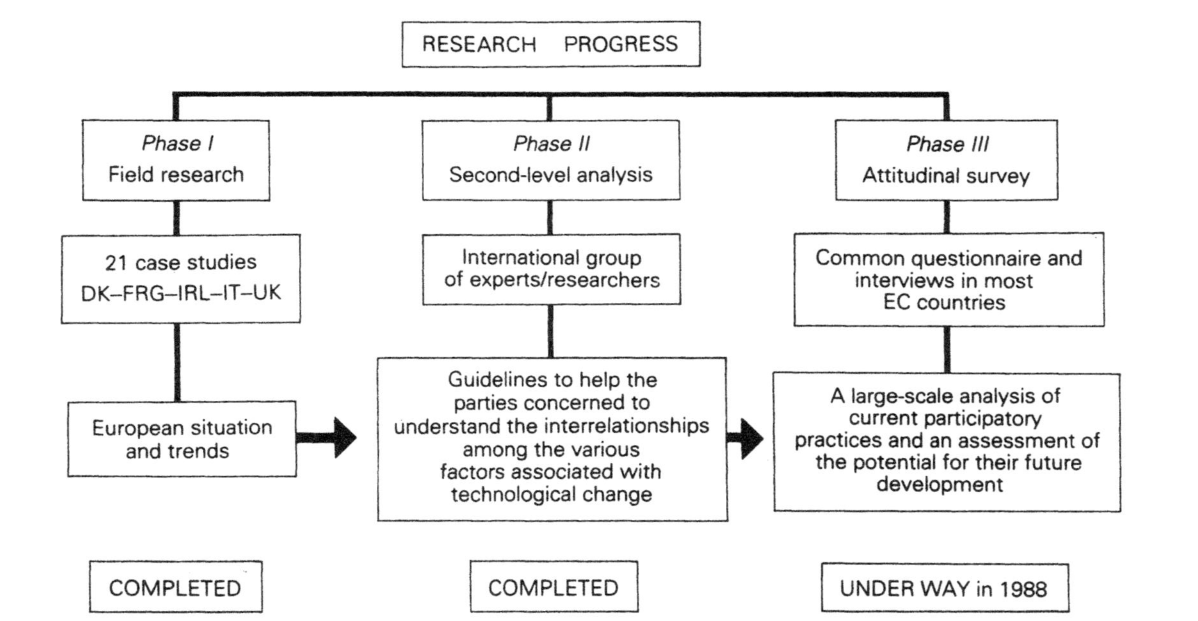

Figure 7.1 *The European Foundation's research programme on technological participation*
Source: European Foundation.

development and adaptability that new technology offers, those involved in the processes of change often seem unable to work out suitable strategies and to develop coordinated effective practices. The uncertainties are compounded by unemployment and loss of skill in large parts of the workforce.

New technology can be used to create new jobs, especially in some rapidly developing sectors. Despite this, in other sectors and in the short to medium term, a high level of unemployment is likely to remain. So far, at least, this situation has been only partly relieved by the various measures adopted (training and retraining initiatives; mobility incentives; rearrangement of working time; search for flexibility in company organization and in work organization, etc.). The solution of this problem will depend on the ability to prepare and implement, in the different countries and at European level, comprehensive programmes of action and development aimed at reducing unemployment. Unemployment will probably be reduced when such initiatives, coupled with the falling European birth rate, eventually bring the labour supply curve into equilibrium with demand.

There are also serious difficulties of occupational readjustment, especially for older workers and for certain types of occupations which are vanishing or undergoing drastic change. A split is thus emerging in the workforce between those who are able to adjust to the new requirements, remain in the system and enjoy its benefits, and those who lack that ability and are becoming increasingly marginalized. Such far-reaching and long-lasting phenomena have a decisive impact on the climate and framework of industrial relations.

Industrial relations are also affected by a 'deterministic' approach, whereby new technologies are seen as inescapable and uncontrollable. This approach, summarized by 'only one way: the best', rejects the process of dialogue between the social partners as being a nuisance, superfluous in the context of technological development, which is strictly governed by precise production requirements, in the face of increasing international competition. Consequently, closed positions are taken up, especially in certain countries or production sectors where the tradition of dialogue is not firmly established, and conditions for development are not favourable. In this setting, the union ability to respond is put to a very severe test.

Unions are having difficulty, more or less everywhere, in translating the technological knowledge that they have acquired into practical policies on technology. Often the unions do not have the technical, organizational and financial resources to analyse and evaluate the information received. In some areas the character of the unions has been transformed by the gradual emerging of a 'new', highly skilled, white-collar workforce. This new workforce can prove less willing to be involved in unions, especially if their leadership is still dominated by blue-collar traditions. Other situations, such as teleworking, drastically affect the whole organizational framework on which union structures are built (see Chapters 10 and 12 in this book).

On the other hand, employers, although they too may suffer from a lack of clear strategy and from a shortage of key skills (on the shopfloor and in management), can use new technology to increase their control over organizational decisions and production processes. The imbalance in strength between the two main social partners promotes further uncertainty in industrial relations.

This uncertainty is aggravated, especially at individual company level, by changes and increases in the centres of decision-making and power, as opposed to the traditional two-party system (employers and unions). The flexibility and pervasive nature of the new technology is facilitating the proliferation of *ad hoc* structures, often informal and temporary ones, which bring together the new actors promoting technological innovation (managers in key positions, software specialists, technicians, consultants, etc.).

In a context characterized by dynamism and uncertainty, the traditional 'balancing' function attributed to statutory regulations is difficult to achieve. These regulations presuppose a certain degree of stability of the conditions in which they have to operate. For this reason prescriptive legislation cannot provide a detailed framework for technological dialogue; that dialogue demands the adoption of more effective and flexible methods together with a different approach to the use of the law.

Attention has therefore shifted towards the collective technology agreements that have been developed in many European countries since the mid-1970s, because of their greater adaptability. At national or sectoral level they appear to be capable of encouraging greater participation, especially if they are used in the context of a well-structured collective bargaining system. At company level, a distinction must be drawn between 'one-off' or 'substantive' technology agreements, by which parties agree on levels of employment, remuneration, etc. for a specific innovation, and 'procedural' technology agreements, which include procedures for information, consultation and involvement of workers and their representatives during the processes of change. The first category, whilst it appeals directly to the workers' interests, is also rather inflexible and somewhat limited in content, whereas the second seems to be more effective and capable of responding more flexibly to technological requirements. In general, however, technology agreements do not appear to have produced, at least so far, the qualitative change in the dialogue on technology that many had hoped for. They show a limited range of contents and are generally confined to certain sectors of industry (see Chapter 1 and the Appendix in this book).

In sum, then, profound changes are taking place, often accompanied by uncertainties and fears, but there is an absence of well-defined strategies or instruments that could meet the challenge of technology.

Technological Alternatives and Options

Against this background, the research has confirmed the inadequacy of the deterministic approach. This approach is based on a mechanical view of the process of change and is clearly insufficient for the management of new technology, which is characterized by such uncertainties. Whilst there are constraints within which employers have to operate, there still remains a wide margin for the formulation and development of valid alternatives, not only in the implementation but also in the design phase (see Chapter 8 in this book).

The possibility of a broader set of choices arises particularly in the design phase. Design may be considered as a *functional* activity. On the basis of a clear set of goals (given explicitly at the start and not subject to change during the process) and a clear set of criteria to evaluate performance, design becomes a scientific process of selecting means for achieving the best solution.

Accordingly, the solution is given a normative value (it becomes the one best way). In this context, the designer (as an individual or a team) is implicitly thought of as behaving rationally and possessing full information about the environment and the system to be designed. In this first view of design, little room is left for alternative criteria and solutions; they must be quantifiable and not too divergent from the dominant criterion of economic efficiency.

A more open conception of design is as a *problem-solving* activity. In this perspective, the designer is not able to specify a single rational course of action and lacks perfect information. The designer can find a satisfactory solution only by searching and learning from experience. The search for a solution is carried out following a set of simple rules (such as examining a tree of alternatives) and is constrained only by time and money; thus it frequently happens that the final solution is just one amongst many that are feasible. The solution is not necessarily optimal (loaded with normative, indisputable value); on the contrary, it is open to modification and '*ex post*' revision. Moreover, as design is a heuristic process of collecting information on the structure and ways of representing the problem, it can easily be adapted to and accept qualitative requirements, such as those related to the working environment. This design strategy tends to lead to minor, though qualitative, modifications or alternative designs of a system.

A third view of design activity overcomes the limitations of the two preceding approaches. This perspective points out that, in most situations, design is a process of collective inquiry and search, taking place through transactions among several actors in cooperation and competition, and often with mixed interests over the problem and solution. Real design situations in organizations are generally confused, puzzling and characterized by uncertainty and by conflicting views and mindsets of the designers. Design is difficult not only because of the internal technical complexity of a given problem, but because people do not agree on what to do; thus the setting of the problem is a much more crucial phase than solving the problem given, or consensually defined. In the *problem-setting* phase, far from following a planned schedule and procedure, various predispositions brought by the various actors compete to establish the point of departure.

Technological innovation should therefore be seen as an open process. It is open in the sense that there are design, human resources and industrial relations choices, and the Foundation research has shown that these are better made through a dynamic of confrontation/cooperation among all the parties concerned. The cases in the Foundation's research did show the importance of both the management's and the union/workforce's attitude to such an open approach to change. How the parties approached change and their correspondence or clash of philosophies did have a great impact. Figure 7.2 illustrates four of the possible outcomes given different degrees of openness or closure to participation.

The Dialogue between the Parties

The parties affected by new technology adopt tactics to pursue particular individual and/or group interests. It is these interests that determine the actions of the parties and represent the real basis for participation. It is sometimes difficult to identify the 'participatory' interests of the different actors, as these are confused in the uncertainties that often accompany the introduction of new technology. The research has shown, however, that employers and workers both have a definite interest in technological participation.

For the employers, it is a question of handling a delicate phase in the life of the organization rapidly and effectively. The consent

Management attitude	Closed	Closed	Open	Open
	+	+	+	+
Union attitude	Closed	Open	Closed	Open
Form of technological participation	Conflict: objectives rigidly defined by both sides	Unilateral decisions by management; little involvement of workers	Consultation; minor areas of negotiation	Shared decisions; joint committees; workers potentially involved in all phases

Figure 7.2 *The parties' approaches and types of technological participation*

Source: European Foundation.

of workers and their representatives constitutes an essential factor in this strategy, and their involvement the indispensable corollary (see Chapter 6 in this book).

For the workers and their representatives, involvement in the processes of technological innovation is a prerequisite for their being able to influence decisions that are important to their own future. Despite defensive positions in some of the more traditional areas of the union movement, there are few signs of neo-Luddite reactions; the general trend, throughout Europe, is to adopt positive policies on new technologies. Unions are becoming more aware that it is no longer possible to confine their activities to a limited sphere of interests (employment levels, remuneration and working conditions), but that they must tackle the whole range of problems connected with the introduction of new technology (e.g. restructuring plans, workforce mobility, productivity and competitiveness). They are realizing that they cannot exploit the enormous potential of new technologies unless they accept a more active role in the management of the change processes. This is a vital challenge for the union movement, and confronts its powers of representation and organization and its negotiating abilities.

In practice, the degree of openness of the parties will depend on a series of specific factors, which can highlight the practical interest of the parties in participatory processes and procedures. These factors include the following.

The Level of Technological Qualification of the Workforce

The higher the level of qualification, the greater the interest in participation. Given the trend towards polarization of the workforce ('skill squeeze process'), managers can be induced to encourage cooperation with the high-tech core workforce (see Figure 1.1), without which any introduction or application of technology would falter, but may progressively reduce dialogue with the peripheral workforce. In search of flexibility, managers may also specially favour participation with the emerging core groups of multi-skilled, multi-role workers, capable of combining different functions (e.g. operators and maintenance workers), thus allowing for higher degrees of mobility, integration, interchangeability and, therefore, productivity.

The Type of Technology Introduced

Participation appears to be correlated with the degree of uncertainty posed by the new technologies. Some technologies develop existing methods merely by the use of more advanced machinery. The machine may be highly sophisticated but it is still an auxiliary to human work, which retains its dominating function – the management of the whole process. Other technology may be designed to supersede human functions, as in robotics, to create a mainly autonomous system, but still be clearly related to traditional methods. In this case, people retain their roles of actively or passively monitoring the production process. But information technology shifts the centre of gravity even further away from people and closer to technology. These systems do not think, at least not yet, but they obviously further reduce the role of operators. In this perpsective the main dialogue is between the creators of the technology and the technology itself, with such systems being capable of extensive self-management.

In these circumstances, we might think that the more advanced the type of technology, the less impetus there is for participation. The more traditional processes of technological development undeniably provide ample scope for a 'factual' type of participation, that is based on knowledge of the machinery rather than of the system. However, the flexibility of more sophisticated technologies creates a range of options not found elsewhere. They offer a broader potential for participation. Decision-making can be decentralized, for instance, and there is new scope for people to be involved, not just as workers, but also as citizens and as users of the new systems.

Management Strategies

The case studies reported a wide range of management rationales for introducing new technology. These could be grouped into four main areas, with potential for participation especially evident when strategies (c) and (d) occur.

(a) *A cost-push pressure for innovation:* this occurred in companies under the influence of adverse market forces. The new technology was introduced to reduce costs and rationalize production in pursuit of market share in a competitive situation.

(b) *A control-push innovation:* here the change sought to re-order the forms of influence that both management and the workforce had over the work process. Usually this meant seeking or strengthening of management control by the reduction of worker skills or demarcation lines.

(c) *A quality-push innovation:* in some cases the prime concern in production was referred to as the quality of the product, the service or the process of production. The technology was installed in order that such levels be maintained or improved.

(d) *A developmental innovation:* here the technology was aimed at providing greater scope for product or service development, either in greater complexity of the product (such as newspapers) or in the methods by which the product could be produced.

Market Situation

In general terms, where market decline was occurring, there was also greater conflict. The thesis that crisis engenders 'participative practices' as a means of survival is not borne out by our evidence. Instead, the pressure on jobs, on gradings and on a host of frictional issues tended to promote defensive postures, with workgroups protecting their area of job skills. Sectional conflicts, such as those between machine tool operators and technicians who programmed machine tools, were illustrative of this type of response inside companies. Few cases were found where the workforce as a whole offered a concerted alternative to management's plans or could sustain a valid position vis-à-vis technological innovation for any length of time.

Where the market position of an enterprise was benign, there was most experimentation with different participative forms. In an expanding market, more risks could be undertaken and resources allocated to management attempts to gain consensus. In an expanding market, the atmosphere was not negatively charged with distrust nor were job reductions a necessary element in the new technology package. This was mostly where we found new technology committees, joint consultative groups and other *ad hoc* arrangements for the introduction of new technology, whereas in the declining-market enterprises the introduction was regulated in the main by traditional collective bargaining or under the aegis of management, with little active participation from the workforce.

The Organization of the Company

Processes of decentralization and organizational segmentation have shifted the centres of operation and decision-making in many companies. This has direct consequences for the possibilities of participation. In such a firm it is obvious that participation, in the form of a sustained influence on decisions taken by management, will be restricted to core groups in the workforce. It would be difficult, if not impossible, for such forms of employee–employer relations to be extended to sub-contract, fee-paid or temporary staffs.

As the Foundation studies showed, it was core groups that exhibited a high degree of work control on whom management relied for their skill and discretion, and it was these groups that were also participating in decision-making.

The Traditions of Industrial Relations

A country's previous experiences of cooperation or confrontation have a substantial influence on its present development. A climate of positive industrial relations and mutual confidence facilitates dialogue among the parties concerned, while conflictual experiences and the use of participation to introduce job losses generate negative attitudes that are difficult to overcome. This is clearly reflected in the successful introduction in Denmark of a Framework Technology Agreement at national level (the first one in the European Community), following a long-established tradition of Cooperation Agreements. This contrasts with the UK, where the hundreds of technology agreements that have been negotiated have been largely unsuccessful because of the defensive attitudes of the parties involved (as discussed in Chapter 1 of this book).

The Capacity of 'Response' from the Unions

This will depend on a number of essential factors such as:

- the degree to which the workforce is aware that it can influence the process of change;
- the ability of the unions to mobilize themselves in pursuit of clearly defined objectives;
- the ability to identify these objectives in a specific and clear-cut fashion;
- the existence of adequate means of representation at the key points of the employers' decision-making structure;
- the degree of independence of the unions in creating real alternatives in relation to largely pre-determined decisions;
- the capacity to make use of information;
- the possibility of access to internal and external expertise;
- a type of organization that is capable of pursuing objectives over a period of time;
- the ability to discuss the merits of problems at the beginning and during the entire course of the innovative process.

The Positive Role of Technological Participation

Within the processes of technological innovation, it is very difficult to evaluate the quality of the dialogue between the social partners, which is an important but not a decisive variable in this context. However, on the basis of our research, we can analyse in which areas participation may play a positive role in the introduction of new technology.

Employment

Despite the growing expectation that new technology will create new jobs, and the positive experiences in some key sectors, it seems unlikely that a dramatic occupational readjustment will occur in the short to medium term. This means that, for some years, millions of workers in Europe will be excluded from employment and a wide stratum of society may be marginalized. A dialogue on technological innovation involving the parties most directly affected would appear to be essential in order to handle this transitional period.

Skills and Qualifications

The introduction of new technology may be accompanied by an upgrading of skills in the workforce. If so, there is a change in the commitment and contribution demanded of the workforce, moving steadily away from a physical/manipulative contribution and towards a mental/conceptual one. This may be accompanied by an inability to modify work practices; this problem arises particularly among older workers and in certain types of processes that are disappearing or undergoing drastic modification. Thus, a split is being created in the workforce between those who enjoy the benefits of technological innovation and adapt successfully to the changed requirements of the job (core workforce), and those who lose and are gradually marginalized in the productive process (peripheral workforce). The type of training demanded is also changing: technological innovation tends to demand general knowledge and adaptability rather than a rigid set of specific abilities, and recurrent rather than once-and-for-all education. Participation can certainly contribute to the search for effective and acceptable solutions to these problems.

Quality of Work

Generally the physical environment and conditions of health and safety in the workplace have improved. There are problems, however, in the use of VDU terminals and in the control of certain hazards associated with industrial robots. On a psychological level, boredom and tension deriving from repetitive tasks, the increasing speed of work, and the attention required by particularly complex systems can create serious stress. Extensive research has been carried out in this area, especially in the field of software ergonomics; problems may arise because of inconsistencies between the phases of design and implementation of automated systems. These inconsistencies arise mainly from a lack of interaction between the people designing the systems and the people using them. A greater degree of worker involvement in the process of technological development could remove these inconsistencies.

Working Time

The potential flexibility facilitates a different distribution of working time. This may result in long working hours (although this may apparently be accepted voluntarily), with possible hazards to workers' health. On a more general level, the introduction of new technology may allow an overall reduction in working hours in the setting of new employment strategies. In this context, technological participation is important, as indicated by the experience of many sets of negotiations in this area.

Productivity and Remuneration

The research shows a clear increase in productivity as a consequence of technological innovation, particularly in cases where innovation has come about in a participatory rather than a compulsory fashion. Pay levels, too, may be increased, made possible by savings on costs and the increased competitiveness achieved by the company.

Industrial Relations

Industrial relations are generally improved where processes of technological innovation take place with the involvement of the workforce concerned. This kind of positive development not only enhances the possibilities for success in these processes of change, but often creates a favourable climate for further understanding between the parties concerned.

The above factors show where technological participation is necessary and has the potential for success. However, it is difficult to measure this success, as we do not have the objective criteria or the analytical tools to analyse the participative influence 'felt' through the process and the outcome of technological change. Case study methods give the best opportunity to assess the process, yet even a longitudinal study that gives a before, during and after view of the variables involved is not easy to evaluate. Evaluation is difficult in view of the lack of acceptable criteria of success, the difficulty of isolating the contributions of each variable and the presence of contradictory evidence. For these reasons, when an index of success is attempted, it tends to be constructed around the actors' own perceptions of satisfaction vis-à-vis their particular interests. We find a positive pattern emerging in the attitudes of both management and the workforce.

This shows that participative forms resulted in a positive evaluation of the process and in a high level of general satisfaction for those involved.

Technological Participation in Action

Significant and clear trends within the existing forms of technological participation are difficult to identify. The context of legislation and regulation would appear to be an important, but not the decisive factor in the development of participatory practices.

Traditional negotiation still plays an essential role and even an extended one, as in the case of the Protocollo IRI (Institute for the Reconstruction of Industry) in Italy. This Protocollo IRI, signed in Italy in 1984 between the largest state holding company and the three main unions, is based on an extensive system of information disclosure and consultation. The workers' organizations participate through joint consultation committees at different levels (sector, enterprise and regional level). These committees are involved in formulating, restructuring and development strategies, monitoring all implementation stages of the programme and designing alternative proposals concerning the programme, work organisation, industrial relations and labour market policies. This system, which represents the most advanced experiment in workers' participation in Italy, has been extended to other state companies and seems likely to be an influence on the negotiations in the private sector.

Technology agreements, following a period of rapid expansion, are now displaying serious limitations because of their restricted content (they have rarely encompassed the full complexities of current technological problems) and their restricted area of influence and diffusion (mainly concentrated on white-collar workers). Informal understandings remain important, especially in some industries. New structures and procedures for participation on an *ad hoc* basis are developing, created specially for the purpose of handling technological innovation. No dominant model is emerging. Instead, a variety of forms of participation, covering a wide spectrum of possibilities, compete with each other or overlap.

Attention and emphasis are increasingly concentrated on effective mechanisms for involving the interested parties. There is a pattern across different European industrial relation systems. This shows how weak forms of involvement, such as notification or consultation, are used in the early phases of the change process, with more intense forms of participation, such as negotiation or joint decision-making, concentrated in the later stages of the innovation. Figure 7.3 illustrates this pattern.

This pattern of participation can be supplemented by looking at the actors involved in the process of change. The process draws on many different groups of actors from both the management and the workforce. There was no indication that company or plant management took charge of the whole process; rather they had

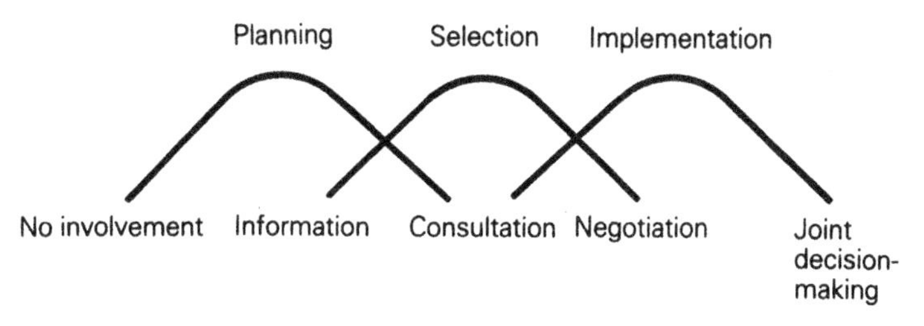

Key

Planning phase: an investment in new technology is discussed, information gathered and options are considered.

Selection phase: specific solutions are discussed and determined, such as make, model, accessories, etc.

Implementation phase: the new technology is installed and operated.

No involvement: decisions are taken by management alone without any involvement of employee representatives.

Information: management provides information through circulars, meetings with employees, etc.

Consultation: joint committees, other than negotiating committees, such as productivity committees, safety or technology commissions, quality circles, *ad hoc* forums for the introduction of new technology, etc.

Negotiation: collective bargaining and agreements at various levels, joint negotiating committees, working parties on new technology, etc.

Joint decision-making: decisions are taken jointly by management and employee representatives.

Figure 7.3 *Intensity of technological participation in the different phases of the process of change*

Source: European Foundation.

responsibility for different elements of decision-making. In relation to the management of human resources, their main involvement tended to be a choice between union action at the company level together with participation in workgroups, or, more often, the use of workgroup participation in local aspects of the innovation and its impact.

During the innovation process, the involvement of the parties and the management did change significantly. The data on this were not easy to evaluate because of the very different structures, gradings and occupations in different sectors. However, where such detail was available, a complementary pattern emerged. Broadly, this showed a shift in level and actors as the innovation progressed and emphasized the importance of experimenting more in the implementation phase (see also Chapter 8 in this book).

We infer that there has been little real employee involvement in technological change outside the implementation phase. The planning phase, in particular, appeared to be management's prerogative: they merely inform the workforce. This was particularly evident in case studies of the introduction of new technology in sectors such as retailing, banking and insurance, where, due to the weakness of the unions, there tended to be no agreed procedures for dealing with the problems generated by the changes and, therefore, no adequate alternative to management's plans was put forward.

However, the studies also reveal instances where involvement succeeded across the different phases and sustained a high degree of workforce participation. These cases emphasized the potential for participation even within the contraints of uncertainty. These strategic cases tended to be concentrated on white-collar work-groups that were highly skilled, enjoyed some autonomy and worked on their own initiative.

There is little participation at the preliminary stages of design and planning, during which fundamental decisions are taken and technological decisions are made that may then be irreversible. If the involvement of the parties concerned is not extended to these essential phases, then workers and their representatives will find themselves merely handling the effects of these decisions on a purely operational level. On the other hand, the formula 'the earlier, the better' will not promote effective technological participation unless early participation is accompanied by specific opportunities to exert real influence in the strategic phase. These opportunities, however, do not arise spontaneously, but require effective and continuous support.

Conclusions

Technological participation should be supported, at national and international level, to improve the understanding of problems by those affected, to equip them with the necessary expertise, and to foster the introduction of new technologies. This could be achieved by *setting up guidelines* at EC or national level through collective agreements or framework legislation. However, no 'one best' model of technological participation should be adopted. Rather, the parties involved should be provided with general advice, which could then be adapted to the specific situations in which they have to operate.

There are at least five ways for promoting this approach, including first, *disseminating information* about the existence and relevance of possible participative techniques for both parties, in various contexts. This could be done by public authorities and/or the social partners inaugurating standing committees for the monitoring of such practices and needs. The EC could usefully coordinate such a monitoring process.

Second, *access to expertise and support facilities* for both parties appears necessary. The lack of access to external resources perpetuates weaker forms of involvement and often confines the influence of employee representatives to the implementation consequences of technological change. Management need for support has sometimes been underestimated; they have constraints, especially of time, which restrict their attention to participation and involvement, especially at the design and planning stages.

Third, *education and training* in this context should be as practical as possible and include awareness of new technologies, as well as encouragement to alter behaviour and attitudes. Overcoming the reluctance of both parties to develop their relationship is a most difficult task, which cannot be achieved by imposing a common legislative framework. Joint forums should be considered; these forums would themselves test the willingness of the parties to develop consensus. Intervention should aim to strengthen awareness of their mutual interests, the options available, the various institutions, and the delicacy of sustained involvement.

Fourth, *suitable incentives*, both direct and indirect, could prompt (without imposing) a search for new and effective forms of participation. In Europe, such incentives for employers could involve modifications to the concessionary mechanisms for EC funds; while on the union side the aid could take the form of training and retraining programmes for worker representatives. Such aid could be supplemented at the national and regional levels by agreed programmes.

Fifth, *periodic joint reviews* could also provide feedback to those who initiate experiments. This mechanism could be supported by EC action to promote awareness and information on experiments throughout Europe.

These five forms of support would encourage the parties to explore the possibilities of technological participation initially by the incentives and benefits being offered, but later and, increasingly, by the intrinsic value of such experiments. The parties would then be more likely to wish to experiment. It would be their responsibility to evaluate the practical advantages of participation programmes, to select the most effective ones, to propose them to the other parties, and in this way to facilitate the spread of participation. They should be assisted in this process by the national authorities and the EC bodies.

It would remain, then, to close the circle of this process by periodically re-analysing the framework of regulations, on the basis of the most significant and most fruitful experiments in participation. Altogether it should be an open and flexible framework, which could enable the parties to introduce new technologies by using participatory processes, but with a minimum of imposition and a maximum of effectiveness.

Further Reading

The references below are all produced by the European Foundation for the Improvement of Living and Working Conditions, Dublin. This paper is based on research carried out by the Foundation.

Butera, F., Di Martino, V. and Köhler, E. (1989), *Options for the Future of Work*.

Cressey, P. (1985), *The role of the parties concerned by the introduction of new technologies – Consolidated report*.

Cressey, P., Di Martino, V., Bolle De Bal, M., Treu, T. and Traynor, K. (1988), *Participation and the improvement of living and working conditions*.

Della Rocca, G. (1984), *The role of the parties concerned in the design and setting up of new forms of work organisation – Consolidated report*.

Di Martino, V. and O'Conghaile, W. (1985), *Worker participation and the improvement of working conditions*.

Di Martino, V. and O'Conghaile, W. (1986), *New technology and the quality of life – The service sector in Europe*.

Dirrheimer, A. (1985), *The role of the parties concerned by the introduction of new technology – Germany*.

Holm, N. J. (1985), *The role of the parties concerned by the introduction of new technology – Denmark*.

Miani, G. *et al.* (1987), *Participation in technological change*.

Murphy, T. (1985), *The role of the parties concerned by the introduction of new technology – Ireland*.

Romano, A. (1985), *The role of the parties concerned by the introduction of new technology – Italy*.

Sievers, B. (1984), *The role of the parties concerned in the design and setting up of new forms of work organisation – Germany*.

Williams, R. (1985), *The role of the parties concerned by the introduction of new technology – Great Britain*.

IV

Managing Change and the Socio-technical Approach

New Technology: International Perspectives on Human Resources and Industrial Relations, Unwin Hyman, London.

CHAPTER EIGHT

Social Factors in the Introduction of New Technology: A Scandinavian Case Study

GERT GRAVERSEN

The chapter is based on a study of the commissioning of a greenfield plant in Denmark, which aimed to integrate technological design and social-psychological considerations. The author uses a socio-technical approach and emphasizes, in particular, the importance of integrating the technical and the social systems in the planning process. He argues that the phasing of the fundamental decision-making about the two systems helps to determine the functioning of the work organization and also influences the quality of industrial relations.

The application of new technology involves not only the technical, but also the social aspects of the organization. As illustrated in Heller's chapter, which follows, failure to recognize the possible effects of technological change on social structures and norms has often led to unfortunate results. A classic case was the introduction of the so-called long-wall coal cutting method in English coal mines, which destroyed the work teams and hence work morale. From this experience, researchers developed the concept of organizations as socio-technical systems. According to this concept, organizations consist of a technical and social system in interaction with each other. In designing work systems, the task is to optimize the joint functioning of the two systems.

In this chapter, the two systems and the interdependency between them are examined in relation to the process of change. It is suggested that all three elements (*the technical system, the social system* and *the change process*), and how these elements interact with each other, must be considered in the design and the introduction of new technology and work systems. The point is illustrated by the planning and construction of a new plant, Fredericia Brewery in Denmark. This chapter is based on a detailed study of the planning and start-up process by a team of researchers from the Technological Institute in Copenhagen.

The Brewery

Fredericia Brewery is an independent production unit under United Breweries Ltd (Carlsberg and Tuborg), a major Danish-owned corporation with its main office and production in Copenhagen. The brewery was built in 1977–8, and production started in the summer of 1979.

When the brewery was commissioned in 1980, its production capacity was 1.1 million hectolitres per year, with a workforce of 250 employees. The capacity was increased in 1981 to a production of 1.7 million hectolitres per year, with a workforce of 400 employees. The entire production is bought by the corporation, which handles all sales and distribution.

Fredericia is a small industrial town in Jutland, the western part of Denmark. It is centrally located for distributing beer to that region. The single-storey buildings are spread over a relatively large area. Their attractive design is in harmony with the surrounding landscape. Likewise, the layout of brewing houses and staff facilities is characterized by high-quality design. The production plant embodies the very latest brewing technology.

The Technical System

The technical system encompasses the task, the production process and installations, and the physical layout of the factory. It can be argued that the task should be separated from the technical system, but for our purpose it is adequate to regard the task as part of the technical system, as it, like the other aspects of the technical system, imposes contraints on and interacts with the social system.

The Task

The task of the plant is to produce two types of beer: 'Hof' and 'Green Tuborg', which are the corporation's two top-selling products on the Danish market. The two brands of beer are bottled in the same type of bottle and packed in the same type of box. The brewing process and the application of raw materials differ slightly between the two products. Both are produced at the same installations and a shift from one product to the other requires only a change in the one standard programme. By limiting the product mix to two standard products, a highly rational production process with a streamlined production flow can be obtained.

The rational and streamlined production at Fredericia is facilitated by the provision of special services and functions from the corporation's breweries in Copenhagen. The Copenhagen breweries can thus absorb unforeseen variations in the production flow (i.e. by delivering or receiving bulk beer, if for some reason the balance between brewing and bottling capacity is disturbed). This means that the Fredericia Brewery can manage with a very low buffer capacity in its production system.

The division of tasks between Fredericia and Copenhagen also means that such special functions as research and development, production control, planning and marketing are carried out in Copenhagen. This implies that a great deal of technical and other expertise is maintained in Copenhagen, whereas only the skills needed to handle the normal production are required at Fredericia. The rationale for this division of tasks between Fredericia and Copenhagen was that the standard production at Fredericia would eliminate the need for additional reserves of staff to cope with variations in the production flow. Whatever was needed in terms of expertise and resources not directly related to the streamlined production at Fredericia would be provided from Copenhagen. As shown later, this division of tasks affected not only the technical, but also the social system at the plant.

The Production Process and Installations

The production process and installations at Fredericia were designed to facilitate standardized production, so the most advanced technology developed in the industry was applied. This included a highly automated computer-controlled brewing process, computer control of bottling lines and automated bottle inspection machines.

In view of the standardized production and the highly automated equipment, far fewer workers are needed compared with the older production plants owned by the corporation. In the brewhouse and beer-processing section, the main work is controlling the process from the two control rooms, but some functions are carried out elsewhere. In the bottling halls, each machine is attended by one or two operators.

Layout

The working area was designed to appear bright and attractive with ample space and easy access. In accordance with the general corporate policy, workshops, stores and employee facilities ('employee houses') were decentralized and located near each production unit (brewhouse, bottling halls and stores). Each 'employee house' attached to a production unit contained a canteen, changing rooms with bath and toilet facilities, sick bays and, in some instances, meeting rooms.

Initially, office space for managers and technical and administrative staff was situated in one large central open office area. A number of meeting rooms were located nearby. A few years after the construction of the brewery, however, the open office area was rebuilt into a number of individual offices for the managers, leaving a smaller open office space for the administrative staff.

The Social System

The social system encompasses the work organization, the management system, job content, and industrial relations.

The Work Organization and Management System

The original plan was to introduce a flat organizational hierarchy involving only a few levels between the rank-and-file workers and the managing director. Accordingly, there was to be only a relatively small group of managers and technical staff. In particular, it was proposed that the plant would do without first-line supervisors. These intentions were associated, in part, with the notion of the standardized production process (with specialist functions and variations being handled in Copenhagen), but also with the objective of establishing a certain degree of self-management in the production units, which would make the supervisor function superfluous.

However, things turned out differently. The need for local management and technical staff proved greater than anticipated, so additional technical and managerial staff had to be employed. Also, the self-management of the production units did not work out as intended, and first-line supervisors were introduced shortly after production start-up.

The failure of the self-management proposal was due to a combination of several factors. First, there was a lack of support from the Brewery Workers' Union. The union was opposed to the idea of self-managing groups on the grounds that, in their view, some brewery workers could come to exert supervisory control over fellow brewery workers. Second, among the local managers, there was an apparent lack of acceptance and belief in the viability of such a proposal. There was little motivation on the part of some of the middle managers to make the proposal work and no attempt had been made to establish a consensus on the issue within the management. Third, no plan was formulated of how self-management should function in practice, and little or no guidance was given to the individual production groups. Fourth, technical and other problems in the production start-up period resulted in pressure on the organization to employ supervisors. Thus, in spite of the planners' intentions and the positive motivation of most of the workers, the idea of self-management was abandoned and the brewery reverted to a more traditional supervisory system.

Job Content

In the Fredericia study, the job content was evaluated by a questionnaire measuring the following dimensions:

1 *self-determination:* the degree to which the job holder can make his or her own decisions;
2 *skill utilization and skill development:* the degree to which it is possible to use and develop skills;
3 *social contact:* the degree to which the job involves cooperation and contact with others.

For each type of job, a job content score based on these three dimensions was calculated, and the results are presented in Figures 8.1 to 8.3. The six different job categories represent the main job types in the brewery. The production jobs are carried out by unskilled brewery workers (with some job training) and comprise *process control operators,* who work in the brewhouse with the highly automated brewing process, mainly in the control rooms; *bottle fillers,* who tend the machines in the bottling halls; and *storage workers,* who transport the beer on trucks in the warehouse. It appears from these results that the process control

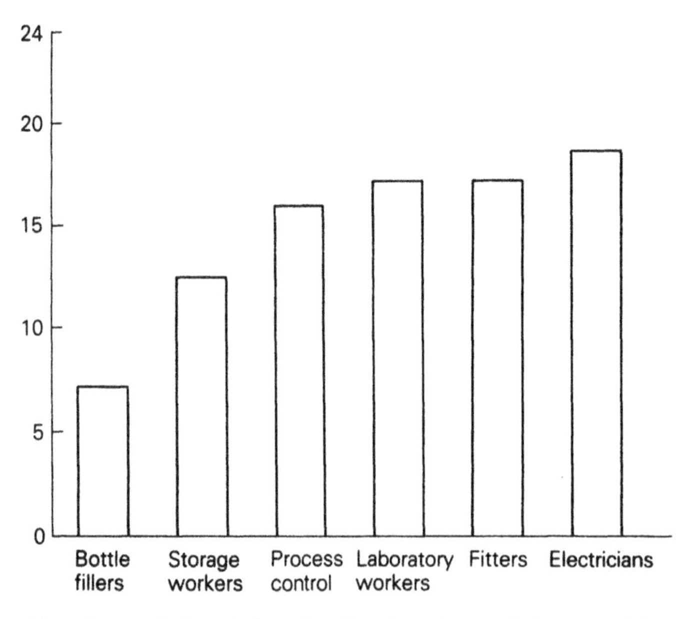

Note: The vertical scale from 0 to 24 is based on an index comprising eight questions about different aspects of self-determination in own job.

Figure 8.1 *Degree of self-determination experienced in the job*

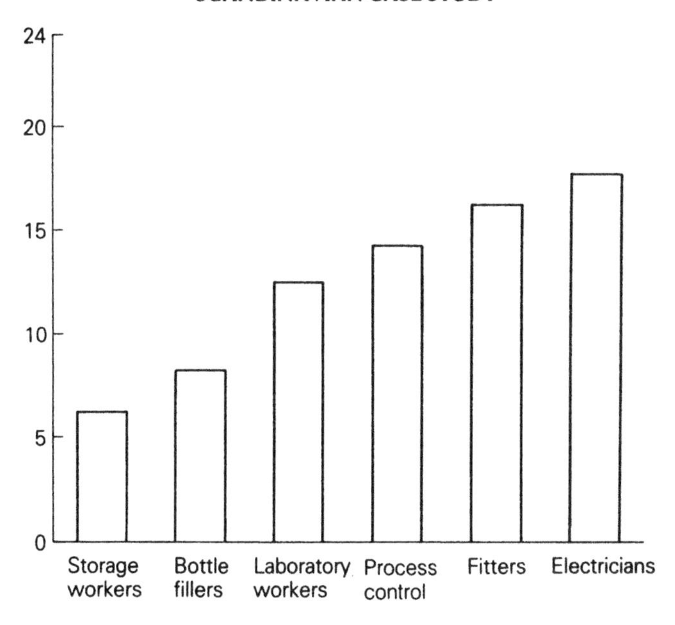

Note: The vertical scale from 0 to 24 is based on an index comprising eight questions about different aspects of skill utilization and development in own job.

Figure 8.2 *Degree of skill utilization and development experienced in the job*

workers have the most skill-demanding and self-determined jobs among the unskilled brewery workers, whereas the bottle fillers' and the storage workers' jobs seem to be rather low on these dimensions. The skilled maintenance workers – the *fitters* and especially the *electricians* – score relatively high on all three dimensions, while the *laboratory workers* are between the skilled craftsmen and the unskilled brewery workers.

These findings correspond with those of studies of comparable production systems. The challenge in the design of work systems is to create jobs with a reasonably high content, as low-content jobs tend to result in a dissatisfied and disengaged workforce. This will, among other things, make it difficult to promote a participative and democratic work organization – as had been intended at Fredericia.

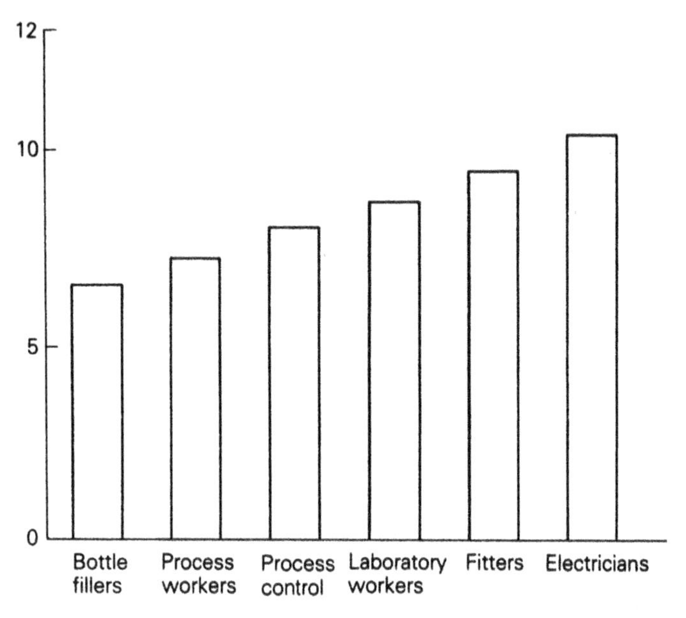

Note: The vertical scale from 0 to 12 is based on an index comprising four questions about different aspects of social contact in own job.

Figure 8.3 *Degree of social contact experienced in the job*

Industrial Relations

In the planning at Fredericia, the promotion of good industrial relations with a high degree of cooperation was to take place at the local level (i.e. directly between the plant management and the employees). Where the unions were involved, cooperation was to be between the local management and the local union branches. At the planning stage, some contact was established with the Brewery Workers' Union at national level, but involvement of the Copenhagen branches was avoided.

Management formulated this policy because industrial relations at the Copenhagen breweries were strained; there was a lack of trust there between the parties. The Copenhagen union branches seemed reasonably strong vis-à-vis the management. The brewery workers wielded considerable power on matters of technical and organizational innovation and rationalization; they were particularly concerned about any consequences of intended changes in terms of staffing levels. They strongly opposed the application of new technology and were also sceptical about the introduction of motivation-orientated forms of work organization. In view of these difficulties, the corporate management saw the building of the new brewery on a greenfield site as an opportunity to establish, from their point of view, higher-trust industrial relations at the local level, away from the Copenhagen industrial relations culture. In spite of these intentions and the introduction of an employee-orientated management policy, industrial relations at Fredericia turned out to be much more troubled than anticipated.

In the initial phase, the new employees were excited about the spirit of cooperation at Fredericia. Expectations were high, and the majority of the workers were in favour of the participative forms of management and cooperation proposed for the brewery. However, the workers were also influenced by the sceptical attitudes held by their Copenhagen colleagues. The shop stewards, especially, felt torn between the wish to cooperate with the local management, and expectations from the Copenhagen branches that they should adopt a more worker-conscious stand against management.

Once production had started, the pressure of work increased. As a result, management control increased and there were disputes between the workers and management. Initially, the workers' demands were met fairly quickly, as in the first wage dispute. But the spirit of mutual support and friendship between management and workers soon deteriorated. One issue of conflict was the balance between the concern for production, on the one hand, and the concern for maintaining good industrial relations, on the other.

The main conflict at Fredericia, however, was about staffing levels. The low staffing ratio, compared with Copenhagen, had been subject to strong criticism by the Copenhagen branches even at the planning stages. They regarded the rational, labour-saving production technology at Fredericia as a serious threat to the workers' jobs in both breweries. The negotiations resulted in a preliminary agreement, subject to review when full production at Fredericia was achieved. When the plant reached full production, this issue was raised again, this time by the local workers. They demanded a considerable increase in staffing.

The demand was rejected by the management, and the workers went on strike. The strike lasted one month, after which the workers resumed work without management having acceded to their demands. The strike, which to some extent was inspired by and supported by the Copenhagen brewery workers, dealt a heavy blow to the initial hopes for cooperative industrial relations at Fredericia. The lack of trust between management and the shop stewards raised further problems. A survey carried out six months after the strike showed that 'cooperation between managers and employees' was seen as most unsatisfactory by workers as well as by managers.

Subsequent developments showed some improvement, but the initially high expectations for good industrial relations were not fulfilled.

The Change Process – Phases and Participation

In the planning, building and commissioning of a new plant, the phasing and sequence of events, together with the involvement of the different parties, can be crucial for the outcome of the change (also see Chapter 7). At Fredericia, minor overlaps occurred between the different phases, though the aim was that each phase should be finalized before the next phase was implemented. Figure 8.4 shows the main phases and the main events. I go on to discuss the various phases.

The Idea and Initiatory Phase

In this phase, the United Breweries' management made preliminary investigations to decide whether or not to build the new brewery. Market analyses were carried out, production capacity requirements were examined, and profitability compared with the investment, operating costs and savings in transport costs, etc. In this phase, the main ideas for the design of the brewery were developed. One of these was to divide the process into small production units with self-managing workgroups. The idea and initiatory phase was concluded with a draft plan, on which the United Breweries' management based their decision to go ahead with the project.

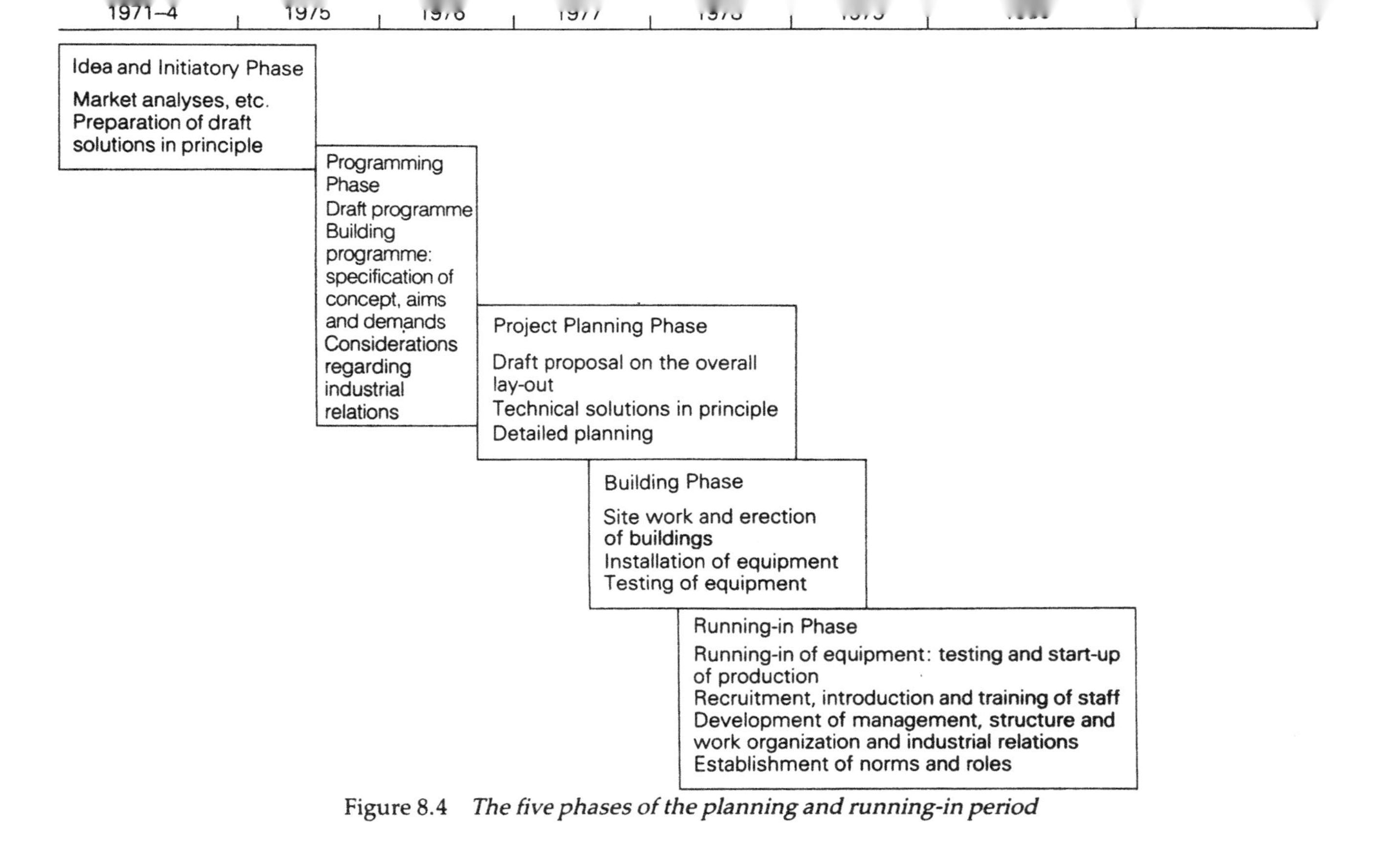

Figure 8.4 *The five phases of the planning and running-in period*

The work in the idea and initiatory phase was carried out by various groups of technicians in the company's planning and project department. The initiative and the inspiration behind the work came from the United Breweries' technical director. The decision to go ahead was made by the management board.

The Programming Phase

In this phase the company specified its objectives and requirements for the new building project. The aims and requirements had to be formulated in sufficient detail to be an adequate basis for subsequent developments. The programming phase for Fredericia comprised the preparation of draft proposals outlining the general ideas, aims and preconditions of the project, and the building programme itself, in which requirements for the brewery were specified in greater detail.

The programming phase also included formulating the major principles and proposals about human resource management and industrial relations. These proposals had been outlined in various working papers, but only marginal reference had been made to them in the building programme itself. The building programme, nevertheless, did reflect the principle of the independent production units which had been outlined earlier.

The work in the programming phase was conducted by a project team chaired by the United Breweries' technical manager. Within this team, a technical group was established to take charge of the programming and actual project work. Its members were recruited from the planning and project department. In the programming phase, this group was composed of selected technical planners. Later, in the project planning phase, the group was extended to include several *ad hoc* working parties, whose members were also recruited primarily from the company's technical staff. The manager of the technical project group was responsible to the building committee for day-to-day management of the project.

An 'employee relations group' was set up to advise on such matters as management, organization, cooperation, personnel policy etc. The group, which was composed of four managers and an external consultant, was established in March 1976 and completed its work in August 1976. During this period, it visited several Danish firms known for their progressive management policies. It also visited the Volvo plant in Sweden to tap their experiences of autonomous workgroups. The group prepared proposals for work organization and the industrial relations arrangements. The group's ideas were communicated to the technical project group via the building committee. However, it is difficult to determine whether these ideas had any impact on the layout of buildings and installations, as the general concepts regarding the independent production units had already been formulated in the idea and initiatory phase. The group's proposals dealt only to a very limited extent with demands regarding the technical system, concentrating instead on the future development of the social side of the organization.

The Project Planning Phase

In this phase, technical solutions were found in response to the requirements laid down in the building programme. The project planning phase can be divided into three sub-phases: first, a *basic planning phase*, setting up the overall design of the buildings; second, a *main planning phase* setting out the main principles in the production installations; and, third, a *detailed planning phase* covering the individual production units of the plant. This detailed planning phase was carried out by, or in close cooperation with, the suppliers.

The main planning phase resulted in a proposal that was finalized in the spring of 1977 and on which the board's approval of the project and the budget was based. Once the proposal had been adopted, the site work went ahead, even though the detailed planning had not been completed. The proposal dealt only with physical and technical matters, excluding such things as organizational structure and human resource management, except where these were directly reflected in the physical design. However, the project planning phase also included proposals for the subsequent recruitment and training of employees.

The work in the project planning phase was carried out by the 'technical project group', assisted by *ad hoc* groups of technicians and architects who had been assigned different parts of the work. The contractors' technicians were also involved in the detailed planning phase.

The various technical groups involved in the project planning phase were responsible for implementing the provisions of the building programme. Although these provisions were fairly detailed, the project planning phase did give scope for choosing alternative solutions. The technical solutions reached at this point had, in some instances, consequences for such matters as work organization, job content and levels of staffing. As an example, the brewing process offered the possibility of locating all the control functions in the central control rooms, or having some functions conducted in the plant.

In the planning phase only one meeting was held between the corporation management and the executive of the national Brewery Workers' Union. At that meeting the union was informed about the plans for the new brewery.

The Building Phase

Construction started at the site in the spring of 1977 and was completed in the autumn of 1979. The erection of the building itself, from the laying of the first stone to completion of roofing, lasted from the autumn of 1977 until the autumn of 1978. Installation and testing of the last bottling line ended in the autumn of 1979.

The building phase was carried out by the contractors and suppliers in accordance with the specifications set down in the project description. Work at the site was managed and coordinated by a firm of consultants chosen by the technical project group. This group ensured that the contractors and suppliers complied with the technical specifications, deadlines and costs stipulated in the contracts.

During the building phase, an external group became involved in the plans of the new brewery. This was the so-called 'Fredericia Committee', which the Brewery Workers' Union had set up in the autumn of 1977, and which approached the project management team to obtain information about the plans for work organization, human resource management, industrial relations and, in particular, staffing.

The Running-in Phase

Following the appointment of the managing director and the head of administration, recruitment of the other employees began in May 1978. The running-in phase was both 'technical' and 'social' in character. The technical side included plant testing and commissioning of production, with modifications and trouble-shooting. The technical running-in phase started with the first trial production run in May 1979 and ended in the summer of 1980 when the running-in problems were solved, and normal production levels had been reached.

The 'social' side included both planned and unplanned activities and procedures that eventually shaped the social structure, norms and roles at the brewery. Thus, recruitment of staff, training, establishment of the work organization and industrial relations, establishment of cooperative arrangements, expectations, attitudes and norms were part of the 'social' running-in phase. It is difficult to set time limits for this phase; it is a continuing process, which becomes more routine as time passes.

The extent to which the development of the project could be influenced in the running-in phase was determined by previous decisions. Some of these decisions were reflected in physical constraints of buildings and equipment. Other decisions were reflected in declarations of intent, which could be changed or modified. The difference in the degree of freedom in influencing the various areas of the project meant that this phase was of crucial importance for several aspects of the social structure, such as work organization, human resource management, industrial relations and associated attitudes, whereas the technical structure was much less susceptible to change.

The sole actors and decision-makers in the previous phases had been the brewery planners, but the patterns of influence became much more complex in the running-in phase. This was the first phase in which the employees took an active part in the development. Figure 8.5 illustrates the involvement of the various parties in the five phases.

Applying the Socio-technical Change Model

The Fredericia case illustrates some central features of the socio-technical change model, especially the interaction of the technical

	The parties involved / The phases	Idea and initiatory phase	Programming phase	Project planning phase	Building phase	Running-in phase
The United Breweries	Board and management	X	(X)			
	Technical manager	X	X	X	(X)	(X)
	Technicians	X	X	X		
The project team	Building committee		X	X	(X)	
	Technical project group		X	X	X	
	Employee relations group		(X)			
	Suppliers/ contractors External consultants			(X)	X	
Fredericia Brewery	Board					(X)
	Management		(X)		(X)	X
	Middle management					X
	Employees					X
External parties	National brewery union Copenhagen brewery workers/Fredericia community (local govt., employers, unions)				(X)	(X)
	The press and other external parties				(X)	(X)

Key

X = primary and direct involvement
(X) = secondary, or indirect involvement

Figure 8.5 *The involvement of the various parties in the individual phases*

and social systems in the design and implementation process. It raises questions such as:

- How can the objectives for the social system be incorporated in the design of the technical system?
- How can the gradual development of the social system be provided for in the technical design?
- What is the significance of the phasing or the time sequence of technical and social solutions of principles in the design process?
- What is the importance of employee participation in the process?
- How early should different parties be involved?
- How can people be involved in the design of the technical system when none have been recruited?

These questions apply in general to the design of work systems and the application of new production technology.

In the Fredericia case, objectives were stipulated for the social as well as for the technical system, but not all the objectives for the social system were met. The extent of the planners' success in reaching their objectives was related to how well the technical and the social systems were integrated in the planning and change process.

In principle, we can identify various different design patterns based on the links between technical and social objectives in the design process, the extent to which social objectives and consequences are considered in the technical design, the extent to which the two systems are integrated in the design, and the time sequence in which the two systems are dealt with in the planning process.

The four typical design patterns shown in Figure 8.6 illustrate specific cases along these dimensions. These design patterns are as follows:

1 Technical systems are designed without setting objectives or considering consequences for the social system.
2 Objectives for, and the design of, social systems are separated from the design of technical systems.

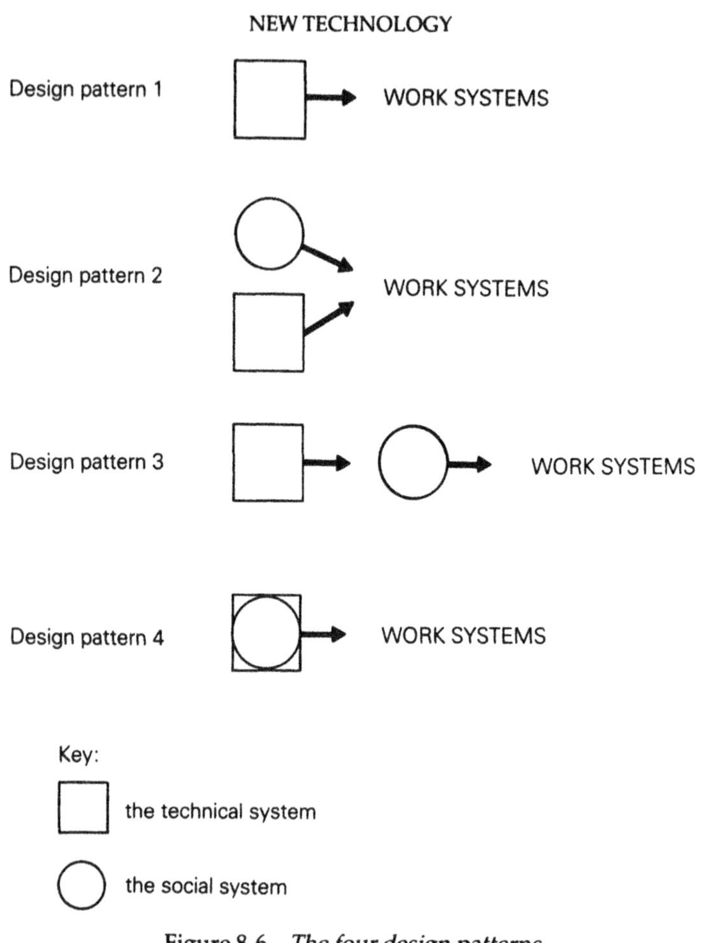

Figure 8.6 *The four design patterns*

3 Objectives for, and the design of, social systems are introduced after the design of technical systems.
4 Technical and social objectives and solutions are integrated in the design process.

In the design at Fredericia, considerable efforts were made to plan according to pattern 4, and the implications for the social system were considered carefully in most aspects of the technical design. As this study illustrates, however, some design problems were reflected in the functioning of the social system in the new plant, such as: reversion to 'traditional' work organization, low job content in certain jobs, and troubled industrial relations. The problems observed at Fredericia can be related to difficulties in integrating technical and social considerations in the design and change process. In some instances, design patterns 1, 2 or 3 were applied rather than pattern 4. In conclusion, I shall further illustrate the four design patterns.

Design Pattern 1: Technical systems are designed without setting objectives or considering consequences for the social system

At Fredericia, many implications for the social system were considered carefully in the technical design. However, it was not anticipated that some aspects of the planned technical system would have consequences for the social system. One example was the task definition, which stipulated a streamlined, standardized production process in which variations in the demand for special expertise and resources should be handled by the corporation's main breweries in Copenhagen.

This task definition had some unforeseen consequences for the social system at Fredericia. First, it created a high degree of dependence on the Copenhagen breweries, which made it difficult to create an independent local plant culture as intended. Second, the minimal room for variation in the Fredericia production system limited the potential for local planning and local managerial discretion and decision-making. Third, possibilities for variation in the functions and the jobs were restricted. Fourth, there was little scope for development of local skills and competence, since the necessary expertise was recruited from Copenhagen.

The tendency to disregard social consequences is a classic problem associated with technological change. The extent to which social objectives are considered in the design and application of new technology often depends upon the demands made by the users, may of whom exhibit a growing awareness of the social implications of technical innovations. However, the possible impact of new technologies on the social structure and attitudes is often poorly anticipated and calls for increased attention to the interrelatedness of technical and social systems.

Design Pattern 2: Objectives for, and design of, social systems are separated from the design of technical systems

In the early design phase at Fredericia, technical and social design were well integrated. One example is the layout of the production halls and the 'employee houses', which meet the objectives of rational production and of the group-oriented work organization. However, later in the planning process, development of the two systems was carried out by two separate groups, the employee relations group and the technical design group. There was some contact between those two groups, but the contribution of the employee relations group had little influence on the technical design. The employee relations group concentrated on the general principles of work organization and industrial relations, to some extent isolated from the technical planning. This separate planning of the two systems meant that the two systems were not jointly optimized. The lack of integration was reflected in the technical system's constraint on job design and in some of the difficulties faced in the new brewery during the running-in period.

The frequent occurrence of this design pattern is a consequence of the compartmentalization of technical and social expertise in our society. Where the engineers' insight and interests are limited to the technical aspects and the social scientists lack technical competence, the two groups are likely to work as separate entities. But with the continuing development of information technology, there seems to be a growing understanding of the necessity for a close cooperation and integration of the technical and social sciences.

Design Pattern 3: Objectives for, and design of, social systems are introduced after the design of technical systems

At Fredericia, the technical system was designed and the physical environment, buildings and production installations were established before employees were recruited and the social system had developed. Even if the social aspects are considered and incorporated in the physical–technical design, as at Fredericia, employee involvement in the design process becomes a crucial factor. When employee participation was introduced at Fredericia, the technical system could not easily be altered and adjusted to fit the requirement of the social system.

In general, a late introduction of 'social' considerations in the planning process tends to limit the available choices about alternative forms of work organization, design of jobs, or other social structures. The principle of the small independent decentralized and partly self-managed production units was decided early in the design process at Fredericia (in the idea and initiatory phase). This early introduction of objectives for the social system made it possible to design the physical layout of the plant accordingly. However, subsequent proposals for the social system (e.g. principles for job content) became difficult to implement in the design.

When there turned out to be a mismatch between the technical design and the requirements of the social system, in general it was the social system that had to adjust to the constraints of the technical system. In a few cases, however, it was possible to adjust the physical–technical structure to demands made by the social system (e.g. when the open-plan office was converted into individual offices).

Design pattern 3 seems to be the rule rather than the exception in the design of work systems, for three reasons. First, much investment in new technology seems to require an optimal utilization of the installations, which gives a lower priority to choices of work organization and human resource management. Second, only in rare cases (like greenfield enterprises) are technical systems subject to fully open choices. More usually, technical systems are restricted by existing buildings and installations. This means that the social system has to adapt to certain physical constraints. Third, the design of social systems is often organic and linked to participation by the members (employees) of the system, and these are not always present until rather late in the design process.

Design Pattern 4: Technical and social objectives and solutions are integrated in the design process

Examples of design pattern 4 are, of course, also found at Fredericia – perhaps to a greater extent than in most other such projects. For example, the small production units with attached 'employee houses' have led to the intended small-group culture. (The fact that the very idea of separated units was opposed by some of the union representatives, on the grounds that it destroyed worker unity, is a different point.) Also, the layout of the installations in the production halls was designed to encourage cooperation and to foster contact within the workgroup.

In general, there is an increasing awareness of the desirability of integrating social and technical thinking in the design of systems and products. Such integration may add a competitive edge for more and more successful companies. None the less, we should caution that not every problem can be solved or avoided by a proper, integrated socio-technical design. In the Fredericia case, for instance, the conflict between the management and the union over staffing, and the consequent troubled industrial relations climate, could not have been eliminated even by the best conceivable integration of technical and social considerations. Where there are such conflicts in the social system, these must be confronted directly, as separate issues.

Further Reading

Davies, A. (1986), *Industrial Relations and New Technology* (London: Croom Helm). This study is based on research in the British brewing industry.

Graversen, G., Holm, N. J. and Clausen, C. (1983), *Ny Virksomhed på Åben Mark – Erfaringer fra Fredericia Bryggeri* [Greenfield Site Plant – Experience from Fredericia Brewery), 2 vols (Copenhagen: Technological Institute Press).

Graversen, G. and Lansbury, R. D. (eds) (1988), *New Technology and Industrial Relations in Scandinavia* (Aldershot: Gower).

New Technology: International Perspectives on Human Resources and Industrial Relations, Unwin Hyman, London.

CHAPTER NINE

Human Resource Management and the Socio-technical Approach

FRANK HELLER

Technological change may create many problems for human resource managers and union representatives. This chapter suggests that a socio-technical approach is appropriate and useful in dealing with at least one set of problems: the range of choices available in the design or adaptation of technology to the skills and aspirations of employees. This approach is based on the requirement that the cost as well as the non-cost benefits should be jointly optimized between technological design on the one hand and socio-psychological requirements on the other hand. Joint optimization is antithetical to 'the technological imperative' which is usually, but erroneously, put forward as the only viable solution when a new technology is launched in a competitive market.

By tradition, the human resource and industrial relations function has not concerned itself with technological innovation and has developed no expertise in the assessment of technological change. This has recently changed under the combined impact of economic recession and the propensity for certain technological developments to displace working people.

Unions have also been uncertain about their role. It is not always clear whether, from the narrow point of view of changes in employment prospects, some unions – particularly those of white-collar workers – may gain at the expense of other unions. This appears to have happened in the newspaper printing revolution in London. Unions that are prepared to collaborate on long-term plans and give up some of their traditional strike-prone practices, have won negotiating rights and some new members, particularly on new sites, like the Nissan plant in Britain (Wickens, 1987). The introduction of new technology is usually part of such deals.

This chapter will suggest that the time has come for industrial relations and union personnel to have another look at what new technology has in store for them. In particular, it is necessary to face the challenge of what has been called the 'technological imperative' and the repercussions of this doctrine on their role in the organizational decision-making process.

Technology itself is neutral. That is to say, it is not necessarily antagonistic to the human condition. In fact, over a wide area of experience, technology has been beneficial to mankind. It has been used to improve the range and speed of interpersonal contact through telecommunication, and to produce rapid, safe transportation on land and in the air. It has been used to make former luxuries more widely available, to improve the quality of medical treatment and, in general, to give people a wider choice over a range of activities.

Much social science literature relating to technology has produced extensive evidence of critical side-effects, ranging from mild pollution and extensive work alienation to serious threats to health and life. These incongruities of beneficial and damaging consequences of modern technology lead to an examination of ways and means for achieving a good measure of the benefits with minimum negative side-effects. It will be suggested that, in many cases, such an objective can be obtained by using a theoretical framework that eliminates the notion of maximizing the technological as well as the human benefits. To achieve an overall optimum solution, both factors have to be sub-optimized to some extent. This blending of the relationship between technology and the people who have to use it can be approached through research, using the 'socio-technical model', as in Graversen's study (Chapter 8). This chapter will further illustrate circumstances where such an approach would have been useful.

Puncturing the Technological Imperative

Most people are familiar with the inhumanity of the assembly line through Charlie Chaplin's brilliant parody in his film 'Modern Times'. Many more systematic investigations have been carried out, particularly in the motor car industry, and the best-known one, by Walker and Guest (1952), has since been followed up several times. In the thirty years since the original plant 'X' was found to have serious problems with low morale, poor working conditions and unsatisfactory interpersonal relations, all attributed to the rigid assembly technology, very little change has occurred in that plant (Guest, 1983, p. 152). Elsewhere, however, particularly in Sweden but also in the USA, substantial positive adjustments of people and machines have been introduced in the motor car industry, demonstrating that technological as well as human organizational redesign is possible at no significant additional economic cost.

The argument about whether technology is a law unto itself (the imperative) or whether the necessary progress in technological sophistication can be tamed and integrated with basic human requirements (as in the socio-technical approach) is not yet settled. Ellul and his followers say that, under the new technological system, machines are no longer isolated entities but become 'unitary and complex, carrying out a whole series of tasks without external intervention . . . a factory now creates a vertical integration of successive machines, each having a different function' (Ellul, 1980, p. 3). He goes on to argue that the main characteristics of the consumer society and the affluent society are that all ancilliary needs, like advertising as well as the production of goods and services, have their own technology and, for economic reasons, integration between them will become inevitable. This all suggests that the human being will inevitably be subordinated to the machine.

There are many counter-arguments. Blauner, as early as 1964, showed that technological progress can liberate working people from the slavery of being insignificant appendices to machines by giving them a sense of control over their daily work activity. Under automation, people are liberated from the stultifying rhythms of machines; it allows them to make their own decisions about where and how to operate the technology: 'continuous process technology offers more scope for self-actualization than machine and assembly-line technologies. The nature of the work encourages a scientific, technical orientation and the changing character of the technology results in opportunities for learning and personal development . . .' (Blauner, 1964, p. 174).

Brzezinski, who coined the term 'technetronic era' is even more optimistic. He foresees that the new combination of technology and electronics will lead to a substantial growth in services that mankind needs; automation will replace routine jobs and require higher qualifications and competence in people, and this will enhance their job security. Knowledge, he believes, will replace wealth as the primary source of power. Universities will become reservoirs of essential knowledge, economic power will be depersonalized, and participation in decision-making by the highly skilled workforce will become routine (Brzezinski, 1970).

Most technological forecasts, even if they oppose the technological imperative, are a little less euphoric about the dawn of a new age of power devolution and universal competence, but, for many, it is a matter of degree. Taylor (1971), for instance, agrees that the shift to automation will lead to higher skill requirements, much improved job satisfaction and substantially greater self-determination at work. Automation, he argues, increases the employee's opportunity for exercising responsibility and discretion. The more sophisticated technology will reduce the need for close supervision by higher levels, because results can be evaluated more objectively by the technology itself. This will reduce the justification for hierarchical control and the exercise of personal autocracy.

Mumford (Mumford and Henshall, 1979; Mumford, 1981) has shown through action research that increased employee participation not only is possible but considerably enhances the effective use of modern technology. Similar conclusions from research have been demonstrated in Scandinavia (see, for instance, Elden *et al.*, 1982).

A working party report by a group of eminent scientists is more cautious about the effect as well as the rate of change, and advises us to remain forever vigilant (CSS, 1981). They show that in the UK, while the proportion of manual workers in the total workforce from 1911 to 1971 declined from 74 per cent to 59 per cent for men and from 77 per cent to 43 per cent for women, the proportion of skilled, semi-skilled and unskilled among the manual workers did not change very much. However, there was a clear increase in the number of professional and technical workers in the same period (from 4 per cent in 1911 to 12 per cent in 1971). It is often assumed that this group of highly trained workers is not subject to the de-skilling process as a consequence of new technology, but the working party was not convinced by the optimism contained in such a belief (p. 34). They also doubt whether optimistic forecasts about automation's negligible effect on unemployment are realistic. At the moment, 8,000 robots replace about 16,000 people, which is manageable; but if the number of robots increases very sharply the replacement problem cannot be ignored. It is perhaps fortunate that the diffusion of innovation is often quite slow, much slower than popular reports have us believe, and this may give time for positive intervention (CSS, 1981, p. 70).

Positive intervention can work only if we believe in the limitations of technological determinism. The problem has been put well by Winner, who discusses the paradox of technological determinism and its reconciliation with free will. 'On the one hand we encounter the idea that technological development goes forward virtually of its own inertia, resists any limitation and has the character of a self-propelling, self-sustaining, ineluctable flow. On the other hand there are arguments that human beings have full and conscious choice in the matter and that they are responsible for choices made at each step in the sequence of change' (Winner, 1977, p. 46).

This is where constant vigilance becomes necessary, even if we believe that man is capable of exercising free will. Vigilance may become a matter of survival if we consider the risks involved in the development of certain new technologies that have a propensity for occasional lapses, even though their 'normal' use appears perfectly safe. After Chernobyl, this may seem obvious, but Perrow (1984) analysed the problem very clearly several years earlier.

Normal accidents are those that should be expected, even

though they occur at unpredictable and very infrequent intervals. This approach is necessarily critical of those recent commentators who argue that the near-misses of the Three Mile Island incident and the Chernobyl disaster were largely due to the stupid interference of technicians who mishandled the warning signals. The disasters, so the argument goes, would almost certainly have been avoided if the built-in automatic safeguards had only been allowed to operate. But Perrow argues on the basis of many examples that we have now entered a period where this kind of technological deterministic argument is demonstrably out of date, because we operate with inherently dangerous systems that go out of control in ways that are not subject to normal predictions or to normal control mechanisms.

Evidence shows that even the most competent designers and managers are hung up on the 'technological fix'. They will design multiple feedback loops and emergency fail-safe devices in overconfident attempts to produce a 'perfect system' and, Perrow argues, political power is often in favour of this philosophy. Against this dangerous alliance of forces, we must demonstrate the need to puncture the technological imperative.

Humanizing Technology

Once we admit that technology must not be allowed to dictate its own terms, it becomes necessary to demonstrate the feasibility of alternative approaches on a level that relates to our everyday experience. The possibility that two nuclear-powered submarines may collide close to an important city like New York, London, Sydney or Tokyo may stir our imaginations for a short time, but the experience of finding a vandalized telephone box when we badly want to make a phone call has – perhaps – greater demonstration value for the vulnerability of the technological fix. Over the last half century at least, telephone companies in most parts of the world seem to have accepted that coin-operated public telephone boxes, which at one time were an advanced technical solution, are still adequate today and that the ever more extensive vandalism that renders them inoperative even for emergency calls is simply due to criminal elements that cannot be controlled.[1]

Many suggestions for alternative, more user-friendly

technological solutions have been proposed. In the early 1970s I made one such suggestion in a letter to *The Times* (24 January 1972) and repeated it with elaboration five years later (*The Times*, 9 November 1977). The idea then was for post offices, banks and maybe other shops to sell booklets of tickets in varying denominations which could be used for all state-run transport systems (buses and underground, as in Paris) as well as for telephone boxes. This would avoid vandalism and the considerable expense of constantly changing the box mechanisms for larger coins to keep up with cost inflation. There was no response.

More recently, a French colleague interested in vandalism carried out research on public telephones with the agreement of the French Post Office, which regularly spends considerable sums on repairing damaged boxes (Levy-Leboyer, 1986, pp. 27–9). The researcher was interested in the motives of people who destroy this type of public amenity. The Post Office thought it knew the answer: it was due to anti-social young delinquents. However, Levy-Leboyer's research demonstrated quite a different situation. Most of the damage to boxes occurred in booths that were very heavily used and the most significant reason was frustration at not being able to use the phone when the box was too full of coins! The technology could not cope with the public demand. When the researchers suggested giving the customer more control over the situation and demonstrated by action research that this was quite possible, the French Post Office refused to implement the more humanized solution.

Technological Over-confidence: The DVLC Case

In a recent report, five cases of interaction of new technologies and their users are analysed (Heller *et al.*, 1984). Two of the examples demonstrate how social and technical relationships can be handled successfully, and two cases describe how designs based on the technological imperative have had disastrous consequences. I will describe one of these cases briefly. It will be called the DVLC case (the initials stand for 'Driving and Vehicle Licensing Centre').

Driving licences have to be issued and renewed regularly and, similarly, every new car is issued with a vehicle licence that has to be re-registered every time the car changes hands until it eventually goes on the scrap heap. Until 1973, all this work had been done in 183 rural and metropolitan authorities all over Great Britain. The local offices used simple manual methods and accounting machines and the procedure was quick, taking about thirty minutes. However, there were problems of standardization between different authorities and the police found this decentralized system very frustrating for locating stolen cars and other delinquencies.

Consequently, the decision was made to centralize all driving and vehicle licensing in an office in Swansea, Wales, with the aid of a large mainframe computer. Swansea was a greenfield site and the experts were free to design the new set-up in any way they liked. In the event, they chose a very traditional Tayloristic method with a detailed division of labour, so that each operator had a very narrow unskilled job to carry out: opening post; examining contents; editing; coding; applying batch numbers; microfilming; key-punching; etc.

The results were nearly disastrous. After delays of years and large capital and operating cost over-runs, the DVLC began problematic operation. Workers were bored, had no view of the larger system within which they were working, needed to learn many computer conventions, and could not understand many computer error messages. Rates of absenteeism, turnover and error were high. Staff who were basically kind and helpful became unfriendly to people making telephone enquiries about delayed applications. Delays were often in the order of months; licence errors were sometimes severe. The DVLC became an object of anger and ridicule for the millions of average people who had to deal with it and did not understand the reasons for its difficulties. It received extensive adverse press publicity.

In order to cope, the DVLC began to reduce its workload. Vehicle licences were never issued from Swansea, as had been planned, and this function was permanently transferred to post offices and local vehicle licensing offices. From 1975 to 1978 the Swansea Centre's share of excise duty collected fell from 80 per cent to 60 per cent. Driving licences, which had been a smaller part of the work than vehicle licences, were still being issued from Swansea, but went from being issued every three years to being 'lifetime', with a review at age 70. This considerably reduced the annual workload from 6 million licences in 1977 to fewer than 1.5

million in 1979 (compared to 8 million licences issued in 1957). Recently, the DVLC has begun to decentralize the enforcement of vehicle excise duty laws, moving the work from Swansea to the Local Vehicle Licensing Offices. (For a more detailed description of the many problems occasioned by the design based on the technological imperative, see Heller *et al.*, 1984.)

The efficiency of the DVLC operation was very low. The original design estimates were for a cost of £146 million and 4,000 employees, but when completed it had cost £350 million and needed 7,900 people to run it. Morale, complaints and absenteeism were so unsatisfactory that a special consultancy unit had to be introduced to analyse the situation. By using socio-psychological job redesign, they were able to achieve very substantial improvements, all of which have lasted to the present day.

As an example, the answering of written correspondence and telephones was at first strictly separated. Every twelve months clerks would change from the correspondence desks to the telephone room, or vice versa. Clerks disliked answering the (often angry) telephone calls, came to hate the telephone room, and were afraid of being transferred to it. With turnover rates increasing sharply, a job satisfaction exercise began in 1976. As a result, by 1982, telephone and correspondence work had been integrated. The first change was for clerks to move from correspondence desks to the telephone room for a few hours each day. This arrangement was disruptive to the areas through which the clerks had to move, and dissatisfaction with going into the telephone room persisted. Finally, an unrelated move of the branch to another location in the building involving telephone rewiring permitted a physical change in the pattern of working. Since November 1982, clerks have been working in teams of eighteen, with each team at a series of correspondence desks that adjoin telephone consoles capable of handling four of the Vehicle Enquiry Unit's twenty-four telephone lines.

There is no longer a telephone room, and clerks move only a few feet when switching to or from the telephone-answering task. This solution had been proposed as early as 1976, but was thought too expensive before the move allowed a relatively cheap redesign of the workplace. Even so, the engineers who planned the new floor layout had once again segregated all the telephones into one area, in imitation of the old way of working. This particular fact is important, because it graphically illustrates the difficulty technical designers as well as senior managers have in thinking in socio-technical terms, even when other changes are going on nearby.

Using Socio-technology

Engineering solutions are often designed to maximize the effectiveness of the technology on the assumption that human beings are almost infinitely flexible and can be relied on to make all the adjustments needed to work the system without too much disturbance. We have seen that such one-sided solutions can fail completely. Elsewhere, I have described how an over-confident engineering design, in the case of the atomic energy plant at Three Mile Island, was responsible for the near-disaster that could have had consequences similar to Chernobyl in 1986.

One of the major contributory factors to the Three Mile Island accident was a technical control design that largely ignored what psychologists know about the human factor. Many control functions, like lights and buttons, were located in places where a single operator (who was supposed to run the whole station in normal times) would be unable to see them. There were many different warning lights, but the colour system was inconsistent. Gauges were put so high on the wall that the operator could not see them without standing on a footstool. Some gauges were on a different wall from their regulatory levers. Alarms of one kind or another were going off most of the time, usually for quite minor malfunctions, such as a burned-out bulb which needed to be replaced. Operators got used to alarms and could not easily differentiate between serious and less serious causes; and so on (Heller, 1984, pp. 3–6).

To a psychologist, as well as the proverbial man in the street, such design errors may seem extraordinary, particularly in an installation where the cost of an ergonomic consultant would have been trifling compared with the total capital expenditure. It is for this reason that the Three Mile Island case is worth detailed study (see Kopec and Michie, 1983). If the human factor can be so blatantly ignored there, we are justified in expecting such 'technology only' errors to occur almost everywhere.

It is also sensible to agree with Perrow that the inevitable occurrence of some disasters and malfunctions must be allowed for in a design. In addition, for major as well as minor projects, the deliberate use of the socio-technical model can avoid many problems, including those I have given as examples here.

One can start with the proposition that, whenever a technology requires the intervention of people, it is unlikely that a solution based on *maximizing* the advantages of technology alone can function without reducing the overall effectiveness of the system, which, by definition, is a system requiring the cooperation of the human component.

It is necessary to create a balance; the socio-technical model is a useful way of analysing the possibility of achieving this. This model is derived from work in the Tavistock Institute in the late 1940s and has since been used in investigations in various parts of the world. Starting with work in British coalmines (Trist and Bamforth, 1951), it is based on two considerations:

1 the production of goods and services normally requires the joint operation of two independent yet correlated systems – one is social, the other technical;
2 the social as well as the technical system must relate to its environment if it is to function and develop (Cummings and Srivasta, 1977).

Although the model was developed by social scientists, it does not attempt to give preference to the social component. Human requirements cannot be maximized without damaging the potential technological contribution in most cases. Usually, both have to be sub-optimized in various degrees, depending on the contingencies of the situation, in order to achieve an overall optimum. In most cases of some complexity, it needs research to discover the appropriate contribution of the two components (Herbst, 1972).

Nearly all past analysis using the socio-technical model has been based on the manufacturing process and, usually, at the lowest level of organization. More recently, office work has been included, but there is no inherent reason why the model should not be applied to broader problem areas, including the relationship of technology to the public at large or specific groups of users, as in the cases described earlier. For this purpose, it is necessary to re-conceptualize some existing notions. Cherns (1976), for instance, has put forward nine principles of organizational design that help to make appropriate choices for socio-technical solutions in the manufacturing process.

For our purpose, these principles can be extended and regrouped into two broad divisions: flexibility and the need for balance; and organic humanism.

Flexibility and the Need for Balance

- In the design of the technology and the corresponding human component, it helps to reduce the number and detail of specifications to a minimum. The more specifications, the fewer options and the less adaptability to external changes. For instance, the minute subdivision of functions in the DVLC case was counterproductive.
- Excessive specialization is counterproductive. In manufacture, this principle leads to the use of multi-skilled employees based on more extensive training giving the organization much greater opportunities for adaptation (for instance, in the case of illness of employees, labour turnover or changes in product design).
- Excessive specialization leads to impermeable boundaries, which reduce flexibility. The typical telephone box has two or three slots for coins of different sizes. If the coins change, the box has to be changed. A more flexible technology gives change for any combination of coins, but the pre-paid ticket system mentioned earlier is even more flexible, is cheaper, and avoids vandalism. A self-shredder could be incorporated to reduce the time needed for frequent servicing. In manufacturing, the principle leads to arrangements like 'group technology' with redrawn boundaries and encouragement for decentralized participation (for other examples, see Sorge *et al.*, 1983).
- Information must be provided where it is needed for action. The most relevant point for the information is often at the lower levels of an organization. The Three Mile Island mishap is one example where neither the appropriate information nor the corresponding training was available in accessible form to the operator. In manufacture this principle is widely ignored (for other examples, see Klein, 1976).

- Anticipating inherent imperfections. There is a constant need to re-evaluate the various features of the design – the interaction between technology and its operators, users or the general public. Every design is capable of improvement.

Organic Humanism

- Designs must be compatible with their objectives. If self-modification is part of the objective (for instance, in response to environmental changes), then the human component – be it customer or employee – has to be trusted and given some influence over events. This applies to all our examples, including the assembly-line system in the manufacture of mass-production articles like cars.
- Elimination of variances or unprogrammed events. This is a core aspect of socio-technical thinking and applies particularly to quality variations. Such variations must be anticipated in all products as well as in services. Unprogrammed events are best handled at the point where they are most likely to occur (and not, as so often happens, higher in the organization).

  The quality circle idea is a way of matching technological needs for quality with the requisite social motivation to achieve this objective. There was an early example in the English Midlands hosiery industry in the 1940s (Scott and Lynton, 1952, pp. 121–5). Adaptations of this system have since been used in many countries.
- Harmonization between technology and organizational or societal support systems. Technologies need support systems. Inside organizations they refer to pay, selection, training and conflict resolution. Outside the organizations, technology and its users require the public's confidence and trust. These were absent in our examples: Three Mile Island, telephone boxes and the DVLC.
- Motivation to use the combined system. The design of cooperation between the social and the technical components must be able to produce an adequate level of motivation on the part of the system users. This requires careful attention to the values that prevail among employees (inside organizations) and the public (for systems that affect one or more constituencies among the general population).

> The telephone box vandalism is an obvious example of this principle. The low motivation of employees on the original flow production in the DVLC case illustrates the advantage of thinking socio-technically at the very beginning of a new design.

I now want to return to my opening statement, which suggested that the human resources management function as well as unions should have another look at the implications of new technology. In the light of the evidence reviewed – and there is a great deal more that could be cited – outright and unqualified hostility to technology is not justified. However, the opportunities for user-hostile and anti-humanistic design will be extensively exploited in the pursuit of the mindless technological imperative, unless somebody keeps a very careful eye on new designs or adaptations of old designs. The human resource management function and unions, in their different roles, can play a useful part in this monitoring process.

Concluding Comments

There are two irreconcilable notions about technology. One supports the view that technology must be designed to maximize its efficiency on a cost–benefit basis. This leads to the manufacture of artefacts and systems that assume that the human component, which has to work with the technology, is always capable of adapting successfully to it. This philosophy is sometimes called the technological imperative.

The second view is that the human–machine adaptation cannot be taken for granted. The theoretically 'best technical solution' will often fail to produce an optimum overall result. The social as well as the technical components of a human–machine system have to be carefully coordinated in terms of physical as well as psychological factors. This often means that, after careful study, sub-optimal solutions for both components lead to an optimally most effective solution. An optimally effective solution is one that produces acceptable results from the point of view of employees at every level, as well as from a technological–economic assessment.

Research evidence shows that such an integrated approach is a realistic objective, which can be achieved in most cases unless the 'technological fix' has been allowed to proceed too far before the sub-optimization is allowed to intervene. Much research also illustrates that the technological imperative, which ignores the requirements of the human factor, fails to achieve the maximum forecast benefits and usually operates at a lower level of overall effectiveness than the optimization solution achieved by means of a socio-technical design.

Note

1 In recent years, card-operated boxes have been introduced in a few locations, but for a long time to come the major part of the population that most needs to use public phone boxes will not use phone cards or credit cards. It is also surprising that special phone token/coin boxes, which exist in some countries, have not been more widely adopted.

References

Blauner, R. (1964), *Alienation and Freedom: The Factory Worker and His Industry* (Chicago: University of Chicago Press).

Brzezinski, Z. (1970), *Between Two Ages: America's Role in the Technetronic Era* (New York: Viking Press).

Cherns, A. (1976), 'The principles of socio-technical design', *Human Relations*, vol. 29, pp. 783–92.

CSS (1981), *Report, New Technology: Society, Employment and Skill*, Chairman of Working Party: Professor Howard Rosenbrock (London: Council for Science and Technology).

Cummings, T. G. and Srivasta, S. (1977), *Management at Work: A Socio-Technical Systems Approach* (Kent, Ohio: Kent State University Press).

Elden, M., Havn, V., Levin, M., Nilssen, T., Rasmussen, B. and Veium, K. (1982), *Good Technology is Not Enough: Automation and Work Design in Norway*, A contribution to the International Labour Office's International Comparative Study of Work Design and Automation (Trondheim: Institute for Social Research in Industry).

Ellul, J. (1964), *Technological Society* (New York: Random House).

Ellul, J. (1980), *The Technological System* (New York: Continuum).

Guest, R. (1983), 'Organizational democracy and the quality of work life: The man on the assembly line', in C. Crouch and F. Heller (eds), *International Yearbook of Organizational Democracy* (Chichester: John Wiley).

Heller, F. A. (1984), *How Technology Affects the Quality of Employment – Part 1: Options Derived from an Assessment of Available Evidence* (London: Tavistock Institute of Human Relations).
Heller, F., Karapin, R. S. and Acuna, E. (1984), *How Technology Affects the Quality of Employment – Part 2: Case Study Evidence and Examples* (London: Tavistock Institute of Human Relations; available from Institute of Manpower Studies, University of Sussex, Brighton).
Herbst, P. G. (1972), *Sociotechnical Design* (London: Tavistock).
Klein, L. (1976), *New Forms of Work Organisation* (Cambridge: Cambridge University Press).
Kopec, D. and Michie, D. (1983), *Mismatch between Machine Representations and Human Concepts: Dangers and Remedies*, FAST Series no. 9 (Luxembourg: Commission of the European Communities, Ref. ERU 8426 EN).
Levy-Leboyer, C. (1986), 'Applying psychology or applied psychology', in F. Heller (ed.), *The Use and Abuse of Social Science* (London: Sage).
Mumford, E. and Henshall, D. (1979), *A Participative Approach to Computer Systems Designs* (London: Associated Business Press).
Mumford, E. (1981), *Values, Technology and Work* (The Hague: Martinus Nijhoff).
Perrow, C. (1984), *Normal Accidents: Living with High Risk Technologies* (New York: Basic Books).
Scott, J. and Lynton, R. P. (1952), *Three Studies in Management* (London: Routledge & Kegan Paul).
Sorge, A., Hartman, G., Warner, M. and Nichols, I. (1983), *Microelectronics and Manpower in Manufacturing* (Aldershot: Gower).
Taylor, J. C. (1971), 'High technology leads to more democracy: Some effects of technology in organizational change', *Human Relations*, vol. 24, pp. 105–23.
Trist, E. L. and Bamforth, K. W. (1951), 'Some social and psychological consequences of the longwall method of coal getting', *Human Relations*, vol. 4, pp. 3–38.
Walker, C. R. and Guest, R. H. (1952), *The Man on the Assembly Line* (New York: Arno Press), reprinted Cambridge, Mass.: Harvard University Press, 1979.
Wickens, P. D. (1987), *The Road to Nissan: Flexibility, Quality, Teamwork* (London: Macmillan).
Winner, L. (1977), *Autonomous Technology: Technics out of Control as a Theme in Political Thought* (Cambridge, Mass.: MIT Press).

V

Gender, Structural Change, Skills and Labour Market Segmentation

New Technology: International Perspectives on Human Resources and Industrial Relations, Unwin Hyman, London.

CHAPTER TEN

Technological Change and Women Workers

ROSE MARIE GREVE

This chapter argues that the concentration of women in a limited number of low status occupations, particularly in the service sector, has made them especially vulnerable to the new wave of technological innovation. Women's employment, job content and terms and conditions of work are all affected, sometimes adversely and women – and the unions which represent them – are beginning to realize that they must acquire the power to influence the direction of such change, as well as the skills to aspire to the new jobs which are being created.

Women have been entering the labour market in increasing numbers since the end of the Second World War. In OECD countries alone their numbers are thought to have increased by 74 per cent in the last three decades; there were 136 million by 1980 (Paukert, 1984, p. 10). On average, women now comprise around 40 per cent of the labour force of the industrialized market economy countries (ILO, 1985, p. 14).

In these countries, two characteristics distinguish women's participation in the labour market and both have important implications for the effects of technological change on women's employment. The first is the concentration of women in certain occupations of the service sector, where they comprise around two-thirds of all employees. The second is that this 'feminization' of the service sector is distinguished by a marked segregation by sex and that women tend to be concentrated in a limited number of occupations, which are themselves characterized by lower skills, status and remuneration. In the USA, for example, women constitute 78.7 per cent of all clerical workers (ICFTU, 1983).

This concentration of women in a few occupations and in the lower ranks of these occupations has made them particularly vulnerable to the recent wave of technological change. This has been directed towards the service sector and the more routine clerical, secretarial and typing jobs that women occupy, and it is probable that they will suffer disproportionately from its effects. While this does not necessarily imply that large numbers of women will lose their jobs, it does suggest that many women, in particular, will be required to adjust to the changes taking place (Werneke, 1983, p. 2).

The Technology

The use of microelectronic technology in offices and elsewhere is fostered by an employer preoccupation with increasing productivity and efficiency, in the interests of competitiveness. What is variously described as 'telematics', 'informatics' or information technology has a wide range of applications in the traditionally labour-intensive service sector, transforming it radically (Rada, 1980).

While the integrated electronic ('paperless') office is still in the future, the applications of new technology include the use of word processors, facsimile equipment, electronic mailing and filing systems, and networking of terminals in the administrative and clerical areas; the use of electronic funds transfer, automatic teller machines and point of sales terminals in banking and commerce; sophisticated cash registers, optical character recognition and automatic telephone exchanges. Some of these developments are already transforming the nature and organization of work in these areas and are influencing their employment potential.

Closely linked with office technology and of special relevance to women workers is the development of home computer terminals and portable computers linked by telephone or cable to central locations, which permit the growth of homework or telework.

In all these areas it is the less skilled, routine tasks, undertaken mainly by women workers, that will be subjected to change and it is feared that the application of microelectronic technology to service sector occupations will have an adverse effect on women's employment in terms of its availability and quality.

Problems Specific to Women Workers

On the premise that women are concentrated to a greater extent than men in the 'at risk' occupations in the service sector, this section examines some areas in which the introduction of new technology is likely to have consequences of particular relevance to women workers.

Employment

It is difficult to distinguish the effects on employment of new technology from those of structural factors. The speed and diffusion of technological change and the capacity of the economy to absorb it will also influence the degree to which technology affects employment and the areas in which it does so.

Opinions are divided about the impact of technological change on women in the service sector. On the one hand, it is argued that, notwithstanding fears that the new generation of office equipment will have a negative impact on employment prospects, the net effect since the 1960s has been the creation of more jobs. According to this argument, new technology, although it can be used to save labour, has resulted, not in widespread female job loss, but rather in considerable relocation of female labour within enterprises and in changes of job content.

On the other hand, some studies support the contention that technological changes will precipitate job losses, which will be particularly dramatic among women workers. For example, the International Federation of Commercial, Clerical, Professional and Technical Employees (FIET) estimates that 20–25 per cent of the existing 15 million office jobs in the European Community will be affected by 1990. The jobs in question are those held mainly by women, i.e. typists, secretarial staff, general clerical and administrative staff, mailroom and filing clerks, supervisors and first-line managers. It can be inferred from FIET's survey of its insurance sector affiliates that new technologies have already caused a 40 per cent reduction in staff in this area (ICFTU, 1983, pp. 28 and 32). In telecommunications, it is estimated that employment levels will fall in areas where women are currently employed and that, while there may be an increase in supervisory and managerial positions, women are either traditionally excluded from such positions or do not have the qualifications specified for these jobs. Estimates of reductions in other service sector occupations are equally dramatic (Nora and Minc, 1978).

While it could be argued that not all of the above instances will affect women, such jobs are particularly liable to be automated and are therefore the most vulnerable to change. This is confirmed, for example, by a further FIET survey of commercial workers, which indicates that women are more affected by technological change than men, since electronic check-out desks in retailing and word processors and visual display units (VDUs) in clerical and administrative areas are primarily staffed by women. The Deutsche Angestellten-Gewerkschaft (DGA) in the Federal Republic of Germany (FRG) estimates that approximately 70 per cent of the women in commerce will be affected by technological change, but only 30 per cent of the men; this 70/30 ratio is confirmed by the other FIET affiliates surveyed. Statistics submitted by these unions show that women already account for around 70–80 per cent of the job reduction in the retail trade in some European countries (FIET, 1983, p. 13). It would appear, therefore, that women are, and will continue to be, the main victims of job displacement.

Job Creation and Women's Opportunities

Proponents of technological change argue, with some justification, that the economic expansion engendered by technological change will lead to considerable job creation. The key question for women is whether the new jobs will be accessible to them. On the basis of existing evidence, one might suggest that this is not the case and that many women lack the appropriate technical background, the requisite skills and the training to adjust to the higher-level jobs that are most likely to be created by new technology. For example, while the proportion of women on computer courses has grown significantly in the last two decades, they still comprise no more than 25 per cent of all participants on such courses (ILO, 1981a, p. 63). There is a similar situation with regard to general managerial and supervisory training, blocking the access of women to the new jobs that are being created.

It could be argued that the present mismatch between the available skills and those required (and therefore between job displacement and creation) is a short-term effect, which will be rectified in time, and that the shift in the balance of opportunities could work as much to the advantage of women as of men. However, at present, 'a disproportionate number of jobs mainly occupied by women seem likely to be either eliminated entirely or reduced in grade. These discriminatory effects are likely to be reinforced by the fact that where highly qualified positions are created these will be largely reserved for men' (FIET, 1983, p. 30).

Polarization and Downgrading

Whether or not this contention is justified, it highlights the fact that the introduction of new technology in the service sector has resulted in a growing polarization of the workforce, with a (mainly) male elite in the highly skilled 'thinking' or 'planning' jobs, and women in deskilled, monotonous and repetitive jobs.

In addition to its obvious effects on work content, this polarization could have important negative implications for remuneration and for the career possibilities of the women who find themselves at the lower levels of the hierarchy. In particular, the tendency for first-line supervision and middle management positions to be occupied by men blocks upward mobility and removes one of the traditional career paths of women workers. For the women occupying the lower levels of this polarized hierarchy, there is the additional danger that the new highly structured and routinized jobs might themselves be easily automated in the future (Bjorn-Andersen, 1983, p. 121).

In its survey of commercial workers, FIET noted that the

majority of its affiliates expected certain jobs occupied by women to be downgraded. One might expect that deskilling and downgrading would have adverse implications for remuneration. This is an area of some concern for the unions; consequently, many new technology agreements include clauses on the maintenance of the pay levels of workers whose jobs have been downgraded. The FIET survey of commercial workers notes that, even where existing staff have suffered no loss in income through deskilling, inferior conditions are being offered to new entrants (FIET, 1983, p. 19).

Scientific Management of Service Sector Occupations

Deskilling and standardization raise the spectre of scientific management, or 'Taylorism in the office' (on Taylorism, see Chapter 1). New technologies should not necessarily be used to create dehumanized working conditions, but with jobs being deskilled (Dy, 1985, p. 3), and work organization being fragmented, clerical work is becoming more and more like an assembly line (Menzies, 1981, p. 61). This is confirmed by other national and cross-national studies and, on balance, most people associate microelectronic technology with negative effects on the content and organization of work (Zmroczek and Henwood, 1983; also see Chapter 11 in this book).

Technology may be used not only to streamline office operations but also to centralize and standardize decisions and to enhance managerial control. Increased monitoring and implicit pressure for greater output result in a further depersonalization of the workplace, thereby increasing the level of stress experienced by many women workers. Such effects could eventually lead to the kind of social problems associated with scientific management and assembly-line occupations.

Safety and Health

Health and safety are an issue of considerable concern for workers – one that features in government, employer and union guidelines on the application of new technology, and in technology agreements.

For women workers, this issue has two dimensions: first, the potential hazards associated with the use of VDUs and other electronic equipment; and second, the psychological effects of the increasing monotony and diminishing social contacts associated with low-skilled, routine jobs that are subject to high levels of centralization and control.

ILO sources suggest that, while the applications of new technologies can lead to increased comfort and reduction of noise and physical work loads, they can also have negative effects – attributable not to the technology itself but to the manner in which it is applied and to the work organization that develops around it. This would appear to be a fruitful and recognized area for joint regulation by management, union and government representatives (ILO, 1981b).

Working Time Arrangements

While it is difficult to separate the effects of new technology from those of structural change, the introduction of labour-saving technologies will probably influence the growth of part-time work. A FIET survey of the banking sector suggests that much of the predicted job growth will be accounted for by part-time workers and that, in the clerical grades, a duality is emerging with the proportion of 'non-career' staff growing considerably (FIET, 1980). There are similar trends in commerce, where the introduction of flexible working hours and particularly of capacity-oriented variable working time in retailing permits the optimal use of employees.

Part-time work and flexible work schedules are attractive for women with family responsibilities. While this has undoubtedly contributed to the high incidence of women among part-time workers, it has its disadvantages for them in terms of remuneration, benefits, training and career development. Part-time workers are also less likely to be unionized.

Homework and Telework

Another area that has important implications for women workers is that of homework and working at other locations that are remote from the employer's main site, but with a link by an electronic network (telework). While it could also be attractive to women with young children, it too has disadvantages. These include isolation, piece-work payment systems, routinized or structured tasks that are subject to detailed control, and the absence of effective labour standards with regard to working conditions, safety and health, and social security provisions. Unions view this development with some concern.

New Technologies, Industrial Relations and Women Workers

There appears to be a growing realization that the issue of technological change should be confronted in the industrial relations arena (ILO, 1985). Technology agreements have been negotiated 'which place explicitly on the agenda of collective bargaining a range of topics which affect all aspects of technological and organisational change' (Evans, 1983, p. 158).

The policies of each of the parties and their attitudes towards the concept of technology agreements depend on the prevailing industrial relations system and climate in a given country. However, an examination of some of the agreements demonstrates that the scope of substantive and procedural issues is greater than in more traditional agreements. The scope sometimes extends to include employee and union participation in the design and application of innovations. While the decisive voice is still that of the employer, unions have developed a more coherent and comprehensive approach towards negotiating about technological change and are moving away from the piecemeal and reactive responses of earlier years.

To what extent are women's concerns reflected in the industrial relations processes and discussed at the bargaining table? While technology agreements do not necessarily refer specifically to women workers, their interests are addressed, at least implicitly. Many such agreements cover occupations in which women predominate, and the substantive issues covered are those that have special relevance for women. For example, provisions concerning job security, limiting staff reductions and avoiding redundancies provide some measure of protection for women whose jobs are particularly open to change. Redeployment and training also feature in many technology agreements, which often carry an equal opportunity clause stating the principle of equality in relation to both retraining and new jobs (Epstein, 1984, p. 42). This, incidentally, has also been the trend of many union policy statements. For example, FIET's *Action Programme for Women Salaried Employees* recognizes the importance of training and further training for women in those fields traditionally reserved for men (FIET, 1981).

Safety and health are probably the areas that have received the greatest attention and in which specific references are made to the possible effects of new technology on women workers. As mentioned earlier, various guidelines on the use of VDUs and other electronic equipment have been issued by governments, employers' organizations and unions. This issue is covered by many technology agreements in the service sector, with particular reference to the potential risks associated with electronic equipment. Agreements can cover standards for the selection of personnel, medical supervision and prophylactic measures, ergonomic standards for the construction and use of equipment, and time spent by individual workers at VDUs.

The main thrust of union policy has, however, been an insistence on information, joint consultation and collective bargaining. This has not generally been welcomed by the employers' organizations; but, even where it has been favourably received, such union goals have not always been achieved in relation to women workers. Women are likely to be at a disadvantage, given their lower levels of unionization and because they are under-represented in the higher levels of the union hierarchy and at the bargaining table. This lack of influence is implicitly recognized by the International Confederation of Free Trade Unions/International Trade Secretariat (ICFTU/ITS) Women's Committee. It proposes that, where women comprise a large proportion of the membership, an appropriate number of women should be included in the negotiating team and in the groups set up to monitor the effects of technological change (ICFTU, 1983).

Several of the major international trade secretariats and their affiliates have recognized that, in spite of all the union policies, guidelines and agreements on new technology, the special problems of women workers have received insufficient attention. While many unions have followed the lead of governments by adopting policies and action programmes on equal rights, there has been less attention to the specific area of women's employment and technology in the industrial relations arena.

Much research has been undertaken by the unions on the most vulnerable women's occupations. The ICFTU/ITS Women's Committee proposes special measures in an attempt to ensure that the introduction of new technology will improve living and working conditions and will not discriminate against women workers. These measures include the involvement of unions at every level of the introduction of new technology, careful monitoring of its impact on women in order to mitigate the risk of sex segregation in computer-related jobs, the safeguarding of career development prospects for women affected by technological change, and equal access to new jobs and to training and retraining, especially for higher-level posts. Similarly, FIET's (1981) *Action Programme* suggests that, while the growing use of technology in the salaried areas must be monitored, women deserve particular attention, both because they are likely to be the first to be affected, and so that they do not continue to be more severely penalized than men by the negative effects of technological change.

Possible Future Developments

If technological change continues as some predict, new issues will emerge. Since many of the occupations currently targeted for automation are predominantly held by women, the issue of their unionization, the protection of their interests and their representation at the bargaining table should assume greater importance, particularly if unions are not to lose a relatively important source of membership. In addition, it is sometimes suggested that the professionalization of clerical jobs has created a new breed of white-collar technical worker who is less receptive to unionization. Hence women who remain in the lower-skilled jobs could become more important if unions are to retain their numerical strength and bargaining power (Gaudart and Greve, 1985, p. 168).

Technological innovations are making possible certain non-standardized patterns of employment, which are of special interest to women and which could also become important industrial relations issues. These include a considerable increase in part-time work, the growth of casual homework and the potential for telework.

While unions have not been especially concerned about part-time work in the past, its growth has encouraged them to review this issue. Unions contend that part-time work should not be allowed to escape union control and must become an issue for negotiation, in order to protect part-time workers (both men and women) to ensure that they enjoy the same rights and benefits as full-time workers. Unions argue that conditions of work, remuneration and fringe benefits for part-time workers should be specified in collective agreements and that workers should also be eligible for promotion. They also fear that employers may, in the interests of flexibility, encourage the growth of part-time work to the detriment of full-time workers.

Telework is not yet widespread but the potential for it exists and the use of remote terminals is likely to increase substantially in the next decade. Most such jobs are not yet covered by collective bargaining, which could constitute a further drain on union strength.

New technology has produced 'typical women's jobs' such as computer operators, check-out attendants and teleworkers. There is a danger that, if deskilled and downgraded, these jobs could form new ghettos in which women will be concentrated. Efforts should be made by both employers and unions to avoid such a development. Training is important, but should be expanded from the prevailing task- and firm-specific training into the more widely applicable skills that engender a greater degree of flexibility and computer literacy. This flexibility would, in turn, be invaluable in promoting equality of opportunity in employment should 'office technologies with more sophisticated software become available [facilitating] the transfer back to clerical workers of some discretion and autonomy on the job' (Dy, 1985, p. 2). Joint consultation and collective agreements on training that incorporate the equality principle will continue to be vital in ensuring that women will be able to benefit from the unique opportunities that are offered by new technologies.

The importance of special policies for women workers cannot be sufficiently emphasized and, as the ICFTU/ITS Women's

Committee suggests, all union policies on new technology and all technology agreements should include the provision that arrangements for the introduction and operation of new technology should not discriminate against women workers, either directly or indirectly (ICFTU, 1983).

Conclusion

The introduction of new technology has had a disproportionately negative impact on the employment of women workers in the service sector, in terms of both the availability and quality of the appropriate job opportunities. While issues that are of relevance to women workers are included implicitly or explicitly in policy statements, technology agreements and legislative provisions, their benefit to women workers still appears to be limited. In the long run, if appropriately handled, new technology could make an important contribution to increasing equal opportunities for women workers and decreasing sex-specific job segregation, thereby allowing women to move into areas previously dominated by men. However, this would necessitate greater attention to the problems of women workers, if the introduction and operation of new technology is not to work to their detriment, and if equality of opportunity and treatment are to be actively promoted.

References

Bjorn-Andersen, N. (1983), 'The changing role of secretaries and clerks', in Otway and Peltu (eds) (1983).

Davidson, M. J. and Cooper, C. L. (eds) (1987), *Women and Information Technology* (Chichester: Wiley).

Dy, J. F. (1985), *Visual Display Units: Job Content and Stress in Office Work* (Geneva: International Labour Organization).

Epstein, E. (1984), 'Negotiating over technological change in banking and insurance', *International Labour Review*, vol. 123, no. 4, July–August.

Evans, J. (1983), 'Negotiating technological change in banking and insurance', in Otway and Peltu (eds) (1983).

FIET (1980), *Bank Workers and New Technology* (Geneva: International Federation of Commercial, Clerical, Professional and Technical Employees).

FIET (1981), *Action Programme for Women Salaried Employees* (Geneva: International Federation of Commercial, Clerical, Professional and Technical Employees).
FIET (1983), *Commercial Workers and New Technology* (Geneva: International Federation of Commercial, Clerical, Professional and Technical Employees).
Gaudart, D. and Greve, R. M. (eds) (1985), 'Changes in economic structures in Europe and their effects on industrial relations: An overview of the debate', *Labour and Society*, vol. 10, no. 2, May.
ICFTU (1983), *New Technology and Women's Employment*, Report to the ICFTU/ITS Women's Committee (Geneva: International Confederation of Free Trade Unions).
ILO (1981a), 'Problems of non-manual workers: Work organisation, vocational training, equality of treatment at the workplace, job opportunities', *Report III*, Advisory Committee on Salaried Employees and Professional Workers, Eighth Session (Geneva: International Labour Organization).
ILO (1981b), 'The effects of technological and structural changes on employment and working conditions of non-manual workers', *Report*, Advisory Committee on Salaried and Professional Workers (Geneva: International Labour Organization).
ILO (1985), 'Equal opportunities and equal treatment for men and women in employment', *Report IV*, International Labour Conference, 71st Session (Geneva: International Labour Organization).
Menzies, H. (1981), *Women and the Chip: Case Studies of the Effects of Informatics on Employment in Canada* (Montreal: The Institute for Research on Public Policy).
Nora, S. and Minc, A. (1978), *L'Information de la Société* (Paris: La Documentation Française).
Paukert, L. (1984), *The Employment and Unemployment of Women in OECD Countries* (Paris: Organization for Economic Co-operation and Development).
Otway, H. J. and Peltu, M. (eds) (1983), *New Office Technology: Human and Organisational Aspects* (London: Frances Pinter).
Rada, J. (1980), *The Impact of Microelectronics: A Tentative Appraisal of Information Technology* (Geneva: International Labour Organization).
Werneke, D. (1983), *Microelectronics and Office Jobs: the Impact of the Chip on Women's Employment* (Geneva: International Labour Organization).
Zmroczek, C. and Henwood, F. (1983), 'New information technology and women's employment', *FAST Occasional Papers*, No. 54 (Brighton: Science Policy Research Unit, University of Sussex).

New Technology: International Perspectives on Human Resources and Industrial Relations, Unwin Hyman, London.

CHAPTER ELEVEN

New Technology, Economic Progress and Employment in Sweden

ANDERS BÄCKSTRÖM

This chapter is an attempt to explain the Swedish unions' very positive attitude to technological change and flexibility. This attitude is based on an analysis of economic and technological progress, and on the Swedish context of co-determination. Less union influence on economic policy and the introduction of new technology might erode their traditionally favourable attitude to new technology.

Two questions have always concerned the Swedish unions: higher wages and employment. From the union movement's earliest days it was realized that, in the long run, higher wages could be paid only if there is more efficient production. So there has never been any widespread union opposition to technological change in Sweden at either the local or central levels; though of course there have been individuals who have held negative attitudes.

Swedish society has undergone very dramatic changes during the last hundred years. The positive element in these changes has been that poverty, which was previously widespread, has been abolished

– through higher wages and a well-developed social safety net. On the whole we have achieved the welfare society of which our predecessors dreamed, though we have since discovered that even the dreams had certain imperfections.

The enormous reorganization of Swedish society has taken its toll. The most notable element on the cost side has been the restructuring of employment that has taken place. As shown in Table 11.1, the proportion of those employed in agriculture, forestry and fishing has decreased from 60 per cent in 1860 to 6 per cent in 1980. Within manufacturing industry, employment levels rose sharply until the middle of the 1960s and then slowly declined. Trade, transport and other private services have increased their share of employment from 5 per cent to over 30 per cent. During the same period public services have grown from 3 per cent to 30 per cent. The domestic employment sector constituted 17 per cent of the labour force in 1860, but has now become too small to be registered.

This restructuring of the workforce has occurred as a result of children choosing different jobs from their parents. They have chosen better-paid, indoor occupations, sheltered from wind and weather, and in urban areas which have better amenities. Throughout the past hundred years, periods of higher and lower unemployment have alternated. However, the trend throughout this period has been for unemployment to decrease and employment to increase. Technological development has, then, led to a restructuring of the workforce and higher wages, while unemployment has declined.

Table 11.1 *The distribution of employment among industries, Sweden, 1860–1980*

Industries	*Years*			
	1860 %	*1900* %	*1940* %	*1980* %
Agriculture, forestry, fishing	60	45	28	6
Industry, crafts, construction	15	25	36	33
Trade, transport, private services	5	10	19	31
Public services	3	5	11	30
Domestic work	17	15	6	–
TOTAL	100	100	100	100

Source: Statistics Sweden, *Various Surveys of the Swedish Labour Force, 1860–1980.*

According to the Swedish union movement, there is no direct long-term relationship between technological development and employment. Rather, employment is determined by economic policy and people's will to work. Full employment has nurtured a very favourable attitude towards technology. With the relative security that characterizes the Swedish labour market, no one need fear a development that necessitates changes. This attitude has also been consolidated through the close cooperation between the Swedish union movement and the Social Democratic Party during half a century of social democratic government. The six-year period of non-socialist government that we recently experienced was negative for the unions in several ways, but did not affect their positive attitude towards progress. Instead, unions feel that the need for rapid technological progress is greater now than it has been for a long time. The simplest and most painless way to redress the imbalances suffered during the period 1976–1982 is through greater technological change. Therefore, the Swedish Confederation of Trade Unions' (LO) representatives on many occasions over the last few years have urged that economic policy must be directed towards stronger support for technological development.

Is Microelectronics Special?

It would, of course, be convenient if one could separate the effects of technological development from all the other factors that also affect economic development. Unfortunately this cannot be done. It is not possible to determine with any great accuracy how the economy is affected by such things as altered consumer tastes, cultural change, new forms of work organization, differences in industrial relations, and so on. It is even more difficult to separate the effects of developments in microelectronics from those of other technological developments. Therefore, it must be with a certain humility that one discusses the significance of microelectronic technology for economic development and the labour market.

An essential question is whether there is anything particularly special about the significance of micro-technology for economic development, compared with earlier technological developments. One often hears that microelectronics is different because it is universally applicable. However, many earlier technical developments also exhibited some universality. The steam engine meant a reduction in dependence on wind and water power; it was portable and could be used everywhere that energy was needed. Nevertheless, in the long run it was superseded by the more cost-effective petrol engine. In the same way, it is easy to demonstrate the universality of electricity, which removes dependency on where energy is transformed, since it is so easy to transport.

Microelectronics may be most significant in the area of information. It is, however, only the latest in a very long series of technological advances. These started with language, which made it possible to transfer information from one person to another. The art of writing made it possible to transfer information more cheaply over longer distances. The art of printing radically lowered the cost of certain types of information. The telephone, radio and television have since made it possible to reduce the amount of time taken to transfer information, with simultaneously declining costs. Microelectronics is a further step in this progression. However, this step is not much more radical than the previous ones.

Developments in microelectronics are merely the latest step in a long process of technological developments, and these do not have any unique qualities compared with the previous steps. We can, therefore, use experience gained from earlier technological developments to evaluate the probable effects of microelectronics.

Employment Trends in Various Industries

To illustrate the effects on the labour market of the technological and economic developments of the last decades, the Economic Policy Department of the LO commissioned Statistics Sweden to analyse data from the population censuses for 1960 and 1980.

Table 11.2 shows how the distribution of employment among various industries has changed between 1960 and 1980. These changes, of course, are only partly the result of technological developments. To a great extent they are an expression of a specific economic policy, which aimed to steer economic development in certain directions, for instance to expand the public services.

Total employment increased by 15.7 per cent during the twenty-year period. No industry, however, has followed the average

Table 11.2 *The distribution of employment among industries, Sweden, 1960–80*

	Change in the number employed 1960–80 %	*Share of total employment 1980* %	*Change in share of employment 1960–80* %
Public administration and other services	123.6	33.2	16.6
Banking, insurance, property, consulting	174.4	6.9	4.1
Commerce, restaurants	–5.5	13.5	–2.5
Electricity, gas & water provision	14.7	0.9	0.0
Mining & quarrying	–32.3	0.4	–0.3
Transport, storage and communication	12.1	7.2	–0.1
Construction	–8.5	7.2	–1.6
Agriculture, forestry, hunting and fishing	–53.8	5.5	–7.9
Manufacturing	–15.6	24.9	–8.3
All industries	15.7	100	. . .

Source: Statistics Sweden, *Various Surveys of the Swedish Labour Force, 1960–80.*

trend. Industries that have diverged from this trend are of great interest. The most significant employment increases have taken place within public administration and other services, which have more than doubled their total employment. This substantial expansion is primarily a consequence of Sweden's welfare-oriented economic policy. Technological developments have probably played only an indirect part in this increase in employment, given that increasing productivity in the entire economy has made it possible to finance public sector expansion.

The banking and insurance sector is interesting because it is the most computerized part of the Swedish economy. Here one could have expected to find a reduction in employment. Instead, this sector has expanded considerably. The increase is even greater than the average. One explanation is that computerization has reduced production costs in the sector, which has had the effect of increasing the demand for the sector's products (more than has productivity). This is one of the most striking examples of how difficult it is to differentiate between the effects of technological development and the effects of economic circumstances.

Electricity, gas and water supply is a small sector from the point of view of employment and it has, moreover, increased at approximately the same rate as the mean value for the whole of the labour market.

Commerce has reduced its share of employment. To some extent this is the result of increased productivity. The role of microelectronics in this context is probably still fairly modest, even though some computerized cash registers had already been introduced by 1980. The political support for expanding the public services was probably crucial, because this expansion has been financed by taxation. Tax increases have meant that private consumption, and thus commercial turnover, have increased less than they would have otherwise. Hence, specific economic policy has influenced the sector's employment trends more than technological developments.

The transport, storage and communication sector has increased in employment, but at a somewhat lower rate than the average. Its share of total employment has fallen somewhat. This sector includes telecommunications, which has perhaps been the most affected by microelectronics development.

Employment in the manufacturing industry has declined by 15 per cent which, because of the size of the sector, means a greater loss of people than within agriculture (which declined by over 50 per cent). The decline in manufacturing is partly a result of the introduction of microelectronics into production processes and products, but most of the decline must be ascribed to increased productivity for other reasons, as well as diminished demand.

The drastic decline in mining employment, by one-third, is hardly a result of microelectronics. Rather, international competition and improved productivity for other reasons have led to the decline. The construction industry has also suffered fairly substantial employment reduction, but it is unlikely that microelectronics has had any major influence in this area.

To summarize, we can observe that the twenty-year period from 1960 to 1980 saw dramatic changes on the Swedish labour market. This was also the period when computerization was first applied on a large scale. It is, however, only in exceptional cases that new technology played a major part in the employment changes. In most cases other factors have had a greater influence.

Occupational Changes

The analysis above concerned the distribution of employment among *industries*. It is also interesting to examine the changing distribution of various *occupations*. As there are a large number of occupations, a full account cannot be given here. Instead, discussion will be confined to those occupations which have increased or decreased most during the period 1960–80.

It is obvious from Table 11.3 that those occupations that have increased most are those that are dependent on the development of the welfare state. Various types of teaching jobs, work within health care, and employment in other parts of the social services constitute the major part of the increase. Systems analysts, programmers and other computer-related occupations increased five-fold, but in relation to all employment their increase is marginal. Clerks have increased by almost 50 per cent (corresponding to 2 per cent of all employment). There were also

Table 11.3 *Occupations that have increased most significantly, Sweden, 1960–80*

	Change in the number employed 1960–80 %	*Share of total employment 1980* %	*Change in share of employment 1960–80* %
Auxiliary nurses	282.7	4.3	3.0
Clerks (i.e. occupation nos 290, 298, 299)	43.7	7.0	2.0
Programmers, etc.	472.5	1.3	1.1
Cleaners	93.9	2.5	1.0
Buyers, etc.	84.8	2.6	1.0
Home helps, etc.	396.9	1.1	0.9
Teachers of theoretical subjects	212.8	1.2	0.8
Social service workers	480.4	0.9	0.8
General social administrative work	300.2	0.9	0.7
Nurses	148.6	1.3	0.7
Nursery school teachers	1176.3	0.7	0.7

Source: Statistics Sweden, *Various Surveys of the Swedish Labour Force, 1960–80*

large increases in the numbers of cleaners and buyers. Of the occupations listed above, it is mainly programmers, administrators and clerks who have come into contact with microelectronics to any major extent. In education and health care, the new technology has been used much more selectively, mainly by specialists.

It is of equal interest to analyse the occupations that have experienced the greatest decline. If microelectronics causes unemployment, the effects should be most noticeable in those occupations where employment has fallen. The considerable decline in the numbers of farmers and farm workers probably has little to do with the effects of microelectronics. It is a continuation of a trend that has been dominant for about a hundred years. The reason is that consumption of agricultural products has not increased very rapidly, while productivity has increased dramatically through mechanization, fertilizers, plant and animal improvement. The decline in the number of forestry workers and unskilled labourers is mainly a consequence of mechanization, as more and more machines have been used to replace human workers.

Table 11.4 *Occupations that have declined most significantly, Sweden, 1960–80*

	Change in the number employed 1960–80 %	*Share of total employment 1980* %	*Change in share of employment 1960–80* %
Farmers	–44.5	3.1	–3.5
Farm workers	–79.0	0.6	–2.8
Forestry workers	–56.6	0.7	–1.3
Unskilled labourers	–59.2	0.6	–1.3
Tailors, sewing workers	–71.0	0.3	–1.2
Shop assistants, etc.	–14.2	3.5	–1.2
Concrete & construction workers etc.	–31.6	1.0	–0.7
Retailers	–35.2	0.8	–0.7
Textile workers	–63.1	0.2	–0.7
Machine tool operators, etc.	–7.9	2.6	–0.7
Bakers & confectioners	–56.3	0.2	–0.5

Source: Statistics Sweden, *Various Surveys of the Swedish Labour Force, 1960–80*

As far as the trend for tailors, sewing workers and textile workers is concerned, one must take account of the conditions of the entire Swedish textile industry. For a long time, this industry has been squeezed between the solidarity wage policy and increasing international competition (especially from some developing countries). As a part of the policy of evening out wage differentials in Sweden, textile workers' wages have been pushed to become the world's highest. This is probably the main reason for the declining employment of tailors, sewing workers and textile workers, rather than the introduction of microelectronics.

One can also examine other occupational groups in the same way and see that there are special reasons for the declining employment in each and every case, except for machine tool operators. For this occupational group, it is probable that microelectronics has played a large part in its decline. For a long period Sweden has been a successful exporter of engineering products, many of whose controlling mechanisms have been based on precision mechanics. In this field, the advent of microelectronics has meant that such controlling mechanisms can be replaced by electronic controls. The production of these requires fewer workers and, moreover, the products are often imported.

The Structure of Education

Microelectronics has been shown to have a relatively marginal effect on the great changes that have taken place in the labour market. However, the significance of microelectronics has increased and will continue to do so in the future. Therefore, it is reasonable to analyse the effects that this technology has had on the labour market's need for skilled labour. In Table 11.5, a socio-economic grouping is used that is mainly based on the length of education. It categorizes blue-collar workers into skilled and non-skilled, and white-collar workers in accordance with the number of years of post-elementary education. It also shows self-employed people and farmers.

Table 11.5 shows that great changes have taken place. All the white-collar groups have increased their share of employment, particularly those with three–six years post-elementary education. Furthermore, non-skilled workers in service production have

Table 11.5 *Changing educational requirements of the Swedish labour market, 1960–80*

Socio-economic designation (SEI)	*Change in the number employed 1960–80 %*	*Share of total employment 1980 %*	*Change in share of employment 1960–80 %*
Medium-level white-collar workers with 3–6 years post elementary education	112.3	15.8	7.2
Lower-level white-collar workers < 3 years	55.5	16.8	4.3
Higher-level white-collar workers/senior managers > 6 years	98.0	7.7	3.2
Non-skilled workers in service production	25.4	21.7	1.7
Skilled workers in service production	12.6	3.6	–0.1
Self-employed (excluding farmers)	–8.1	5.8	–1.5
Skilled workers in goods production	–1.1	13.0	–2.2
Farmers	–43.9	3.3	–3.5
Non-skilled workers in goods production	–34.9	11.3	–8.8
Total	15.7	100	. . .

Source: Statistics Sweden, *Various Surveys of the Swedish Labour Market, 1960–80.*

increased their share. Other types of workers, skilled and non-skilled, in goods and service production have decreased their employment share, as have the self-employed and farmers. The decline in non-skilled workers in goods production corresponds to almost 10 per cent of total employment. Nevertheless, it is important to note that these changes depend on technological development only in part, and that economic and political factors have also been influential.

Attitudes to Microelectronics

The preceding analysis has attributed a fairly marginal role to microelectronics in the major changes that have taken place in the

Swedish labour market since 1960. One could infer from much public debate, however, that microelectronics is the main explanation for the changes taking place. Why? This paradox has been illuminated by an investigation of the Swedes' computer habits, undertaken by Statistics Sweden in 1984. The investigation had several purposes. It sought to survey the skills and experience of the population in this field, to examine whether and how people use computer equipment, what educational requirements existed, and what were the prevailing attitudes to computers and their use. As can be seen from Figure 11.1, the use of computers had increased substantially in the previous 20 years and in 1984 affected one-third of the population of working age.

How had computerization affected people's jobs? Table 11.6 shows that only 0.6 per cent had been made redundant as a result of computerization, while over 90 per cent stated that their work had not changed to any great extent or that they had no experience of computerization. Seven per cent had experienced substantial changes in their work as the result of computerization (5 per cent considered that the change was for the better, 1 per cent that it was for the worse, while 1 per cent thought that it was neither for better nor for worse).

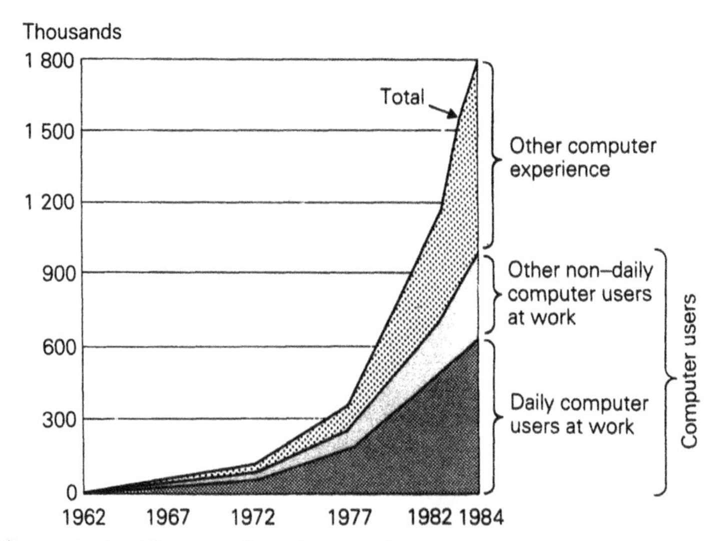

Figure 11.1 *The growth in the use of computers in Sweden, 1962–84*
Source: Statistics Sweden, *The Growth and Use of Computers in Sweden, 1962–84.*

Table 11.6 *Experience of computerization at work in Sweden*

	Thousands: Men	Women	Total	Share %
Made redundant	12	21	33	0.6
Considerable changes in own job	200	161	361	7
Of which:				
made no difference	39	31	70	1
for the better	134	104	238	5
for the worse	27	26	53	1
No experience	2,455	2,426	4,881	92
No reply given	7	5	12	0
Total	2,674	2,613	5,287	100

Source: Statistics Sweden, *Folkets Datavanor*, 1985.

Few reported negative experiences of computerization: 1 per cent of the workforce had been given worse tasks and 0.6 per cent had lost their jobs. In answer to another question, 50 per cent stated that they considered that the experience of computerization was predominantly positive, while a quarter considered it to be negative and a quarter had no opinion on the matter.

These positive experiences can be contrasted with the evaluations of the future effects of computerization, which the survey also covers. One can infer from Table 11.7 that people

Table 11.7 *Expectations of computerization in Sweden*

Do you believe that computerization leads to:	*Yes* %	*No* %	*Don't know* %	*Total* %
Increased employment	65	23	12	100
More jobs	19	67	14	100
Simplified tasks	75	12	13	100
The disappearance of heavy, dirty monotonous jobs	65	24	11	100
Increased control of the individual at work	69	16	15	100
Increased control of the individual by the authorities	78	11	11	100
Increased vulnerability of society	80	7	13	100

Source: Statistics Sweden, *Folkets Datavanor*, 1985.

foresee more negative than positive effects. The negative evaluations of the future, however, do not appear to be founded on past experience. Instead, the survey shows that the greater one's own direct experience of computers, the fewer risks one foresees in the future. The chief explanation for the gloomy expectations may be that much of the population lacks experience of computers at work and that people are frightened of the unknown. Unfortunately, the information in the mass media, upon which people's expectations tend to be based, often lacks objectivity. The more fantastic the forecasts or the more frightening the pictures that are presented, the larger the headlines in the media. Furthermore, computer and computer equipment salesmen have always had a tendency to exaggerate the rationalization made possible by new technology.

Conclusions

Swedish unions have traditionally had a positive attitude to new technology. Their analysts infer that microelectronics does not differ fundamentally from earlier developments in new technology. For more than a hundred years, the Swedish labour market has been subjected to dramatic changes. From an analysis of recent developments, it is concluded that most of them have not been caused by new technologies, even though these have been of considerable significance. The structural transformation of the Swedish economy has had predominantly positive effects for the population. It has generally been possible to overcome any negative effects that have occurred by means of economic and labour market policy measures.

Many people feel great anxiety about what technological developments will bring in the future. The anxiety is keenest among those who have little or no personal experience of the new technology. As the new technology continues to affect more of the labour force, such anxiety will decrease. There is no reason for the Swedish unions to abandon their traditionally favourable view of technology. The restructuring of the Swedish labour market will not proceed much faster than before, or be any more difficult to live with.

The general view that technological developments are

progressing at an increasing rate is difficult to substantiate. The consequence of a new and more effective technology should be that productivity increases. If technological developments are taking place at an accelerating rate, productivity should also be increasing faster and faster, yet this is not the case. In Sweden, and in most other Western countries, the rate of productivity increases has dwindled from the levels of the 1950s and 1960s. The 'accelerating rate of technological development' is an illusion – at least in certain respects.

Swedish unions will continue to exercise strong political influence. There is no alternative in a country where 90 per cent of employees are unionized. The unions will therefore take part in and influence future developments, including the introduction of new technology and the formulation of economic policy. It is not strange, therefore, that Swedish unions have a positive attitude to technological change. They shared the fruits of such developments. Full employment is the most important goal for economic policy. Sweden has a well-developed labour market policy, which the unions have helped to formulate, whereby 3–4 per cent of the labour force are retrained annually.

It is understandable that unions in some other countries have a less positive attitude to technological progress. If full employment is not a political priority and unions lack the opportunity to influence developments, then it is almost inevitable that unions will oppose all changes in a desperate attempt to protect existing jobs. Swedish unions have demanded that a greater proportion of the training needed as a consequence of the new technology should be directed towards those in the labour market who have less education. In this way, previously repetitive and monotonous occupations can be enriched and thereby benefit both the employees and the national economy.

Note

This chapter refers to official statistics. This does not mean that we lack relevant union information. On the contrary, we have a great deal. However, as there are no discrepancies between union and official sources I have chosen to make reference to the latter, as they may be regarded as more reliable by an international audience.

References

Statistics Sweden (1985), *Folkets Datavanor* (Stockholm: Swedish Government Printer).

Sehlstedt, K. and Schroder, L. (1985), *Datateknik och Omställnings-problem* (Stockholm: Swedish Government Printer).

CHAPTER TWELVE

New Technologies: Skills 'Mismatch' and the Challenges ahead

HEDVA SARFATI and MARGARET COVE

This chapter attempts to identify the possible effects of new technologies on employment in industrialized countries. It reviews the responses of employers and unions through the collective bargaining process and discussions in international forums. It also outlines government employment policies and the findings of several researchers. It is suggested that new patterns of industrial relations are emerging under the combined pressure of the recession and new technologies. Emphasising the importance of education, training and human resources allocation, this chapter advocates greater consensus between governments and both sides of industry, particularly in relation to training.

The problem of understanding the changes being brought about by the introduction of new technologies and how to alleviate their negative effects is preoccupying policy-makers at national level throughout the industrialized world, whether in government, industry or trade unions.

On the basis of opinions expressed by the ILO's tripartite constituents (governments, employers' and workers' organizations) and independent researchers, this chapter gives an account of the positions of both sides of industry towards the introduction of new technology in industrialized market economy countries. It tries to identify the main areas of disagreement, and in some cases agreement, between the parties involved. While considerable uncertainty still surrounds the 'job displacement' and 'job creation' impact of new technology, an attempt will be made to clarify some of the policy implications involved. Source material, unless otherwise indicated, is drawn from articles published in the ILO's quarterly *Social and Labour Bulletin*.

Impact on Employment

It has generally been agreed that most applications of computer-based technology, in both offices and factories, tend to reduce the amount of labour required in relation to a given volume of work. However, the introduction of new technologies has opened up new industries, new types of jobs and an even greater growth in services associated with technological innovation. The question is whether these developments will be enough to offset the employment displacement effects. So far there is no consensus. Nor is it clear whether some of the new services are really new, or have merely been transferred within sectors, or to outside specialized services.

The ILO *World Labour Report* (International Labour Office, 1984) argues that no one is yet in a position to make reasonable forecasts on technological innovation. There are several reasons for this: technological change is not yet integrated into macro-economic analysis; immediate repercussions overshadow long-term potential; and no way has been found to separate the influence of the prevailing economic climate, particularly the effects of recessions.

In spite of this, there have been more and more studies of the impact of technological change in many countries. As conditions differ from country to country, it is difficult to generalize, but the overall conclusion is that the net balance of employment resulting from the introduction of information technologies (IT) will be negative at least in the immediate future, particularly if there is no sustained economic growth. Even assuming the most optimistic scenario, most countries will have to resolve serious labour-displacement problems.

Despite this, at least one leading economist, Leontief, has concluded that overall unemployment in the USA will not rise because of automation (Leontief and Duchin, 1984). He estimates that by the year 2000, professionals (especially computer specialists and engineers) will account for nearly 20 per cent of all jobs, compared with 15.6 per cent in 1978. The demand for clerical workers will fall to 11.5 per cent, from 17.8 per cent in 1978.

The impact of robots is at present seen as being fairly modest. While robots will displace about 400,000 semi-skilled jobs by 1990 and nearly 2 million by the year 2000, roughly the same number of jobs will be created to make the necessary capital goods, particularly hardware, for the new technologies.

Total demand for labour in the private sector, according to Leontief, will increase from 88.2 million workers in 1977 to 156.6 in the year 2000. But with labour force growth slowing down, his study implies a shortage of labour in the next fifteen years, rather than unemployment. However, as the use of computers increases, it is estimated that the proportion of managerial and supervisory staff will decline from 9.5 per cent in 1978 to 7.2 per cent by the year 2000. In pointing to major changes in the demand for skills, the study emphasizes the need for a major education and training effort over the next twenty years without which a number of vacancies could not be filled.

Similar conclusions are reached in a report by the Upjohn Institute for Employment Research in the USA. Looking at the significant changes in skill requirements brought about by factory automation, the institute argues that, while robots will eliminate low-skill jobs, more than half the jobs they create will require a minimum of two years' post-secondary education.

In terms of employment, the Upjohn report predicts that some 100,000–200,000 unskilled jobs will be eliminated by 1990 while some 32,000–64,000 additional jobs are expected to be created, mainly in robot manufacturing, direct suppliers and systems engineering (Hunt and Hunt, 1983). Thus, automation necessarily results in fewer jobs. However, by increasing productivity, each company or industry should reduce costs, allowing it to reduce prices, and thus boost sales. Therefore the end result should be more production and, therefore, more jobs. None the less, certain occupations will be dramatically affected. In the US car industry Upjohn predicts that 5–10 per cent of assembly jobs and 30–40 per cent of painters will be displaced by 1990. Other studies include similar results, and substantial displacement is also expected in iron and steel, consumer non-durables and aerospace. However, the speed of diffusion of the new technology cannot be forecast and depends on many factors, as shown by the initial troubles experienced in developing computer-integrated manufacturing systems.

Repercussions in the car industry have been clearly illustrated at the Rivalta plant of Fiat, the leading Italian car manufacturer. Following the introduction of robots, the proportion of direct production workers declined dramatically from 70 to 10 per cent while the proportion of indirect service workers rose from 9 to 12 per cent and of maintenance workers from 17 to 71.5 per cent (Treu, 1984). It is these *indirect* employment effects that have importance in the job creation debate and have yet to be incorporated effectively into a macroeconomic model.

Another factor is that technology has been used to create a world market. Increasingly, workers have to compete for jobs with workers in other parts of the world. Some industries gravitate towards the world's low-wage, low-tax, cheap capital regions. In the USA, more manufacturers are buying parts or finished products from other producers, both at home and abroad. This breaks down manufacturers' integrated vertical structure, whereby they make many of their own components, and replaces it with a network of small suppliers. While flexible and efficient, some experts fear that, if expanded further, such fragmented manufacturing practices will leave countries without a sound industrial base.

In Japan, robots (an estimated 80 per cent of the world total) have been introduced apparently with few growing pains. A 1985 White Paper by the Ministry of Labour shows that the reduction in employment of production workers has been more than offset by an increase in employment of other workers, such as engineers, electronic engineering technicians, electronic data-processing staff, and maintenance workers. As far as skill requirements are concerned, it appears that alternative work processes may lead to additional requirements rather than complete obsolescence of existing skills (JIL, 1985).

The Japanese experience is, in fact, often cited as an example to other industrialized countries. While Western Europe and the USA have experienced shrinking markets in traditional industries, there has been a significant growth of employment in Japan. And while growth in manufacturing slowed down during the 1970s, an additional 700,000 jobs have been created in Japanese manufacturing since 1979. However, a case could be made that this pattern of rapid technological progress and employment growth can only be maintained in the long run by the significant inroads Japan has made in international markets (Freeman and Soete, 1985). In a similar way, it has been argued that, in the case of Japan, indirect employment effects have occurred elsewhere in other countries. Japanese automakers, for example, have been striving to enlarge their share of the US market and, according to the *Wall Street Journal* (6 June 1986), the number of employees of Japanese operations and joint ventures in the US is expected to double by 1989.

With regard to the impact of robotics on labour, the OECD (Organization for Economic Co-operation and Development, 1983) foresees a reduction in the number of work posts, but points out that robots are still being used in a comparatively narrow range of industries and applications in its twenty-five industrialized member states, with the automobile industry being the major user. Moreover, the proliferation of incompatible systems and machines, unable to speak a common 'language', presents a major obstacle to the fully computer-integrated manufacturing system, the so-called 'unmanned' factory.

Many companies are worried about a sufficient return on investment. Automation projects are invariably delayed or exceed budgets because of serious software and coordination problems. Users tend to experience initial problems when commissioning simple electronically controlled robots. Any attempt to reconcile systems that were meant to be incompatible for competitive reasons are bound to be fraught with difficulties. This emphasizes that people and their skills are still necessary inputs. Widescale introduction will also depend on costs, as robots are expensive (Ebel, 1986). According to many consultants, if you have 'just the right amount' of technology, you end up with lower investment yet high productivity. Nevertheless, the potential for computer-integrated manufacturing certainly exists and it would be unreasonable to assume that it will never be realized.

Office Automation

The first civilian jobs to be affected by mainframe computers were in offices. It is therefore not surprising that the new technologies involving microelectronics are again profoundly affecting the nature of office work. Basic computer skills are becoming essential for all office workers from secretary to manager. And not only inside the office – 'lap-top' computers are accompanying many managers and executives when travelling. The falling cost of computers and the development of user-friendly software will accelerate the process. As in manufacturing, there is widespread concern that computers may eventually oust some skilled labour, including clerks, from offices. Once more, proper debate is hampered by lack of an accurate information base on which to draw conclusions. The optimists see services and clerical work offsetting job cutbacks in other sectors, and base their conclusions on past trends of substantial growth among these categories.

The Office of Technology Assessment (OTA), an advisory body to the US Congress, has forecast that by 1990 one out of every three office workers will use a computer terminal, and by the year 2000 terminals may be as commonplace on office desks as telephones are in the 1980s (OTA, 1985). That OTA report is slightly less optimistic about office jobs than it was in an earlier study. By 1985, it considered that the increased efficiency offered by office automation would be likely to slow the growth in office employment in the next few years; and during the 1990s it might even decline. The OTA concluded that any possibility of reduced job opportunities in office work, which has been the strongest source of job creation throughout the century, should be closely watched by Congress. However, this outcome is not certain. Strong growth in the US economy and continuing growth in demand for information and information-based products and services may outweigh the labour saving achieved through office automation (OTA, 1984).

The Institute of Manpower Studies (IMS) at Sussex University (UK) also refutes the idea of any strong growth in the clerical labour market. It suggests that the loss of 250,000 clerical jobs in the production sector alone in 1980–2 is unlikely to be offset, although much will depend on the trend toward part-time, temporary and short-term contract employment (IMS, 1985). This is another current development, with employers covering peak periods by taking on temporary staff. Regular staffing levels are related to low-activity periods.

There are also other changes. The 'underground' economy is booming and 'home' and remote-site working are becoming controversial issues. Will such practices force workers back into a socially unprotected status either at home or outside the main work centres? There are other indications that we may here be dealing with a new 'high-tech' form of 'labour-only sub-contracting' combined with the even older 'putting-out system' – which have long been criticized by organized labour as well as by those who manage employment-related social security and pension schemes.

Significantly, the more recent ILO standards such as the Termination of Employment Convention (No. 158) and Recommendation (No. 166) adopted in 1982 attach much more importance to dismissal for economic, technological, structural or similar reasons than did the 1963 Recommendation on the subject.

Against the background of other changes, new technologies are being used to break down many currently accepted employment patterns, including the arrangement of working time and the notion of the 'full-time' worker. An example of this is the 'networking' at Rank Xerox, in the UK. The arrangement of working time depends on the computer terminals in the networkers' homes. The networkers are not employed by Rank Xerox but work as consultants for 50 per cent of their time. Under a pilot experiment, some state postal services in the Federal Republic of Germany are also organized in such a flexible way. The unanswered question is whether such patterns will develop into definitive trends.

Computer-associated technology is also having a significant impact in the services sector. The most dramatic employment effects are in offices, banking, insurance, retailing, telecommunications and printing. Most insurance companies have developed a major processing capacity and introduced integrated computer systems for the creation, storage and adjustment of policy records. According to the Geneva-based International Federation of Commercial, Clerical, Professional and Technical Employees (FIET), this means that traditional insurance skills are no longer required and some jobs have disappeared (FIET, 1983). Workers in lower-grade jobs have fared worst, notably women employees (as discussed in Chapter 10). Furthermore, experiments in some countries with home-based and self-service banking and insurance have become a reality: the PRESTEL system in the UK permits a customer to acquire information, manage a bank account or purchase insurance via a small terminal attached to the family television set. Similar systems have been introduced in other countries.

Since 1965, job creation in most industrialized countries has occurred in the service sector. This raises the question whether the service sector will continue to make up for jobs lost in manufacturing. The large-scale introduction of automated tellers and cashless shopping is also seen by FIET as a serious threat to jobs in banking and commerce. Moreover, according to FIET, the spread of electronic funds transfer (EFT) will also be dramatic.

Collective Bargaining

The issues concerning technological change have affected labour–management relations and will continue to do so. Not only do the new technologies have profound implications for the jobs and working conditions of union members but there are many signs that the traditional 'adversarial' relationship is changing on both sides (see Chapters 2 and 3). Many managements have realized that involving the workforce can smooth the introduction of new technology (see Chapters 6 and 7). Simultaneously, unions have been rethinking ways and means of offsetting the negative effects on employment.

Hitherto, unions in all countries have accepted the need for change to maintain national or company competitiveness in world markets. But they have argued that, inasmuch as technology leads to higher productivity and profits, the workforce should benefit through improved working conditions. Unions in Australia, Belgium, Canada, France, the Federal Republic of Germany, Japan, Switzerland, the UK, the USA, the Nordic countries and

Asia agree at both national and international level that workers must be fully involved in planning for technological change (Sarfati and Cove, 1985). Technological change is also seen by unions as a means of achieving their long-term aim of reduced working time; although in some instances, such as printing in the Federal Republic of Germany, successful pressure to cut hours has speeded up the introduction of new technologies.

Particularly in Western Europe, the result has been the negotiation of technology agreements (see Appendix). Almost all agreements contain a clause on joint consultation. Most of them have some provisions covering redundancy, voluntary leaving and early retirement. While this is not always the case, most unions would like to see a comprehensive approach covering consultation on planning, investment, manning levels, redundancy, retraining, work organization and reduced working hours. They are also concerned about computerized personnel files and data privacy, both within countries and across borders, as well as with the monitoring of work performance.

The Nordic unions have been especially ready to respond to technological change. Norway adopted a national agreement in 1975. Under a Swedish agreement (1982) local unions can consult outside experts, normally paid for by the employers. In 1986, Denmark updated its 1981 agreement to include wider provisions on disclosure of information and also lowered the employee threshold for setting up works councils from fifty to thirty-five employees.

Underpinning all union approaches is the need to try and strengthen the notions of joint responsibility and control. The Brussels-based International Confederation of Free Trade Unions (ICFTU) and its affiliated international trade secretariats (ITSs) are pressing for international standards on the social protection of workers affected by technological change. They have asked for such an item to be included on the agenda of a future session of the annual conference of the International Labour Organization. Accepting the need for new technology, the Prague-based world Federation of Trade Unions also sees the need for safeguards. At its 21st Congress in 1985, the World Confederation of Labour at Brussels also called for prior consultation, disclosure of information and retraining rights.

According to the European Trade Union Institute (ETUI),

central technology agreements can be useful in establishing procedures for handling change and for providing a mechanism for resolving conflicts. These can also include the main issues to be negotiated at plant and company level, while the central organizations can provide back-up services to the (decentralized) negotiators. It is more difficult to regulate the non-quantitative but potentially more significant questions of systems design, work organization and job quality. Therefore, the ETUI argues that the development of local participation in the systems design process and influence over work organization has become important, especially in relation to attempts to extend joint regulation of the introduction of new technology (ETUI, 1982).

It is not only the unions that are taking initiatives. Many employers have adopted policies on the introduction of new technologies. Under the impetus of technological change, new alignments are taking place on the labour relations scene. Generally new technologies have been introduced more efficiently where there is a long tradition of collective bargaining and a social partnership approach to industrial relations such as in the Nordic countries and the Federal Republic of Germany (Bamber and Lansbury, 1987).

Rather than seeing technological advances wiping out jobs quicker than they can be replaced, the International Employers' Organization (IOE) points to the indirect employment creation effects of higher productivity injecting additional purchasing power into the economy, which translates into increased demand and job creation. The IOE wants an overhaul of outdated collective bargaining practices, which it sees as impeding industrial changes that might eventually restore growth (IOE, 1985).

Union Responses

Many unions are on the defensive, but there are signs of a new responsiveness, a desire to think of new ideas on how to deal with a changing society, including changing technology. While criticizing the employers' emphasis on reducing labour costs, the Italian General Confederation of Labour (CGIL), one of the three leading Italian trade union confederations, accepts that the unions' concentration on wage claims ignores several pertinent issues. Subsequently, a crucial three-year framework agreement was negotiated at the beginning of 1986 between Confindustria, the main Italian employers' organization, and the three main trade union confederations, CGIL, CISL and UIL. The agreement deals with economic growth, improved productivity, competitiveness and reduced inflation. It also includes union aspirations for job creation, cuts in working time, and the maintenance of purchasing power 'so long as these are compatible with the aims of growth' (*International Report* 266, 20 May 1986). This agreement is all the more significant in that it was reached without the government intervention that has characterized Italian negotiations in recent years.

There is a growing awareness among many unions that, if the union movement is to remain a vehicle for social change, it must renew itself and confront the problems of economic crisis and change. In France, Edmond Maire, Secretary-General of the French Democratic Confederation of Labour (CFDT), initiated such a debate at the 40th Congress of the CFDT in June 1985. While ready to negotiate on more flexible work organization, the CFDT sees a need to develop a workforce that is more qualified, more creative and able to accept more responsibility – including involvement in the design and introduction of new technologies.

While the earlier emphasis was on higher wages and better working conditions, it has been shifting also to emphasize information, consultation and participation in decision-making (Monat and Sarfati, 1986). Hence, works councils (as in the Federal Republic of Germany), special *ad hoc* bodies (Denmark) and even special union delegates (Norway) are often involved in the introduction of new technologies. In contrast, Australian unions were slow to develop a more pragmatic response to the issue of new technologies; it was not until 1979 that, concerned with the high level of employment, they adopted a concerted strategy covering planning, consultation, redundancy, training and shorter working hours.

In several countries, through either national, sectoral or enterprise-level agreements, workers have managed to get employers to agree to job security guarantees or no dismissal when new technologies are introduced. The parties concerned and independent observers generally see this type of guarantee as a legitimate way of sharing the benefits of new technologies. Many studies confirm these views. Not only does consultation lead to higher productivity, it leads to better motivation. The willingness of management to notify and consult unions could be seen as an indicator of the quality of labour–management relationships and company performance.

As the introduction of new technologies that lead to skill changes may cut across occupational classifications, the unions will need to acquire the support of the emerging groups of employees 'spawned' by new technologies, especially engineers and technicians. If their support is not harnessed by the unions, then the union role will be seriously affected. Workers who owe their employment to technical innovation and their expertise in operating complicated microelectronic equipment are not likely to support unions that do not recognize the crucial importance of high productivity and competitiveness.

In its 1985 report, the American Federation of Labor–Congress of Industrial Organizations states frankly that the unions 'have fallen behind the pace of change'. But it is optimistic about the ability of the unions to adapt. The report lists a series of recommendations for experiments in organizing techniques that should be introduced immediately. These include representation geared to the needs and concerns of particular groups, greater sensitivity to new concerns and members' demands, new categories of membership, more services and benefits to attract workers beyond the collective bargaining structure, better media campaigns to publicize the unions and above all to stress the benefits of collective bargaining as a stabilizing influence (AFL–CIO, 1985).

The combined pressure of new technological and structural change and tough international competition is not only raising demands from employers for greater labour market flexibility, but also prompting fundamental changes in industrial relations practices. And unions are showing increasing signs of joining the search for novel industrial strategies.

Joint Understandings

A major step has been a joint statement by the employers' and labour's advisory committees to the OECD – namely the Business and Industry Advisory Committee and the Trade Union Advisory Committee (BIAC/TUAC, 1986). This joint statement was presented to ministers of OECD governments in 1986. While recognizing that structural and technological change is required to create new job opportunities, the statement underlined the need 'to devise together the means of achieving non-inflationary high growth and full employment'.

A series of significant talks began in 1985 between the Union of Industrial and Employers' Confederations of Europe and the European Trade Union Confederation. The talks, dealing with new technology and job creation, led to a common position paper in March 1987 (EC, 1987). Both sides recognize the need to make use of the economic and social potential offered by new technologies in order to improve the competitive position of European firms. Employers accept the need for some degree of information and consultation on technological change, while the unions agree that discussions should not hold back innovation. Both sides agreed that training to acquire new skills should be the top priority in collective bargaining, to ensure the smooth transition to new technology.

There have been similar tentative developments in the USA. A record number of participants attended a 1985 National Labor–Management Conference in Washington, DC, under the auspices of the Department of Labor, to discuss how labour–management cooperation could be a successful means of dealing with mutual concerns and result in new approaches to collective bargaining. The department is carrying out a study of labour laws and practices that may inhibit improved labour–management relations. It accepts that current labour legislation may not be able to deal with the new issues raised by technological change.

The Workforce of the Future

Whether or not unions take a leading role in industrial restructuring, 'business as usual' for both management and unions is no longer a viable strategy. Tremendous changes are taking place, which may seem like a 'race against the clock'.

Factory and office automation requires changes in skills and working practices among the workforce, changes in organizational structures and new demands on management expertise. While many talk about a 'polarization' of skills, 'deskilling' and 'dehumanization', there is general consensus that different jobs will result from new technology. Many forecasters, including the OECD, see a reduction in the proportion of low-skilled blue-collar workers, clerical workers and lower managerial and supervisory occupations, with an increased proportion of the labour force installing, operating and carrying out maintenance work on high-tech equipment. Those displaced by new technology will not have the requisite skills to move to new jobs. Similarly, the majority of school leavers lack the appropriate skills. Under such conditions the expression 'knowledge is power' takes on a new meaning.

Most studies have concluded that there is a 'mismatch' between the skills that are needed for the efficient exploitation of the new technologies and the available supply of labour. Governments, managements and unions all need to work faster to change the orientation of education, training and vocational guidance to bring the skills mix into line with the new requirements. Moreover, as technological 'know-how' will rapidly become outdated, steps must be taken to avoid training specialists in the obsolete.

Practical Training Measures

The European Communities programme on forecasting and assessment in science and technology (FAST) underlined the vital importance of education and training. France introduced a comprehensive computerization programme into its schools as far back as 1979. A recent agreement between the French government and the Federation of Metallurgical and Mining Industries, representing employers in the iron and steel industry, provides for the joint implementation of training projects to support the modernization schemes that have been launched in French shipyards and in the automobile industry.

Two trend-setting French agreements on training were negotiated in 1986. The first, negotiated at Sacilor, a leading steel company, describes training as 'one of the strategic variables for company development'. Under the agreement, covering some 65,000 employees in 160 plants, vocational training will become an integral part of company policy and will be treated as an investment, decided in consultation with the workforce. The aim is technological expertise and 'upskilling'. The second, a framework agreement in the banking industry, contains guidelines for offsetting the negative effects of technological change. It contains extensive provisions relating to retraining and updating of employees and managerial staff. All major changes will be discussed with the employee representatives, and the union consensus is that the agreement heralds a more realistic approach to dealing with the problems of job adaptation.

Sweden has introduced a direct levy on companies to finance research and training projects connected with the introduction of new technology. In 1985, it amounted to 10 per cent of company profits and its use was decided in consultation with the unions.

In the UK, the high levels of unemployment together with the shortfall in the new technological skills have led to a series of measures ranging from a Youth Training Scheme, which offers 300,000 two-year (previously one-year) industry-linked training opportunities for jobless young people, to a new national vocational qualification framework.

Seeking the Right Training

There has also been a series of British reports. The UK government's Advisory Council for Applied Research and Development calls for a national forum to rethink funding and attitudes towards research and education (ACARD, 1980). The Institute of Manpower Studies (IMS) has also produced a report commissioned by the government, which assesses the major trends in the supply of and demand for information technology specialists (IMS, 1986). A survey by the Confederation of British Industry showed that a lack of professional engineers is British industry's most serious skill shortage problem. Over 38 per cent of employers expect the situation to worsen. The survey shows that most employers react to most types of skill shortage by trying to recruit new staff, often by 'poaching' from other companies, rather than by retraining existing employees (CBI, 1985).

An even more pertinent report by the IMS was commissioned by British empoyers (*Financial Times*, 13 June 1986). Based on a survey of over 3,000 firms, it emphasizes the need for 'qualitative changes as a result of changing market pressures, new technologies and better working methods'. The study finds that, between 1985 and 1990, UK production industries and agriculture will reduce their workforce by 8 per cent. Much of this will be caused by large employers sub-contracting parts of their business to specialists, often small companies. This movement could account for nearly half of the jobs lost in production industries. Service industries are expected to increase employment by 3.6 per cent. The advent of computerization and the continuing erosion of job demarcation mean that engineers, scientists and multi-function craft workers will be in demand; unskilled workers of all kinds will not.

It is not only the lower echelons that must change. Management and professional staff must also adapt. Poorly trained managers, including those in the boardroom, are seen as one of the causes of poor industrial performance. Future managers will have to have a high level of technological literacy to cope with changes taking place in the labour market (International Management Institute, 1985).

Widespread concern about the need for a more adequate output of highly educated personnel and skills aligned to industry needs does not mean that it is easy to find solutions. In most OECD countries there are problems of 'mismatch' and many Europeans are talking about a crisis in education, because there is not only a mismatch but also a shortfall. While this will certainly boost the salaries of certain categories (such as engineers and programmers), it will, according to some employers, put a brake on investment (*Industrial Relations Review and Report* 365, 1 April 1986). This would be unfortunate for any country of the European Communities, where over 10 per cent of the workforce is unemployed.

Most countries are trying to initiate and improve their educational programmes, but the development and assessment of viable 'high-tech' education programmes is taking a long time, and is being resisted by the teaching profession. Moreover, the skill shortage militates against highly computer-literate teachers staying in the schools – many are poached by industry. Eventually, however, the provision of cost-effective instruction for a technologically oriented society will have to be met.

It is significant that, in the USA, employers themselves are increasing their own educational activities to provide employees with the skills and knowledge to do their jobs. And in several cases, particularly in the Nordic countries and in the USA, the unions are cooperating with industry or initiating their own training.

In 1986 the Clerical and Distributive Workers' Union (HK) in Denmark set up the most comprehensive, modular computer science training programme in the country. The scheme is intended to prepare their membership for both existing and emerging occupations related to microelectronics, including personal computers, terminals and mainframe functions, and electronic cash registers (*HK Bladet*, April 1986).

While no one has yet been able to predict which will be the new jobs, there are some signposts. The demand for labour is changing, especially in the older manufacturing industries, in response to the employers' need to become more competitive. This has meant introducing new technology, which, in turn, leads to fewer workers and a premium on the skills that remain. Adaptability to change is becoming a skill in its own right. In general, there will be more scientists, engineers and skilled workers. Relatively unskilled workers (both in production and services) will be less in demand. There is expected to be growth in the service sector, particularly in distribution, financial and business services, and leisure industries.

According to a 1986 report by the OECD's Centre for Educational Research and Innovation on the management of technological change in the automobile industry, the 'process of innovation itself is experimental' (OECD, 1986). The assumptions about deskilling and the polarization of employees by automation that predominated during the 1950s and 1960s are now changing. Automation introduced in the 1980s seems to affect skills in different ways. In the Federal Republic of Germany it has been shown that automation of production does not necessarily guarantee an optimization of production by a maximum reduction of staff. People are discovering the productivity potential of collective, individual and acquired skills, which can best be realized through new integrated approaches, as opposed to the fragmented Taylorist approach that went with much earlier automation (Kern and Schumann, 1984).

Many observers see emerging technologies reducing, rather than increasing, the skills that are needed by many workers. Moreover, while in the past economic growth offset job losses through technological change, this may no longer be so. It is easy to understand the concerns of those who worry about polarization and the move into service jobs, when, according to a Stanford University study, the greatest number of new jobs in the 1985–95 period will be for janitors, cashiers, clerical workers, secretaries, truck drivers and others in low-paid jobs (Rumberger and Levin, 1984). The fastest-growing occupations will be high-paying, high-tech jobs such as computer service technicians, systems analysts, programmers and electrical engineers. However, while the number of such jobs is expected to increase by 46 per cent, they will account for only 6 per cent of new jobs. Most of these high-paying jobs, together with accountants, lawyers, doctors, technicians and engineers, are in service industries, though professional and technical occupations have increased their share in manufacturing.

Though not yet conclusively documented, the shifts in employment are changing the work people do. Computers will continue to play a dominant role in this shift. Unless steps are taken to change the orientation of education, training and vocational guidance, the 1990 skill-mix among the workforce will correspond to outdated technologies. The present systems of education and training were not designed to cope with the needs of the 'information society'. They are geared to coping with the narrowly defined skills of industrial society, not the emerging broadly scoped or multi-skilled jobs of the future.

The Need for Consensus

If management, unions and workers are successfully to resolve the challenges of new technology, there must be a realignment in their relations and a greater understanding of the issues involved. Training is the most obvious way to adapt a labour force to changing demands. Management benefits because they acquire the skills that are needed. Unions benefit by their members having better employment prospects. But few benefit in a society characterized by growing inequalities, with the workforce divided into highly skilled/high paid, unskilled/low paid and employed/unemployed.

The computer is pivotal in the changing organization of society and work. The relations between people and machines are radically changing. But as the former Xerox Corporation vice-president Paul Strassman notes, it is the person, not the tool, that is important (Strassman, 1985). While computers are important tools for assuring the future growth of productivity, he also sees them as the 'basis for improvement of the quality of life in the workplace'. Much depends on how we organize, educate and train managers and other employees; how we design the working environment; how we justify and monitor capital investment; how we deal with issues of morale, motivation, privacy and displaced employees; how we define and measure productivity. In short, we must ensure that machines become an accessory to people, rather than vice versa.

Companies often invest a lot of money to develop and maintain machines and even special environments are created so that capital assets do not depreciate too quickly. As a computer-based society will depend upon the knowledge and skills of its workforce, it makes sense also to develop and maintain people.

Skill bottlenecks exist in schools, among teaching staff and at the workplace. A study by a French technology consultant (Lasfargue, 1985) cites two key conditions for realizing the economic and social potential of new technologies: 'mastery' of these technologies by the greatest possible number of people, and 'negotiations' on their introduction starting at the pre-investment stage. This, in turn, implies training. Dealing intelligently with the issues requires that managers and union officials keep themselves up to date on automation techniques.

While the debate on new technologies continues, most studies emphasise the vital importance of education and training. A mobile and better-educated workforce is essential for the survival of industrialized societies, regardless of the accuracy of the particular sectoral shifts predicted in different studies.

The future promises continuing and accelerating changes. These changes will give rise to a different landscape, including new products and services, higher levels of technology, new patterns of labour–management relations, and a need for new and vastly different skills and abilities. This is borne out not only by the material on the subject published in the ILO's *Social and Labour Bulletin* but also in the reports on the tripartite discussions that have taken place during ILO Industrial Committees, technical meetings of experts, and similar forums within the ILO.

Although there is still no consensus among the ILO's constituents on how to solve all the problems posed by new technologies, the general view is that, if the ILO is to succeed in its task of promoting social justice throughout the future world, then 'negotiated', rather than imposed, solutions must be found to the problems posed by the introduction of new technologies.

References

ACARD (1980), *Technological Change: Threats and Opportunities for the United Kingdom* (London: Her Majesty's Stationery Office/Advisory Council for Applied Research and Development).

AFL-CIO (1985), *The Changing Situation of Workers and their Unions* (Washington, DC: American Federation of Labor-Congress of Industrial Organizations, February).

Bamber, G. J. and Lansbury, R. D. (eds) (1987), *International and Comparative Industrial Relations* (London: Allen & Unwin).

BIAC/TUAC (1986), *Full Employment and Growth as the Social and Economic Goal: A Joint Statement* (Paris: Business and Industry Advisory Committee/Trade Union Advisory Committee, Organisation for Economic Co-operation and Development, April).

CBI (1985), *CBI-MSC Special Survey: Skill Shortages* (London: Confederation of British Industry).

Ebel, K. H. (1986), 'The impact of industrial robots', *International Labour Review*, vol. 125, no. 1, January–February, pp. 39–51.

EC (1987), *Joint Opinion of the Working Party 'Social Dialogue and the New Technologies' concerning Training, Motivation and Information and Consultation* (Brussels: European Communities, March).

ETUI (1982), *Negotiating Technological Change* (Brussels: European Trade Union Institute).

FIET (1983), *Commercial Workers and New Technology* (Geneva: International Federation of Commercial, Clerical, Professional and Technical Employees).

Freeman, G. and Soete, L. (1985), *Information Technology and Employment: An Assessment* (Brighton: Science Policy Research Unit, University of Sussex, April).

Hunt, H. A. and Hunt, T. L. (1983), *Human Resource Implications of Robotics* (Kalamazoo: Upjohn Institute for Employment Research).

IMS (1985), *Clerical Labour Markets: Changes and Trends in the UK* (Brighton: Institute of Manpower Studies).

IMS (1986), *UK Occupation and Employment Trends to 1990* (London: Butterworths/Institute of Manpower Studies).

ILO (1984), *World Labour Report*, vol. 1 (Geneva: International Labour Office), pp. 175–93.

International Management Institute (1985), *Report of the Commission for the Year 2000* (Geneva).

IOE (1985), *Adapting the Labour Market: A Debate among IOE European Member Federations on Freedom of Enterprises and Freedom of Choice of Employees in Today's and Tomorrow's Market* (Proceedings of a meeting held in Oslo, 12–13 September). (Geneva: International Organisation of Employers).

JIL (1985), *Rodo Ilakusho Gijutsu Kakushin ka no Rodo to Noryoku Kaihatsu* (Labour and Development of Human Resources under Technological Change) (Tokyo: Japan Institute of Labour, 10 July).

Kern, H. and Schumann, M. (1984), 'Vers une professionalisation du travail industriel', *Sociologie du Travail*, vol. 4, pp. 398–406.

Lasfargue, Y. (1985), 'Formation et nouvelles technologies', *Liaisons sociales, politiques sociales et pratiques d'entreprise*, troisième trimestre, pp. 35–52.

Leontief, W. and Duchin, F. (1984), *The Impact of Automation on Employment, 1963–2000*, Abstract and executive summary of final report, New York University, April.

Monat, J. and Sarfati, H. (eds) (1986), *Workers' Participation: A Voice in Decisions, 1981–85* (Geneva: ILO).

OECD (1983), *The Impact of Industrial Robots on the Manufacturing Countries* (Paris: Organisation for Economic Co-operation and Development, 31 January, Doc. DSTI/IND/82.44, 1st revision).

OECD (1986), *New Technology and Human Resource Development in the Automobile Industry* (Paris: Organisation for Economic Co-operation and Development).

OTA (1984), *Computerized Manufacturing Automation: Employment, Education and the Workplace* (Washington, DC: US Government Printing Office/US Congress, Office of Technology Assessment).

OTA (1985), *Automation of America's Offices, 1985–2000* (Washington, DC: US Government Printing Office/US Congress, Office of Technology Assessment).

Rumberger, R. W. and Levin, H. M. (1984), *Forecasting the Impact of New Technologies on the Future of the Job Market* (Stanford University: Institute for Research on Educational Finance and Governance, February).

Sarfati, H. and Cove, M. (eds) (1985), *Technological Change: The Tripartite Response, 1982–85* (Geneva: ILO).

Strassman, P. A. (1985), *Automation Payoff: The Transformation of Work in an Electronic Age* (New York: Free Press).

Treu, T. (1984), 'The impact of new technologies on employment working conditions and industrial relations', *Labour and Society* (Geneva: International Institute for Labour Studies, April–June), pp. 109–26.

APPENDIX

Model Technology Agreement, International Federation of Commercial, Clerical, Professional and Technical Employees (FIET)

The International Federation of Commercial, Clerical, Professional and Technical Employees (FIET) includes many unions in a wide range of countries. In general, its affiliates are non-communist in orientation and represent white-collar employees. This Model Technology Agreement taps their varied experiences of confronting technological change, to produce a practical negotiating guide for unions. It contains provisions covering procedural and substantive aspects of new technologies.

This Model Agreement was compiled by the FIET Technology Working Group and presented to the 20th FIET World Congress (Tokyo, November 1983) for adoption.[1] Their objective was to express in collective bargaining language and in some detail the basic principles on the introduction of new technology which were set out in FIET's Computers and Work Action Programme in 1979 and which were refined in the work of the various FIET trade sections and regional organizations.

The clauses contained in the Model Agreement are not intended to be transferable without alteration into the collective agreements negotiated by FIET affiliates at national level. In view of the enormous variations that exist between industrial relations systems as well as the legal, social and political environments in the eighty-six different countries where FIET has affiliates, this would be an impossible objective. The Model Agreement should rather be seen as a checklist of the main items that should be included in collective agreements on new technology, together with an indication of the kind of approach that should be adopted in relation to each item. Individual unions must choose whether to include in their own agreements some or all of the clauses provided by FIET, and how to adjust the wording to fit their own national circumstances.

In some countries collective agreements already exist dealing with new technology, and the unions probably have little or no need of a Model Agreement. Indeed the provisions in existing agreements concluded by FIET affiliates have formed the main source for the clauses reproduced here. For the vast majority of FIET's affiliates, however, the question of technology is a relatively new one. For those unions, this Agreement is designed to give guidance as to what can be achieved through collective bargaining. FIET recommends that the following specific points need to be borne in mind about the model.

Is it a 'model' agreement from the union standpoint?

The clauses contained in the FIET Model Agreement are those that unions should aim to have included in their collective agreements. In the real world of industrial relations, employers may not always accept these clauses, and any final agreement reached may well be a compromise reflecting what is practically achievable. The principles laid down in the Model Agreement represent a *starting point* for negotiations and can be used to present union demands to employers. In a number of places, alternative formulations of clauses are given where choices will have to be made on the basis of factors such as the economic environment and the relative bargaining strength of the union and employer.

Collective bargaining takes place at various levels

It is not possible to summarize here the many different collective bargaining systems that exist in the world. In some countries negotiations take place mainly at national level, in others at industry and/or regional level, and in others at the level of the individual enterprise. In some countries national framework agreements are supplemented by agreements at enterprise level. In others, collective bargaining results in binding arbitration awards. Not all the clauses in the Model Agreement will be relevant at every level of collective bargaining. In particular those that make reference to a particular type of technology and that give undertakings on behalf of the enterprise are relevant to enterprise-level rather than national- or industry-level agreements. Negotiators must therefore adapt each clause to match the level at which they are negotiating.

Not all countries regulate technology issues through technology agreements

The publication of this Model Agreement is intended to assist those unions that wish to conclude a technology agreement, not to force technology agreements on unions which prefer to regulate these matters in some other way. In some European countries, for example, wide-ranging industrial democracy legislation or cooperation agreements already exist which enable unions to exert influence over many of the issues dealt with here. In such cases, although separate technology agreements may not be needed, the unions concerned may still need to ensure that all the important subjects listed in the Model Agreement are covered in their existing arrangements, or that amendments or annexes to their agreements are made accordingly.

The term 'union' covers all representative bodies of workers

The wide variations in collective bargaining in different countries means that the term 'union' can sometimes be confusing at national level. In some countries the party to a collective agreement may be the national union, in others it may be a federation or cartel of unions acting together. In still others it may be the works council, the local union branch or some other statutory body representing the workforce. The term 'union' in this document means any appropriate body which takes part in collective bargaining on behalf of the workers in accordance with national law and practice. It does not constitute a preference by FIET for any particular form of industrial relations.

Structure of the Agreement

The text of the Agreement is in three sections: Section A deals with general questions, Section B with procedural matters and Section C with substantive matters. The procedural section deals with setting up machinery for exerting union influence over technological change. The substantive section gives suggestions as to how major policy issues might be tackled.

Section A: General

Objectives

1 The parties to this agreement (.................................. [employer] and .... [union/works council]) accept that the introduction of new forms of technology into the areas covered by

this Agreement can be beneficial both for the company and for its employees, provided the conditions under which that technology is introduced are correctly regulated. They accept that the evaluation of new technology must be based not only on its technical and economic effects but also on its social effects on employees.

2 The objective of this Agreement is to regulate the introduction of all forms of new technology so as to maximize the benefits to both parties while avoiding or minimizing to the greatest extent possible any negative implications.

Commitment to Negotiate

3 The parties to the Agreement commit themselves to the principle of negotiating and reaching agreement on all matters relating to the introduction of new technology as laid down in the Agreement, including the choice of equipment, the method and speed of its introduction, and the method of work organization to be used with it. They also agree to negotiate on all matters affecting the employment and conditions of work of the employees affected by it.

Status Quo

4 It is accepted by both parties that no new equipment or systems or changes to existing equipment or systems will be implemented in the workplaces covered by this Agreement until joint agreement has been reached on such implementation. In the absence of agreement between the parties, the present methods of working and conditions of employment shall continue to apply/the normal procedures for the resolution of disputes shall be invoked.

Scope of the Agreement

5 The Agreement covers all categories of worker for which the union is recognized for collective bargaining purposes.

Alternative A. It refers to all new technology or changes in existing technology used in the workplaces covered including data processing, text processing, telecommunications and other electronic equipment, and associated systems and software as well as the methods of work organization associated with it.

Alternative B. This Agreement refers to the .... [manufacturer] .... [model number] ....

[description of system] including a maximum of .... processing units, ...VDU terminals, ... printers, ... laser scanners [etc. etc.] hereafter referred to as 'the system' at the following locations: .... [list of departments and/or sites]. No alteration or addition to this list of equipment will be made except by joint agreement.

Section B: Procedure

Technology Committee(s)

6 The parties agree to establish a committee/committees to supervise and control the process of implementation of the new system(s). This committee shall be called the Technology Committee and shall be composed of equal numbers of employer and union representatives. Decision-making by the Technology Committee shall normally be by consensus. Where appropriate joint bodies already exist, these may instead be given all or some of the tasks designated as being the responsibility of the Technology Committee.

Information Disclosure

7 The employer undertakes to make available to the union all relevant information including internal documents relating to the decision to consider the implementation of new systems including, as appropriate, feasibility studies, consultants' reports, etc. The information provided should include the following items:

(i) The reasons, both technical and financial, for considering the introduction of new technology.

(ii) A detailed technical explanation of the nature and scope of the technological change proposed.

(iii) A detailed financial assessment of the costs involved in obtaining the new technology (hardware, software and consultancy fees), the financial benefits anticipated from the change and the expected market position of the enterprise both with and without the proposed technology.

(iv) Details of the proposed method of operation of the new system(s) and the tasks it/they will perform.

(v) Details of all alternative systems that have been under consideration together with the reasons for choosing any particular system being proposed.

(vi) The proposed timetable for the introduction of the new system(s).

(vii) A detailed assessment of the personnel needs of the enterprise both in terms of absolute numbers and in terms of skills required with the new system(s) as compared with the existing situation.

(viii) An estimate of the effects on workflow, working methods, workplace layout and working hours that may result from implementing the proposed system(s).

(ix) Any proposed changes in systems of performance measurement or of individual control or supervision implied by the new system(s).

(x) Details of plans for the further introduction of new types of technology or of extensions to existing technology being considered by the employer.

(xi) Details of the persons responsible for the implementation of the system(s) within the company, within the manufacturer, and within any consultancy being used by the employer.

8 The information set out in the preceding paragraph should be supplied by the company:

(a) at the earliest possible stage in the decision-making process so that the union is in a position to influence decisions on whether to implement the change, the type of system to be chosen, and the way in which it is to be implemented;

(b) in a form that is clear and understandable to the union representatives involved.

Technology Representatives

9 The union agrees to appoint/elect (in accordance with its own established procedures) a pre-determined number of new technology representatives. These representatives, who will normally have previous experience of union work, will receive the same facilities as other staff representatives, including time off for union activities and office facilities. They will also receive (in working time and at the employer's expense) special training in matters relating to new technology. The content of these training courses will be determined by the union in consultation with the employer.

Access to Outside Experts

10 Where it considers it necessary, the union will be entitled to request independent outside experts to assist it in the assessment of proposals for the introduction of new technology made by the employer. The terms under which such experts are consulted will be agreed jointly by the union and the employer. The employer will bear all costs involved.

Rights of Technology Representatives

11 The employer will, on request by the union, make available to the technology representatives and to any outside experts who may be involved, access to the manufacturer of the equipment, and any consultants involved in implementing the system, as well as the opportunity to visit other workplaces where the proposed system is in operation in order to gain first-hand experience of its effects on the workers concerned.

Access to Employer Research

12 The union will also be given full access to any continuing research on the possible application of new technology being carried out by the employer and will be invited to participate in any feasibility studies that are undertaken either directly or by consultants acting on the employer's behalf.

Monitoring of Personal Data Collection

13 The parties to the Agreement will jointly establish procedures governing the collection and use of personal data within the new system. These procedures will specify the types of data that can be collected, the length of time for which they can be stored, who is permitted access to them, and for what purposes they can be used. The procedures will allow individuals access to all data that relates to them, will prohibit the collection of data on sensitive personal matters (e.g. religious or political convictions, membership of organizations, private life) and will restrict access by third parties to the data and/or the cross-referencing of them with data collected from other sources. Data referring to disciplinary offences will be removed from personnel records after an agreed period, and data relating to work performance, etc., will be used only for purposes agreed in advance with the union.

Information and Consultation

14 During the period of development of the new system, meetings will be held with the employees likely to be directly affected by changes in work organization, work load, etc. Each employee concerned will be given all the available information on the direct effects on his/her job of the proposals under consideration and will be given the opportunity to contribute to the process of developing the system. Full information will also be provided on the likely implications for job grading, pay levels and other working conditions. All meetings with employees will be held with the participation of union representatives.

Review of the Effects of the System

15 The Technology Committee (or other appropriate body) will conduct at regular intervals a review of the effects of the new system on employment levels, workflow, work organization and working conditions to ensure that the terms of this Agreement are being fully met.

Section C: Substantive Issues

Employment and Job Security

16 *Alternative A* There will be no reduction in the total number of staff employed as a result of the implementation of the new system. Where the use of the technology results in a reduction in the employees required in a particular area, compensatory action will be taken to redeploy employees elsewhere, to expand the overall level of business and to negotiate appropriate reductions in working time. Where any reductions in the total number of staff employed take place within (..........) months of the introduction of the new system, the employer will be responsible for demonstrating to the union that these reductions are unconnected with the technological change. In order for the union to be able to monitor the implementation of this clause, the employer will provide on a quarterly basis details of all staff numbers (both full time and part time). All staff vacancies occurring during the period of implementation will be filled.

Alternative B There will be no compulsory redundancy (lay-offs) as a result of the implementation of the new system. Where any redundancies are declared within (..........) months of the introduction of the new system, the employer will be responsible for demonstrating to the union that these redundancies are unconnected with the technological change. Any reductions in the overall demand for employees arising from the introduction of the new system will be carried out by:

(i) natural wastage (attrition)
(ii) voluntary redundancy
(iii) early retirement.

Alternative C If, after full examination of all other possibilities there is no alternative to making employees redundant, the employer will cooperate with the union in order to minimize the number of jobs affected. The criteria for the selection of employees to be made redundant and the compensation payable to them will be agreed by the employer and the union according to established principles and according to clause 23 of this Agreement.

Temporary and Casual Work and Sub-contracting

17 There will be no increase in the use of temporary work or homeworking without the written consent of the union given in advance. Sub-contracting of work or use of consultants for tasks currently performed within the enterprise will not be undertaken except in exceptional circumstances with the union's written consent.

Redeployment

18 Any employee whose job is eliminated or substantially altered as a result of the introduction of the new system will have the right to be redeployed in an equivalent job within the enterprise, with status, pay and working conditions no less favourable than those currently enjoyed.

19 Redeployment of staff will normally be in the same department or field of work as the current job. If this is not possible, redeployment should be at the same geographical location. No employee will be compelled to relocate to another place of work as a result of the introduction of the new system. Where employees agree voluntarily to relocate, the union and employer will agree suitable allowances and conditions of service.

20 Where a suitable equivalent job is not available for an employee, the employer will offer reasonable alternative employment. If the employee objects to the terms of the offer, a joint committee of union

and employer representatives will determine whether the alternative offered is 'reasonable'.

21 Employees who are redeployed or relocated will be given the opportunity in worktime, and with the payment of reasonable expenses by the employer, to inspect their new workplace and job. Should they accept redeployment, they shall continue to have the right to withdraw their acceptance of the new job within a period of (..........) months after the transfer without loss of entitlement to redundancy compensation.

22 Any employee for whom suitable alternative employment in accordance with the above clauses cannot be found or who, after a trial period, declines to accept redeployment shall be compensated for redundancy in accordance with the criteria established in clause 23.

Redundancy

23 Compulsory redundancies will take place only if all other possibilities have been exhausted. The employer undertakes to cooperate to the fullest extent with the union to minimize the financial hardship to any employees made redundant. This will be the case whether the redundancies involved are voluntary or compulsory. The employer undertakes in particular to:

(a) provide the longest possible periods of notice to the individuals concerned;
(b) pay adequate financial compensation related to length of service, age and other factors according to arrangements to be worked out in detail with the union;
(c) provide adequate paid time off to employees and pay fares and reasonable subsistence allowances for employees searching for new jobs elsewhere;
(d) cooperate fully with other employers, employers' organizations and the public employment authorities to find suitable alternative jobs for employees made redundant;
(e) provide continuing financial support on terms agreed with the union to those employees, particularly older ones, who experience special difficulties in finding new jobs.

Job Content, Skills and Qualifications

24 The parties to the Agreement undertake to ensure that the overall quality of jobs covered by the Agreement measured in terms of both the level of skills and qualifications necessary to carry them out and

the degree of satisfaction derived from them does not deteriorate as a result of the introduction of the new system. The Technology Committee will therefore carry out a review of each job affected by the introduction of the system against criteria to be established in advance, and will recommend the redesign of any job that is downgraded in terms of skills or qualifications, or that becomes clearly less demanding and satisfying.

25 Priority will be given, in the process of redesigning jobs, to improving the overall content of those jobs involving simple and repetitive tasks where the new system has brought about a deterioration in job quality. Amongst the criteria that will be used in designing new jobs will be: interchangeability of tasks (mixed work), the avoidance of over-specialization, the opportunity for workers to use higher skills and qualifications, and the maximum possible control over work content and pace of work by the individual employee or group of employees.

26 Where the qualification or skill level of a job is reduced and the job cannot be redesigned to bring it to an equivalent or higher level, the individual carrying out the job will be offered equivalent or reasonable alternative employment elsewhere in the enterprise at the same or a higher qualification level, and will be provided with all necessary retraining to enable him/her to carry out the new job.

Job Grading, Salaries, Working Conditions

27 No employee will suffer a deterioration in job grade, salary or other working conditions (hours of work, annual leave, etc.) as a result of the implementation of the new system.

28 Where jobs are substantially changed by the introduction of the new system, existing methods of salary determination (such as job evaluation) in use will be re-examined by the parties to the Agreement. Adjustments to salary levels and pay structures will then be negotiated to take into account any increases in the skills and qualifications necessary to carry out the jobs concerned or in the demands placed on employees by those jobs.

29 No piecework, payment by results or similar schemes will be introduced during the life of this Agreement. Schemes linking improvements in productivity to improvements in wages and other conditions may be negotiated separately if considered desirable by both parties. In such cases, the parties will give priority in reaching agreements to measures that have a positive effect on employment, and that avoid any deterioration in physical or psychological working conditions.

Work Environment

30 The parties commit themselves to ensure that no job directly or indirectly affected by the introduction of the new system will, as a result, be subjected to an increase in the overall workload, pace or intensity of work that might lead to increases in stress for the employees concerned. The Technology Committee will examine on a regular basis key jobs selected in advance to ensure that this paragraph of the Agreement is observed in practice.

31 The parties further agree that there will be no increase in the level of shiftworking, or other change in the pattern of working time (for example increases in part-time work or overtime or the introduction of flexible working hours), without the written agreement of the union in advance.

32 The employer agrees to observe the highest possible standards of industrial hygiene and safety and ergonomics in relation to the use of the new system. It will make available to the workforce qualified medical advice and will strictly observe all relevant codes of practice issued under national health and safety legislation that may have an effect on the health of workers in the areas affected by this Agreement.

33 In relation to the ergonomic standards and methods of work organization associated with . . ., the employer undertakes to observe the standards set out in the attached annex(es). Further annexes setting out standards for other aspects of occupational health and safety may be added to this Agreement by joint agreement at any stage. These annexes in no way alter the employer's responsibility to ensure a healthy and safe working environment for its employees.

Training

34 In the interests both of gaining the maximum possible benefit from the system for the employer and of giving employees the greatest possible opportunity for increased job satisfaction, all employees associated with the new system will be given sufficient training to enable them to understand the broad principles of the system and the purpose of their own task in relation to the system as a whole.

35 All employees whose tasks are altered as a result of the introduction of the new system will be given sufficient on and off the job training to enable them to carry out their new tasks fully. Where employees are judged unsuitable for such training, they will be transferred to other suitable jobs without loss of pay or status.

36 All employees who are redeployed in accordance with clauses 18–22

will be given adequate training to enable them to carry out their new jobs.

37 Union representatives involved in negotiating the introduction of the new system will be provided with special training under the control of the union.

38 In all the cases mentioned above, the training provided will be in working time, will be financed by the employer, and adequate cover will be provided during the period of absence of those undergoing training to ensure that neither they nor their colleagues are faced with an excessive workload as a result.

Equal Opportunities

39 The parties reaffirm their commitment to the principle of equal pay for men and women employees. They undertake to ensure that all the rights provided for under this agreement are available equally to men and women.

Reduction in Working Time

40 The parties to the Agreement recognize that, if the new system is implemented properly, the result will be substantial economic benefits flowing from improvements in productivity, product quality, etc. They therefore commit themselves to negotiations at an appropriate stage on the fair distribution of any such economic benefits between employer and employees, recognizing the important role that a reduction in working time can play in the preservation and creation of employment, in the context of technological change.

Notes

1 This influential Model Agreement has not been published previously, though it was first circulated by FIET in 1983. We are grateful to FIET for allowing us to publish a slightly edited version of it. FIET also compiled a set of notes that accompany the Model. These explain the reasoning behind each clause and give advice on bargaining tactics. However, there is insufficient space in this book to reproduce these notes, which are longer than the Model itself.

2 On model technology agreements in the British context, see TUC (1979) and Bamber (1985).

References

Bamber, G. J. (1985), 'Some "knowns" and "unknowns" about management, industrial relations and technical change', in B. R. Williams and J. A. Bryan-Brown (eds), *Knowns and Unknowns in Technical Change: Conference Papers* (London: Technical Change Centre/Policy Studies Institute), pp. 131–51.

TUC (1979), *Employment and Technology: Report Adopted by the 1979 Congress* (London: Trades Union Congress).

Index

For Product Safety Concerns and Information please contact our EU representative GPSR@taylorandfrancis.com Taylor & Francis Verlag GmbH, Kaufingerstraße 24, 80331 München, Germany

Printed and bound by CPI Group (UK) Ltd, Croydon, CR0 4YY
11/04/2025
01843977-0001